THE WRITTEN WORD
LITERACY IN TRANSITION

THE WRITTEN WORD

LITERACY IN TRANSITION

Wolfson College Lectures 1985

EDITED BY

GERD BAUMANN

CLARENDON PRESS · OXFORD

1986

Oxford University Press, Walton Street, Oxford OX2 6DP
Oxford New York Toronto
Delhi Bombay Calcutta Madras Karachi
Kuala Lumpur Singapore Hong Kong Tokyo
Nairobi Dar es Salaam Cape Town
Melbourne Auckland
and associated companies in
Beirut Berlin Ibadan Nicosia

Oxford is a trade mark of Oxford University Press

Published in the United States
by Oxford University Press, New York

British Library Cataloguing in Publication Data
The Written word: literacy in
transition.—(Wolfson College
lectures; 1985)
1. Literacy—Social aspects
I. Baumann, Gerd II. Series
302.2 LC149
ISBN 0-19-875068-4

Library of Congress Cataloging in Publication Data
The Written word.
(Wolfson College lectures; 1985)
Includes index.
1. Writing—Addresses, essays, lectures.
2. Literacy—Addresses, essays, lectures. 3. Books
and reading—Addresses, essays, lectures. 4. Publishers
and publishing—Addresses, essays, lectures.
I. Baumann, Gerd. II. Series.
Z40.W75 1986 001.54'3 85-28508
ISBN 0-19-875068-4

Printed in Great Britain by
The Alden Press Ltd,
Oxford

PREFACE

FOR the past fifteen years, the Wolfson College Lectures have provided a forum in which scholars of diverse disciplines can address the public on a subject of general interest. This book contains the revised versions of seven of the eight lectures delivered in the 1985 series entitled *Literacy and the Written Word.*

To organize and edit a series of lectures is always a co-operative enterprise, and I owe thanks to the President of the College, Sir Henry Fisher, and to several Fellows, members of staff, and students. Mr Julian Roberts, Vicegerent at the time of the lectures, has encouraged this series from its beginnings and provided generous support throughout. Dr John Penney has helped me with indispensable sound advice at various stages and made most valuable comments on the Introduction. Mrs Janet Walker has, as College Secretary, lent me her efficient help with unfailing friendliness. I am greatly indebted to Mr Tom Cheesman who first alerted me to the subject, sustained my interest by generously sharing his knowledge, and invaluably spurred the drafting of the Introduction.

Most directly, my thanks are due to the lecturers for their welcome participation, and their kind co-operation in the process of editing and publishing.

August 1985   GERD BAUMANN

CONTENTS

NOTES ON CONTRIBUTORS

WALTER J. ONG, SJ, is University Professor of Humanities and Professor of Humanities in Psychiatry at Saint Louis University. His most recent books are *Orality and Literacy* (London: Methuen, 1982) and *Fighting for Life: Contest, Sexuality and Consciousness* (Ithaca, NY: Cornell University Press, 1981). He has lectured widely in the Americas, Africa, Europe, the Middle East, and East Asia. He is a past President of the Modern Languages Association of America, has received the Ordre des Palmes Académiques, and is a Fellow of the American Academy of Arts and Sciences.

ANNA MORPURGO DAVIES was trained in Classics and Comparative Philology at the University of Rome and is currently Professor of Comparative Philology in the University of Oxford and a Fellow of Somerville College. She has taught as a Visiting Professor at the University of Pennsylvania and at Yale University. In 1975 she was Collitz Professor of the Linguistic Society of America. A Fellow of the British Academy, Professor Morpurgo Davies has published widely on historical and comparative Indo-European linguistics, especially in ancient Greek, Mycenaean Greek, and Anatolian, as well as on the history of linguistics.

GEZA VERMES is Reader in Jewish Studies in the University of Oxford and a Fellow of Wolfson College. He was the first President of the British and the European Associations for Jewish Studies, and is a Fellow of the British Academy. His books include *The Dead Sea Scrolls in English* (Harmondsworth: Penguin, 1962, 1965), *The Dead Sea Scrolls: Qumran in Perspective* (Ohio: Collins World, 1978), *Scripture and Tradition in Judaism* (Leiden: Brill, 1961, 1973), *Post-Biblical Jewish Studies* (Leiden: Brill, 1975), *Jesus the Jew* (London: Collins, 1973) and *Jesus and the World of Judaism* (London: SCM, 1983).

KEITH THOMAS is Reader in Modern History in the University of Oxford and a Fellow and Tutor of St John's College. He is the author of *Religion and the Decline of Magic* (London: Weidenfeld & Nicolson, 1971), *Man and the Natural World* (London: Allen Lane, 1983) and many articles on the social and intellectual history of early modern England. Mr Thomas is a Fellow of the British Academy, and will take up the position of President of Corpus Christi College, Oxford, in October 1986.

IOAN LEWIS is Professor of Social Anthropology at the London School of Economics, and Honorary Director of the International African Institute. He has taught at universities in Europe, Africa, and the United States, and was Hitchcock Professor at the University of California in 1977. Among his books are *A Pastoral Democracy: pastoralism and politics among the northern Somali* (Oxford: Oxford University Press, 1961, 1982), *Somali Poetry* together with B. W. Andrzejewski (Oxford: Oxford University Press, 1964), *A Modern History of Somalia* (London: Longman, 1965, 1980) and *Social Anthropology in Perspective* (Harmondsworth: Pelican, 1976, 1985).

ADAM HODGKIN read philosophy at the Universities of Oxford, Calgary, and Cambridge. After joining Oxford University Press, he has been editor of philosophy and law books. In 1979, he became interested in the effect of computers on publishing when an author delivered a book written on a word processor. Mr Hodgkin drafted the *Oxford Rules for the Preparation of Text on Micro-computers*. Currently he is manager in charge of the academic journals and periodicals list, and has taken additional responsibility for research into, and applications of, new forms of academic publishing.

ANTHONY SMITH is Director of the British Film Institute, having previously been a Director of Channel Four Television Company. He has been a Fellow of St Antony's College, Oxford, and has published numerous books, including *The Shadow in the Cave—the Broadcaster, the Audience and the State* (London: Quartet, 1975), *Television and Political Life* (London: Macmillan, 1979), *Goodbye Gutenberg: The Newspaper Revolution of the 1980s* (Oxford: Oxford University Press, 1980), and *The Geopolitics of Information: How Western Culture dominates the World* (London: Faber, 1980).

GERD BAUMANN read musicology and linguistics at the University of Cologne, and ethnomusicology and social anthropology at the Queen's University of Belfast. He has taught at Belfast and London, and conducted anthropological field research in the Sudan. He is currently a Junior Research Fellow of Wolfson College.

INTRODUCTION

GERD BAUMANN

I

WHEN a German educational magazine recently asked a group of primary-school children to imagine their world if no one could read or write, their replies revealed a surprising awareness of the impact of literacy: in the absence of cookery books food would revert to spit-roasts in prehistoric fashion, and political parties campaigning for votes would have to rely on the trustworthiness of their candidates' faces, instead of the persuasiveness of printed slogans. Poets would be unemployed and replaced by painters, or turn to producing comic strips without the 'bubbles' of speech. The lack of printed programme schedules would spell interminable hours of television since nobody could plan when to switch off (Eltern 1984).

Even an age-group whom Germans used to call 'ABC-recruits' (*ABC-Schützen*) imagine the end of literacy either as a return to a simple or even primitive culture, or as the final departure into a (tele-) visual future. The engaging precision of their replies has something to commend itself beside the speculative scenarios sometimes sketched of a future without literacy in an age of computers and audio-visual media. Still more arresting than their replies, however, is the fact of the question having been put to them at all. It is hard to imagine that an educational magazine would have raised it twenty, fifty, or eighty years ago. An 'end' to literacy has become conceivable, if hard to imagine, and even less adventurous observers see present-day forms of literacy as in a state of transition under the impact of new information technologies. Literacy studies, a recent concern though they are, may also seem to find themselves in such a state of transition.

Literacy has emerged as a topic of academic interest only within the past three decades or so. It has first come into its own in North America rather than Europe—in societies, that is, which have been predicated on mass literacy almost from their beginnings, have taken full advantage of it in processes of cultural formation and integration, and are now in the forefront of spreading 'post'-literate technologies. Simultaneously, scholarly interest has been aroused as many Third World countries have experienced an unprecedented surge of both literate and 'post'-literate technologies of communication. To ask what it is, and what it does to a person, or people, or a society to 'be literate' has become a question of wide interest. The political, cultural, and cognitive effects of literacy are as yet open issues, but issues of crucial importance.

One of the first and most influential scholars to have conceptualized the changing roles of literacy and its impact is Professor Walter Ong, the first contributor to this collection. Building on his earlier studies of Renaissance thought and rhetoric, and developing the pioneering ideas of Innis (1950), Lord (1960), and McLuhan (1962), of Goody (1968), Parry (1971), and Havelock (1973), Walter Ong has outlined a general framework for the systematic study of literacy at its various stages. According to this framework, the invention of script marked a momentous departure from the noetic and social structures associated with 'primary orality', the orality of cultures unaware even of the possibility of writing. The chirographic culture associated with handwriting practices and the typographic culture of print have entailed fundamental reorientations of human thought and perception. Our awareness of these has increased in line with our experience of a further transition when our typographic culture is rivalled by the 'secondary orality' of the new electronic technologies. From radio to the computerized information retrieval system, and from television to the electronic text, these technologies rely on the achievements of writing, but at the same time rehabilitate oral forms of communication in new ways.

Literacy has been recognized as a phenomenon warranting scholarly analysis at a time when its supremacy seems threatened by secondary-oral modes of communication. This may evoke the stockbrokers' axiom that a phenomenon widely discussed is invariably at the end of its effective run. On a less dramatic note, it seems likely that the transition to secondary orality has helped us to sharpen our minds to the impact of literacy and typographic culture.

To explore the impact of literacy, is of necessity an open-ended and at times evasive enterprise. It is not even self-evident that 'literacy' is the most useful general term, or can be studied as one phenomenon. The question is raised by several of the contributors, and this Introduction will return to it. To give form to this exploration, therefore, several plans of procedure seemed useful in organizing the series of lectures and their publication. One of these was to draw into the debate on literacy scholars who define themselves less as comparative students of literacy than as specialists who view the practices of literacy in one specific cultural and historical setting. Further, the contributors have focused on the effects of literacy at junctures of historical transition, rather than stability. These cover a wide range between the shift from syllabic to alphabetic scripts in the Ancient Mediterranean and the transitions from minority to incipient mass literacy in early modern England and in a part of the modern Third World; between the movement from oral to written tradition in inter-testamental Judaism and the transition to new technologies in present-day publishing and in the visual media.

To focus the study of literacy on points of transition, and to anchor it in detailed specialist scholarship, may help us the better to assess the importance of the contemporary transitions from typographic to electronic media. It may further help us to minimize the dangers of hypostasizing literacy, that is, to treat it as an agent in itself, rather than as a technology that is practised, used, and given purposes by human beings according to their specific social objectives and cultural outlooks. None the less, such a plan of study risks fragmentation and the aimless pursuit of detail if it is not unified by shared reference to a theoretical proposition.

Such a proposition is offered by Professor Ong, and the chapters that follow can be read as a series of detailed disputations addressed to it. Professor Ong's proposition argues that *writing is a technology that restructures thought*. Writing is not merely an exterior tool, but a practice that alters human consciousness to the degree to which it is, as Walter Ong says, 'interiorized'. Writing is 'interiorized' psychologically as the subject's experience is mediated to a significant degree by literate forms of discourse. One might perhaps also think of it as socially interiorized as literate practices come to form a basis of social institutions. Writing, proposes Walter Ong, takes language out of the evanescent act of speaking and fixes oral utterance, an event in time, to written signs, objects in space. It thus removes language, and with it, thought, from an immediate personal, social, and cultural contingency. Such 'diaeresis' makes possible a progressive separation of knowledge from interpretation, of logic from rhetoric, of past record from present-day reconstruction, and of cumulative factual learning from the judgement and wisdom acquired by experience. Such a restructuring of thought is embedded, as Walter Ong has stressed throughout his work, in 'the actual history of writing, its growth out of orality' and all the social and 'sociopsychological complexities that history presents us with'.

In his present contribution, Walter Ong warns again that 'in treating of the effects of writing one has to guard against reductionism. All changes in social and noetic structures are not due simply to writing. Writing itself has social causes. . . . But if there is no warrant for reductionism, there is more than ample warrant for relationism.'

All contributors agree in their rejection of reductionism, or of what Street (1984) has called the 'autonomous model' of literacy. Instead, they strive to relate the impact of literacy to the impact of other social practices in specific cases of historical transition. These cases make full use of the historical width and the interdisciplinary range of Walter Ong's proposition.

Professor Morpurgo Davies' contribution rectifies one of the shortcomings in literacy studies that Walter Ong's essay draws particular attention to: 'Most studies investigating psychic, intellectual, and cultural contrasts between oral and writing cultures have looked only to contrasts between orality and alphabetic writing.' These contrasts, moreover, have been drawn in stark colours by most researchers citing the hypothesis of Havelock (1963, 1976, 1983), who has attempted to trace the development of pre-Socratic and Platonic philosophical logic to the Greek invention of the alphabet. In less able hands, these historical hypotheses have been further tinged by evolutionist ideas of progress, as though the succession of scripts followed an evolutionist logic from pictographic writing ('primitive'?) through logographic ('simple-minded'?) to syllabic systems ('clever but clumsy'), only in order to achieve alphabetic perfection. The misconception matters, for it has wide-ranging consequences when applied to literacy programmes, especially in the Third World. It is impossible in some of the most influential designs of literacy policy to distinguish between the anticipated benefits of spreading literacy and the assumed inherent qualities of alphabetic writing.

Anna Davies adduces the evidence that refutes simple-minded ideas of evolutionary progress in the history of Ancient Mediterranean systems of writing, and disputes Havelock's emphasis on the Greek alphabet as the only begetter of a literate trust in the written word, of linear logical argument and grammatical abstraction. Such cultural developments as these cannot be reduced to being effects of one particular system of writing, nor can they be appreciated by isolating the practice of writing from the continuing practices of oral communication. 'The written text, for all its permanence,' states Walter Ong's chapter, 'means nothing, is not even a text, except in relationship to the spoken word.' Dr Geza Vermes explores this seeming paradox in relation to the text that has become known as 'Scripture' or 'The Book' itself. Judaism was the first of the universal religions to define itself by a written text, the Torah. Yet for the Torah to be accorded its ascendancy over the spoken word required a slow and gradual process of transition. It neared completion only after the disintegration of the Kingdom and through a process of 'canonization': the definition of a single complete text, and its elevation to representing the whole of a faith and its doctrine. Even then, and particularly then, the doctrinal understanding of the text and its practical application to changing circumstances required continuing oral scholarship and exegesis; which, in turn, grew into the codified written form of the Talmud Torah.

The same interdependence of the written and spoken word can be recognized also in the following two contributions. They are concerned with the transition from what Goody (1968: 11–20, 198–264) has styled 'restricted literacy' to beginning mass literacy. Early modern England and the present-day Third World are of course cases of immediate interest to present-day English literates, but they are cases also of the greatest general significance: they allow for an unusually discerning appraisal of the interpenetration of oral and literate modes, and of the complexities involved in the spread of the literate technology until it is 'interiorized' to such a degree as to transform social reality and individual thought.

The advance of the written and the printed word in early modern England has spurred literacy studies to an exceptional degree of discernment in the last few years. The popular image is of a period in which Protestantism, and soon afterwards post-Tridentine Catholicism, exalted the faithful to practise reading Holy Writ, printing presses mushroomed to provide not only psalters and family bibles, but unprecedented numbers of popular political pamphlets and gazettes, not to speak of the learned treatises that spread humanist ideas and a new variety of scientific thought. These associations have been refined by a scholarship hardly to be expected only ten years ago. Furet and Ozouf (1982) have traced three centuries of alphabetization in France; Johansson (1981) has begun to elucidate the exceptional case of Sweden where an uncompromising literacy campaign succeeded, without the help of a developed school system, in forcing the ability to read on long unparalleled numbers of people unable to write; Eisenstein (1979) has shown the *printing press as an agent of change* in Renaissance humanism, Reformation thought, and early modern science; for early modern England, Cressy (1980) has painstakingly used available sources to compute the growth of popular literacy rates.

Between such quantitative reconstruction on the one hand, and the tracing of long-range historical dynamics on the other, there is now room for a more confident understanding of what literacy actually entailed, what it meant and did, to the people alive at the time. Keith Thomas's contribution examines the definition, the spread, and the effects of literacy in regard both to those who mastered it, and to those who did not. The hierarchical divisions of Tudor and Stuart England are mirrored in a hierarchy of literate skills that ranges from the ability to read black-letter print to the facility of mastering specialized hands. Increasing rates of literacy tend to follow these hierarchical divisions. The spread of literacy must thus be understood in intimate conjunction with the resilience of oral modes, the different uses of the new technology both in reading and writing, and in the varying contexts of religious, political, scientific, and administrative domains of use. For all the diversity thus indicated, literacy did not necessarily serve to emancipate political opposition or religious dissent, but tended to consolidate power relationships and divisions, albeit in a new form.

Conversely, ideas of liberation have for long been associated with the spread of literacy in Third World countries. Depending on the ideologies invoked, literacy was to serve the 'modernization' of economies deemed 'traditional' or 'backward', or to emancipate new nations from the cultural alienation and political dependency imposed by colonial rule. Economists reiterated the claim that a literacy rate of 40 per cent was the threshold for development take-off (Anderson 1966), and the UNESCO Secretariat saw 'functional literacy' as a prerequisite for the spread of abilities and attitudes conducive to economic growth (Bataille 1976). As the hopes for development led by literacy turned out a grave disappointment, the theoretical foundations of the claims made for literacy came under radical scrutiny. Paulo Freire (1972, 1976) produced an influential reassessment of what literacy meant, and what it could mean, in developing countries. Literacy programmes that merely serve economic expediency are but another tool of oppression; to work for liberation, literacy should serve an aim of 'conscientization' that raises the learner's political consciousness. 'The very decision to bring literacy to the masses is already a political act' (Freire 1979: 29). In the late 1970s, Freire's ideas were applied in newly-independent Guinea-Bissau, where the work of Amilcar Cabral (1975*a*, 1975*b*) had laid firm foundations for a liberationist view of literacy.

The political objectives even of radical literacy campaigns, however, remain precariously poised between a broadly socialist aim of overcoming the colonial heritage of exploitation and class division, and a broadly nationalist aim of overcoming the pre-colonial heritage of ethnic divisions by the propagation of a national culture and national sentiment. The two aspects are often intertwined. Undoubtedly, the most determined literacy campaigns have been carried out by socialist governments; but literacy campaigns being governmental initiatives easily lend themselves to the propagation of nationalist, rather than liberationist ideas.

The implications of mass literacy for the unity of states and the growth of national sentiment have been recognized in numerous cases. Ernest Gellner (1983) sees widespread literacy as a prerequisite of effective national cohesion. Ioan Lewis's contribution to this collection challenges Gellner's view through a case study of the Horn of Africa.

The Horn of Africa presents a most favourable vantage-point from which to reassess the role of literacy in processes of nation-building. Ethiopia is among the oldest independent states of Africa, and its Christian church as well as its dominant groups have for long sustained and cultivated their literate traditions in Ge'ez, Amharic, and Tigrean. None the less, ethnic diversity and conflict were not overcome by the imposition of Amharic as the national language before the 1974 Revolution, and have since been exacerbated by the imposition of the Amharic script for writing other regional languages. Somalia, by contrast, ethnically and culturally far more homogeneous, has traditionally relied on a highly sophisticated oral tradition, and has achieved political independence and incipient mass literacy only recently. Two determined campaigns have spread mother-tongue literacy in a nationally accepted Latin script. This new literacy has succeeded in rivalling its only traditional precursor, the Arabic literacy of Muslim religious specialists, and in nurturing a burgeoning national press and literature. Its effects, however, have been all but overtaken by the impact of a new, secondary orality: radios and cassette recorders have given the most vigorous impetus to traditional forms of oratory and oral poetry.

If literacy is widely seen at present to be undergoing a momentous transition, then the evidence from the Third World cannot fail to heighten that impression. Within the past decade, literacy has spread on an unprecedented global scale, Western ideas about it have been radically challenged, and its impact has been rivalled by new media of secondary orality. Simultaneously, the place of literacy has undergone fundamental change in industrial societies. Schoolchildren can readily imagine a future without writing, pundits conjure up an 'end' to literacy, and academic observers design 'the new literacy' (Pattison 1982). The last two contributions address the present-day transition in Western literacy and typographic culture.

They do so from two contrasting angles: Adam Hodgkin writes from inside one of the long-established academic publishing houses, Anthony Smith from inside the new audio-visual dominion of television and film. But their approaches converge on a common concern, the new electronic technologies, and they link up closely with motifs first introduced in Walter Ong's essay. Walter Ong has pointed to the similarity between the way in which people raised in oral cultures criticized literacy, and the way we ourselves, raised in a late typographic culture, conceive of the dangers of electronic technologies and their 'secondary orality'. Such similarities, far from being historical curios, evoke a basic similarity postulated by Ong: that writing, just like computing, is not merely the use of a tool to a predefined purpose, but the practice of a technology that engages its users in exploring new ways of thinking.

The technologies of writing and printing have for some time developed beyond the use of pen in hand and hot metal print with movable types. Most of the essays in this book were drafted on typewriters, and multiplied for lecturing, editing, and marking up by photostatic means. Two of the contributors have hardly written on paper at all, preferring to key in, delete, and shift electronic signs on the screen of a word-processing micro-computer. Their 'papers' now appear in 'print' with the help of computer setting and photo-lithography.

The most recent processes of producing texts are justly compre-hended to amount to a whole new technology: a practice by which authors, printers, and publishers are led to rethink the purposes and aims of their respective jobs, and obliged to redefine their relationships among each other and to the reader.

Adam Hodgkin discusses the new technology of the printed word as a factor in the intellectual operation of creating texts, and in the social equation of producing, marketing, and consuming them. It is only in the past century or so that new mechanical techniques have made for the emergence of a specialized role for the publisher. With the spread of electronic technology, the functions of this new role have been all but reversed. When previously it was the pub-lisher's role to match scarce material resources and long-winded labour processes with a fairly stable supply of texts, it has now become his task to match an ever-expanding supply of texts and an ever-increasing technical potential to print, to the limited resource of the reader's time and attention. At a stage when not some, but most published texts are never read by most of those for whom they were written, the publisher has turned from being a broker to being an arbiter. The quantitative potential of printing by computer has made for qualitative change in the process of publishing.

Even greater changes are involved when texts are not only multi-plied by computer technology, but written and multiplied to be read on a computer. Imagine a book that, on pushing a button, turns translucent but for those pages dealing with a particular matter—one selected by the reader himself. Envisage a book that yields to the reader confused over one passage a glimpse at com-parable passages selected from later chapters, or an index to which one may add a word of one's own choice. Visualize a book illus-trated not by static diagrams and photographic stills, but by images that move in order to demonstrate the sequence of processes implied in a flow chart.

Promising to readers and terrifying to authors as these specu-lations may be, they sound fanciful only because they attribute to a 'book' the possibilities of a videodisc. One could be forgiven for fighting shy of a word processor and computer talk, and yet feeling excited by the thought of how new electronic technology might allow one to think. Nobody can reasonably predict how electronic technologies will in future affect the written word and literate thought; it is possible, however, to get an idea by looking back at the past, and tracing their impact on the media to which they were first applied, those of the moving image in film and television.

As Anthony Smith points out in his essay, the pioneers of primitive cinema were aware of the possibility that their new technology could restructure perception, and adamant in their desire that it should. The best of them aimed not at a more refined illusion of movement as we are used to seeing it, but at new ways of perceiving it, and at discovering a new visual sensitivity. Cinema was a technology explicitly planned to restructure perception and create a new experience of visual thinking. Even after the invention of sound movies and the commercialization of illusionist cinema, new cinematic techniques have continued to develop and spread a keener visual sensitivity, and the television has had a noticeable effect on the way viewers can think of fiction or fact, distance or proximity, temporal sequence or synchrony.

The new visual media, argues Anthony Smith, have marshalled our perceptions into a new order, and have imposed a different bias and hierarchy on the way we use our senses and on the ways we think. It is a perceptual revolution that warrants comparison with the cognitive revolution ascribed to philosophical innovation among the Greeks at a time of spreading alphabetic literacy. None the less, such parallels must be pursued with a broad appreciation of the differences between literate and visual technologies: film and television share a highly corporate organization and widely collaborative labour processes, both of which deny the individualist, author-centred ethos of typographic culture. They both differ from writing and print also in their information strategy: unlike Gutenberg's strategy of multiplying complete copies of which all owners could make their own, usually incomplete use, electronic information technology is concerned not with physical multiplication but with access and interrogation: it aims at putting information at the user's fingertips when, and in so far as, it is required. Both the visual and the information media have ceased, finally, to rely on the five biological senses, and have created a sixth of their own: the process of digitization. Of course the human user continues to rely on his sense of vision, hearing, or touch when decoding or 'reading' information that has been electronically stored and organized. But as any computer programmer knows, the efficient handling of an electronic machine requires him to think himself in the digital mould, a 'perceptual artifice', as Smith calls it, that intervenes in the process of organizing information into 'bits'.

Given such fundamental differences between the literate technologies and electronic ones, their mutual relationship may well appear to be contrary and irreconcilable. But both Walter Ong and Anthony Smith stress how deeply print culture has left its imprint on the way in which we acquire, organize and use information. Literacy continues to be not only the technical foundation without which no society could build even an adding machine; it also remains the cognitive and perceptual seed-bed on which the new technologies feed. It is more than a figure of speech that lies behind such concepts as the 'video library', or visual or computer 'literacy'. Anthony Smith thus sees the future of the printed word not as a choice between book and screen, but as a question of convergence. Shadows of that convergence are already distinguishable within the distance of the next few years.

All contributors concerned with our present-day transition to new media approach it from clearly distinct angles. But whether speaking of it in the framework of a general proposition or from the experience of an academic publisher, whether describing literacy and 'secondary orality' in a part of the Third World or tracing the impact of visual media and digitization: they all agree in rejecting any simple idea of a pending choice between typographic and electronic culture. Rather, they emphasize that technological change demands a revaluation by which oral, literate, and secondary oral modes are recognized as interdependent, and with the help of which they can be creatively combined.

II

To think about the new audio-visual and information technologies thus necessarily involves thinking about literacy. There are numerous points at which Walter Ong's terminology, and his approach to writing as a technology, are reciprocated in the later contributors' assessments of the present transition. Such reciprocities are not all due to the contingent custom of one author referring to another. They may well reflect a reciprocity that underlies all our present attempts to grapple with literacy: it is only at the threshold of the electronic transition that we have become aware of what literacy means, represents, and may have done, to our ways of thinking.

Given that our conception of literacy and our conception of electronic technology thus condition each other, the enquiry has assumed a historical dimension. It must therefore be asked how far our knowledge of previous transitions may help us to form a more detached view of the impact of literacy in general. The question is tempting, but of doubtful legitimacy. There is ample room for doubt whether a generalized statement on literacy as such, let alone on its impact as such, is possible or useful. These doubts have been theorized in an exceptionally coherent way by Brian Street (1984).

Street takes issue with a number of students of literacy and with the protagonists and planners of literacy programmes and campaigns, who have argued that literacy invariably imparts such cognitive facilities as rational thought, critical analysis, and a systematic separation between personal judgement and disinterested, abstract argument. The theorists and the practitioners alike share one fallacy: that of imputing to literacy a set of supposedly inherent and unchanging qualities. To speak of 'the potentialities', 'the consequences', or the 'nature' of literacy, implies a view of literacy as an independent variable, a thing of itself, and an autonomous entity.

Street exposes the ethnocentric and ideological bias of this approach: its definitions of rationality and logic are circular, deriving from a self-validating equation of literacy and Western varieties of rational thought, and proceeding to define literacy in general as a source of rationality as such. Its ideological bias is untenable in the face of social-anthropological evidence, just as its view of language runs counter to recent trends in linguistics and socio-linguistics. All these shortcomings are characteristic of an approach that Street identifies as the 'autonomous model' of literacy.

Against this 'autonomous model', Street advances his own alternative, which makes use of such work as Smith (1978), Clanchy (1979), Graff (1979), and Cole and Scribner (1981). It is called the 'ideological model'. This model envisages literacy as an essentially ideological practice in that it only ever exists as a social practice in the context of other social practices, institutions, and power structures. In these contexts, the meaning and impact of literacy are never autonomous, but are constructed and used according to the specific practices of reading and writing—practices that are socially imparted and socially controlled. They depend on such factors as stratification, power differentials and ideological hegemony. Literacy thus cannot be discussed as one unified phenomenon and defined by inherent characteristics; it can be studied only as a highly variable social practice. Street indeed suggests: 'We would probably more appropriately refer to "literacies" than to a single "literacy"' (1984: 8).

Street's book is a timely and coherent challenge to a certain approach to literacy, although it remains difficult to assess precisely how widespread this approach has been. His refutation of the 'autonomous model' concentrates on two articles and an unpublished manuscript; the far more substantial work of Goody (1968, 1977) is criticized as much for having laid itself open to being misread as for having been misconceived. Street is certainly right in preferring the detailed textual criticism of selected sources to a sweeping treatment of the entire academic field of literacy studies; but it must remain difficult therefore to decide how far the proposed 'autonomous model' represents more than the failings of students given to adventurous generalization. Street, however, is fully aware that the 'autonomous model' 'is more often implicit in [the literature] produced as part of practical literacy programmes' than in the discourse of academics (1984: 1), and that both 'models' serve in a sense as 'ideal types' in order to emphasize different 'perspectives' on literacy (1984: 3). Certainly the influence of an autonomous perspective is most strongly felt in the implications and policies of official literacy programmes. In many of these, Street argues, it provides a spurious rhetoric of 'liberation' that is to cover the use of literacy as a means of consolidating ideological control. Such rhetoric is effectively demolished by Street's penetrating use of field data from an Iranian village and his poignant assessment of literacy campaigns in the Third World, the United States, and the United Kingdom. This practical orientation only increases the importance of Street's study, and the shadow of an 'autonomous model' is a timely warning also for academic students of literacy and their readers.

Literacy studies cannot progress unless they resist the temptations of 'reductionism' and of hypostasizing literacy as an autonomous agent. The contributors to this book agree that the consequences of literacy can be assessed only from specific historical evidence, and that it is up to empirical research to determine how far, and in which directions, literacy produced social and cultural effects. This is a difficult enterprise; both Walter Ong and Keith Thomas cite the work of Luria (1976) among Soviet peasants in the 1930s: in understanding cultural and mental changes, the effects of spreading literacy proved inextricable from other factors of social and economic change working simultaneously. Ioan Lewis stresses that the heightening sense of ethnic identities in Ethiopia may have as much to do with religious and political developments as with the existing literate traditions and their recent shifts. Literacy can certainly work as a liberating influence, as the process of cultural decolonization in Somalia shows (Andrzejewski 1981, Andrzejewski and Lewis 1964); but it can equally reinforce hierarchical divisions, as Keith Thomas shows for early modern England. Literate practices may not indeed gain any prominence even when they are relatively widespread. Thus Geza Vermes finds no evidence in Scripture or in Palestinian archaeology 'that the written word exerted much influence before the exile'. Texts may be declared charters and canonized as such, as was the Torah or, in Ethiopia, the Amharic *Kebra Nagast*; they are as often pushed aside as dead letter void of relevance.

Historical circumstances come in single sets, not in neatly comparable pairs; so do cultural practices of literacy. Literacy in general exists, after all, as a concept only—a concept, at that, of limited currency: there is no precise equivalent to the word in German, French, Polish, and probably other literate languages. How then can the effects and impact of literacy be approached? Should one speak, as Street (1984: 8) suggests, of literacies, rather than literacy? The new ending by itself does not of course spare us the question what class of phenomena the plural refers to. It is a useful reminder none the less of the task on which the further development of literacy theory may depend: a task of distinction between grades of literacy on the one hand, and domains of literacy on the other.

This collection can be read, as has been pointed out, as a sequence of proposition and disputations, or as a concerted approach to literacy in transition. A third way to read it may be as an enterprise in recognizing and applying these distinctions. Thus, Anna Davies stresses the need 'to enquire about the purposes for which each script is used and about the individuals who use it. Here we shall distinguish for example between scripts which are in use merely as reckoning or list-making devices and scripts with a wider range of uses; we shall also want to know for each script how many people were literate in it at any given moment, what grade of literacy they had, and what proportion they were of the community which used the script.' The distinction of grades of literacy may deserve particular emphasis. It is tempting for the usually highly literate reader of literacy studies to impute to the term his or her own experience of literacy. But historical computations of rates of literacy do not establish rates of literati. Similarly, Walter Ong's proposition that 'writing is a technology that restructures thought' should be kept separate from the experience of the academic who likes to think that the act of writing objectifies and refines his thoughts.

This distinction of grades of literacy necessitates a distinction of domains of literacy. Thus Geza Vermes's contribution on the Torah rightly begins by setting this text into the context of other uses of literacy, ranging from agricultural calendars to commemorative inscriptions and military communications. Ioan Lewis clearly distinguishes the differential impact of writing in different cultural spheres. Thus the Arabic literacy of Muslim religious specialists in Somalia has developed an entirely different dynamic from the schooled literacy in colonial languages and the recent spread of mother-tongue literacy over a wide range of domains. Keith Thomas rests his approach to the impact of literacy on a consistent distinction of abilities in reading and writing, and of attitudes to literacy and the written word. Thus he remarks on the emergence of an increasingly 'introspective relationship with the written word' which can be recognized in 'the greater prevalence of two distinct psychological types: the silent reader . . . and the private diarist'.

Such psychological types of literate personalities hold a key to a more discriminating view of the impact of literacy in any one period or culture. They are culturally specific, and they are images and collective representations of that culture itself. They may allow us to trace the effects of literacy on thought by tracing specific, culturally constructed forms of literate cognition. There are parallels to this venture of discernment in recent research on reading that has not yet penetrated literacy studies to its full extent. Engelsing (1973) has traced the social history of reading from feudal to industrial society in Germany, and has stressed the transition of reading patterns from the 'intensive' perusal of a few habitual texts to the 'extensive' practices of the browser, the subscriber to a journal, or other 'types'. Schenda (1977) follows the social history of popular literature and reading attitudes in the nineteenth century. Göpfert *et al.* (1975) have initiated an entire field of studies on current motivations and attitudes to reading, on the competition of printed matter with the new media of mass information and entertainment, and the changing role of booksellers and publishers—issues taken up from the angle of literacy studies by Adam Hodgkin and Anthony Smith in this collection.

The design of a sociological history of reading and reading attitudes has its roots, by and large, in literary history. Since the pioneering work of Leavis (1932) and Hoggart's seminal *Uses of Literacy* (1957), new perspectives on reading have been advanced from the field of media and communication studies; and the work of Williams (1961, 1962) and of the Centre for Contemporary Cultural Studies at Birmingham (Hall and Whannel 1964, Hall *et al.* 1980) have greatly furthered our understanding of the uses and reception of reading matter. Literacy studies, on the other hand, seem to be in a transition towards a tightly empirical history and sociology of writing as a cultural practice. They are, moreover, acutely aware of the importance of orality in understanding the effects of literacy—an awareness that is spreading also in folklore studies concerned with processes of interference between oral and literate modes (Wehse 1975, Assmann 1980).

'Literacy' and 'orality' are abstract concepts necessary to guide research, but, as Walter Ong has insisted, they must be studied in their interaction, and related anew in each cultural context. From their different angles, the contributors to this book can be seen to engage in a common project, one of differentiation and distinction. Taking them together, it seems possible to distinguish the practices of literacy according to a distinction of cultural domains in which literate and oral practices relate to each other in culturally specific ways, and according to a comparative typology of psychological and cognitive types of reading and writing, conceptualized in terms recognized in each culture itself.

Such a project of discernment is not the end of speaking of literacy in general. Rather, it allows us to see the dialectical relationship between literacy as a social fact and an individual act. This relationship is contained in the term 'literacy' itself. The word subsumes two distinct meanings, and this ambivalence may merit a brief note in conclusion.

III

The words 'literate' and 'literacy' refer to the individual ability or the social practice of reading and writing. Their current meanings, however, are a relatively recent development. The noun is a neologism of late nineteenth-century American origin; simultaneously the adjective was subjected to semantic shift. For most of its history, the word 'literate' was a synonym of 'literary', and to speak of a 'literate' person in English meant a man of letters, or a person of a literary turn of mind.

The invention of the noun and the shift of the adjective are of obvious historical interest. They occur some three hundred years after the words 'literate' and 'literacy' had been established in usage. These, however, meant both ignorance of literature and an inability to read or write. It was only at a time when mass illiteracy was being tackled and was crumbling, but when mass 'literacy' was not expected to produce 'literary' masses, that the new concepts began to circulate and spread. 'Literacy' and 'literate' were to express that new opposite of illiteracy which entailed an ability to read and write, but did not entail literary interests.

Similar neologisms appeared in French and German, but were there not based on such terms as *écriture* or *littéraire*, *Schrift* or *literarisch*, but were derived from the word for alphabet, producing such new words as *alphabétisme*, *analphabétisme*, *alphabétisation* in French, and *Analphabetentum* and *Alphabetisierung* in German. There is room for a comparative history of the circumstances, educational policies, and social concerns that gave rise, at certain junctures in the spread of 'literacy', to these new concepts. More importantly here, the contrast may serve to highlight the ambivalence implicit in the terms 'literacy' and 'literate'.

We speak of 'literacy' as a person's ability to master reading and, usually, writing. We also speak of 'literate cultures' or 'literate societies'. But a 'literate' society is hard to define. It would be simple if there were agreement that a certain number of literate individuals, however defined, would qualify a society as being 'literate'. It would be so simple that few have ever seriously suggested it. 'Literacy' is not an absolute quality. The thought of dividing human societies or cultures into literate and illiterate is attractive but useless. Ruth Finnegan (1973) has effectively refuted the notion of *Literacy versus Non-Literacy* as *the Great Divide.* Austro-German ethnologists, raised on the distinction between *Schriftkultur* and *Naturvölker*—thoughtful enough at least to name a positive opposite of literacy—have similarly discarded it as the oldest hat in the dusty wardrobe of evolutionist ideas.

We know little of any society that is totally illiterate, let alone unaware of the existence of scripts elsewhere; and we do not know of any society that is totally literate. Virtually all societies allowing detailed investigation are somewhere in between. It is probable that literacy rates of, say, 8 per cent and 80 per cent have different consequences in any society or culture. But what kind of texts would a person have to master to qualify as 'literate'? Patently, the answer depends on the specific historical, cultural, and social circumstances.

Different cultures produce different kinds of texts, and attach different weight even to ostensibly similar kinds of texts. To speak of 'literacy' thus involves speaking of more than individual ability to read and write ('literacy'). It involves culturally specific patterns of the circulation of texts. A society is 'literate' by virtue of its members entrusting certain social relationships to the circulation of texts. The circulation of texts is no longer merely an individual matter. It establishes social relationships that are controlled by consensus or by power, in much the same way as the circulation of spouses for marriage across social groups, or the circulation of money establish social relationships.

'Literacy' in any society is thus not defined by the mere presence of people able to read and write, but by the presence of patterns that regulate the circulation of texts. In an enquiry into the effects of literacy, this distinction between individual ability and social institution can be of help. In practice, the effects of a person's mastery and practice of reading or writing, and the effect of his or her society having entrusted particular social relationships to the circulation of texts are of course intimately connected and dependent upon each other. None the less, they need to be distinguished.

Crucially, changes in literacy rates or in the social distribution of particular literate skills can only be explained in terms of complex and dialectical relations obtaining between patterns of circulation and socially constructed meanings and uses, and the competences, needs, and desires of individuals. Rising literacy rates would be hard to understand if it were not for a disparity between the number of individual literates and the felt need for an increased or widened circulation of texts. If the circulation of texts were merely an immediate result of individual literacies, that is, if literacy were not also defined as a social institution, the desire to spread literate skills would hardly arise. A decline in literacy rates is similarly explicable only with reference to this distinction.

This distinction helps to make sense of the seeming paradox, implied by Walter Ong and substantiated by Keith Thomas, that literacy also affects illiterates that live in partially literate societies. It is the social patterns of conducting particular social relationships through the circulation of texts ('literacy') that affect even those who have no ability to read and write ('literacy'). In speaking of the effects or the impact of literacy, we thus speak of two things at once: the effects of a social institution, and the impact of an individual ability or practice. The ambivalence is implicit in the word 'literacy' itself; it is of the essence of the concept, and cannot even be avoided by substituting the word 'writing'.

'Writing' most obviously refers to the act of writing, an act which, however defined, is carried out by individual action. The word is also used, however, to stand for the existence or use of script in any one society. The ambivalence does not of itself cause confusion. When reading an article called 'Writing in China', we know from the context whether it is a scholar's examination of the social uses of scripts or texts, or a novelist's essay on his individual experience. The ambivalence, however, can take its toll when speaking of the effects or the impact of 'writing'. There are consequences of writing as an individual act, none of which illiterates are likely to suffer or enjoy, and other consequences that flow from writing *qua* the social uses of scripts and texts, many of which affect illiterates too. These consequences need to be distinguished all the more as the crude dichotomy between 'literate' and 'illiterate' is refined.

Both terms, 'literacy' and 'writing', thus span the conventional division between social institution and individual ability, or between cultural fact and individual act. To research into the impact of literacy or of writing, is *perforce* to research into a relationship between social fact and individual experience, or in anthropological parlance, between culture and personality.

The two pairs are not of course pairs of opposites, but functions of each other. Individuals are not microcosms of their societies, and culture is not a xerox machine turning out cloned personalities; the effects of reading or writing oneself, and the impact of living in a society predicated on the circulation of texts are closely related to each other. The ambivalence of the word 'literacy' in subsuming both these aspects is anything but a semantic misfortune. It may remind us that the social and the cognitive impacts of literacy, 'interiorized' as an institution or as a habit of thought, are in practice tied to each other. None the less, they must be distinguished in analysis. The task that may face literacy studies is that of differentiating between the two aspects of 'literacy', and of distinguishing the different kinds of behaviour and social relations that particular cultures have developed under their impact.

The task is a new one, and by no means straightforward. The approach which many of the following essays exemplify, and which seems likely to prove most fruitful, is the study of literacy at periods of transition—periods when, quantitatively or qualitatively, the social uses of literacy and individual literate abilities seem to be out of step. It was in such a period that *literati* were moved to recognize literacy as an object of enquiry and to coin a new word for it, and it is our own period of transition to new media that has sharpened our perception of the consequences of literacy for our ways of thinking. It is inescapable that whatever we say about literacy is tied to our own preconceptions and experiences of using literacy. It is possible, however, to become more aware of these preconceptions by a historical approach to literacy in other phases of transition.

REFERENCES

Anderson, C. A. 1966: 'Literacy and Schooling on the Development Threshold: Some Historical Cases', in C. A. Anderson and M. Bowman (eds.), *Education and Economic Development*. London: Cassel.

Andrzejewski, B. W. 1981: 'The Survival of National Culture in Somalia during and after the Colonial Era', in *N.E.A. Journal of Research on North East Africa*, I. 1: 3–15. Oxford.

—— and I. M. Lewis 1964: *Somali Poetry: An Introduction*. Oxford: Clarendon Press.

Assmann, A. 1980: 'Mündlichkeit, Schriftlichkeit. Folklore und Literatur.
—Grenzen und Übergänge'. Paper delivered at Conference 'Mündlichkeit und Schriftlichkeit', University of Bielefeld, 20–22 Nov. 1980.

Bataille, L. (ed.) 1976: *A Turning Point for Literacy. Adult Education for Development. The Spirit and Declaration of Persepolis.* Proceedings of the International Symposium for Literacy, Persepolis, Iran, 1975. Oxford: Pergamon Press.

Cabral, A. 1975*a*: *L'Arme de la théorie.* Paris, Maspero.

—— 1975*b*: *La Pratique révolutionnaire.* Paris, Maspero.

Clanchy, M. 1979: *From Memory to Written Record, England 1066–1307.* Cambridge, Mass.: Harvard University Press. London: Edward Arnold.

Cressy, D. 1980: *Literacy and the Social Order: Reading and Writing in Tudor and Stuart England.* Cambridge: Cambridge University Press.

Cole, M. and S. Scribner 1981: *The Psychology of Literacy.* Cambridge, Mass.: Harvard University Press.

Eisenstein, E. 1979: *The Printing Press as an Agent of Change: Communications and Cultural Transformations in Early-Modern Europe,* 2 vols. New York: Cambridge University Press.

Eltern 1984: 'Nix lesen, nix schreiben—Urmensch bleiben', in *Eltern,* 4: 157–9, ed. Kurt Gessl. Munich: Gruner & Jahr.

Engelsing, R. 1973: *Analphabetentum und Lektüre. Zur Sozialgeschichte des Lesens zwischen feudaler und industrieller Gesellschaft.* Stuttgart: Metzler.

Finnegan, R. 1973: 'Literacy versus Non-Literacy: The Great Divide?', in R. Horton and R. Finnegan (eds.), *Modes of Thought.* London: Faber.

Freire, P. 1972: *Pedagogy of the Oppressed.* Harmondsworth: Penguin.

—— 1976: *Education: The Practice of Freedom.* London: Writers' and Readers' Publishing Cooperative.

—— 1979: 'Letter to Adult Education Workers', in M. D. de Oliveira (ed.), *Guinea-Bissau '79: Learning by Living and Doing.* IDAC Document no. 18. Geneva: Institute of Cultural Action.

Furet, F. and J. Ozouf 1982: *Reading and Writing. Literacy in France from Calvin to Jules Ferry.* Cambridge: Cambridge University Press.

Gellner, E. 1983: *Nations and Nationalism.* Oxford: Blackwell.

Goody, J. (ed.) 1968: *Literacy in Traditional Societies.* Cambridge: Cambridge University Press.

—— 1977: *The Domestication of the Savage Mind.* Cambridge: Cambridge University Press.

Göpfert, H., R. Meyer, L. Muth, W. Rüegg (eds.) 1975: *Lesen und Leben.* Frankfurt-on-Main: Buchhändlervereinigung.

Graff, H. J. 1979: *The Literacy Myth: Literacy and Social Structure in the 19th Century City.* New York: Academic Press.

—— (ed.) 1982: *Literacy and Social Development in the West. A Reader.* Cambridge: Cambridge University Press.

Hall, S. and P. Whannel 1964: *The Popular Arts*. London: Hutchinson.

——, D. Dobson, A. Lowe, P. Willis (eds.) 1980: *Culture, Media and Language*. Birmingham University Centre for Contemporary Cultural Studies series. London: Hutchinson.

Havelock, E. A. 1963: *Preface to Plato*. Oxford: Basil Blackwell.

—— 1976: *Origins of Western Literacy*. Toronto: Ontario Institute for the Study of Education.

—— 1983: 'The Linguistic Task of the Presocratics. Part One: Ionian Science in Search of an Abstract Vocabulary', in K. Robb (ed.), *Language and Thought in Early Greek Philosophy*, 7–82. La Salle, Ill.: Hegeler Institute Monist Library of Philosophy.

Hoggart, R. 1957: *The Uses of Literacy*. London: Chatto & Windus. Harmondsworth: Pelican.

Innis, H. 1950: *Empire and Communications*. London: Oxford University Press.

Johansson, E. 1977: 'The History of Literacy in Sweden, in Comparison with Some Other Countries', in *Educational Reports*, Umea, no. 12: 2–42. Umea University. Reprinted in Graff, H. J. (ed.) 1981: 151–82.

Leavis, Q. D. 1932: *Fiction and the Reading Public*. London: Chatto & Windus.

Lord, A. B. 1960: *The Singer of Tales*. Harvard Studies in Comparative Literature, no. 24. Cambridge, Mass.: Harvard University Press.

Luria, A. R. 1976: *Cognitive Development: Its Cultural and Social Foundations*. Cambridge, Mass.: Harvard University Press.

McLuhan, M. 1962: *The Gutenberg Galaxy*. Toronto: Toronto University Press.

Parry, M. 1971: *The Making of Homeric Verse: The Collected Papers of Milman Perry*, ed. Adam Parry. Oxford: Clarendon Press.

Pattison, R. 1982: *On Literacy. The Politics of the Word from Homer to the Age of Rock*. Oxford: Oxford University Press.

Schenda, R. 1977: *Volk ohne Buch. Studien zur Sozialgeschichte der populären Lesestoffe, 1770–1910*. Munich: DTV Deutscher Taschenbuchverlag.

Street, B. V. 1984: *Literacy in Theory and Practice*. Cambridge: Cambridge University Press.

Smith, M. 1978: 'Vai Literacy Project: Working Paper I'. Unpublished manuscript, cited in Street, B. V. 1984.

Wehse, R. 1975: 'Broadside Ballad and Folksong. Oral Tradition versus Literary Tradition', in *Folklore Forum*, viii. 1: 324–34. Bloomington, Ind.: Folklore Forum Society.

Williams, R. 1961: *The Long Revolution*. London: Chatto & Windus.

—— 1962: *Communications*. Harmondsworth: Penguin.

WRITING IS A TECHNOLOGY THAT RESTRUCTURES THOUGHT

WALTER J. ONG, SJ

I

LITERACY is imperious. It tends to arrogate to itself supreme power by taking itself as normative for human expression and thought. This is particularly true in high-technology cultures, which are built on literacy of necessity and which encourage the impression that literacy is an always to be expected and even natural state of affairs. The term 'illiterate' itself suggests that persons belonging to the class it designates are deviants, defined by something they lack, namely literacy. Moreover, in high-technology cultures—which, more and more, are setting the style for cultures across the world— since literacy is regarded as so unquestionably normative and nor- mal, the deviancy of illiterates tends to be thought of as lack of a simple mechanical skill. Illiterates should learn writing as they learned to tie their shoe-laces or to drive a car. Such views of writing as simply a mechanical skill obligatory for all human beings distort our understanding of what is human if only because they block understanding of what natural human mental processes are before writing takes possession of consciousness. These views also by the same token block understanding of what writing itself really is. For without a deep understanding of the normal oral or oral-aural con- sciousness and noetic economy of humankind before writing came along, it is impossible to grasp what writing accomplished.

Recent research work, however, in the field and in the library, is offering the opportunity to overcome our chirographic (and typo- graphic) bias. This work has deepened our understanding of what I have styled primary orality, the orality of cultures with no knowl- edge at all of writing, as contrasted with what I have styled second- ary orality, the electronic orality of radio and television, which

Some material in the first part of this article has been adapted from the author's 'Writing and the Evolution of Consciousness', in: *Mosaic* (University of Manitoba), xviii (1985), 1-10, with the permission of the editor.

grows out of high-literacy cultures, depending for its invention and operation on the widespread cultivation of writing and reading. Classical scholars, from Milman Parry—the prime mover in the orality–literacy universe—through Albert Lord, Eric Havelock, and others, sociologists and linguists such as Jack Goody, Wallace Chafe, and Deborah Tannen, cultural anthropologists such as Jeff Opland, historians such as M. T. Clanchy, and many others from even more diversified fields, including the late Marshall McLuhan, the greatest diversifier of all, have opened vistas into primary orality which enable us better to understand differences between the oral and the literate mind. My own work in opening such vistas, for whatever it is worth, began deep in Renaissance and earlier intellectual history, and has moved into the present, without, I hope, losing live contact with the past. We can now view in better perspective the world of writing in which we live, see better what this world really is, and what functionally literate human beings really are—that is, beings whose thought processes do not grow out of simply natural powers but out of these powers as structured, directly or indirectly, by the technology of writing. Without writing, the literate mind would not and could not think as it does, not only when engaged in writing but even when it is composing its thoughts in oral form.

Functionally literate persons, those who regularly assimilate discourse such as this, are not simply thinking and speaking human beings but chirographically thinking and speaking human beings (latterly conditioned also by print and by electronics). The fact that we do not commonly feel the influence of writing on our thoughts shows that we have interiorized the technology of writing so deeply that without tremendous effort we cannot separate it from ourselves or even recognize its presence and influence. If functionally literate persons are asked to think of the word 'nevertheless', they will all have present in imagination the letters of the word—vaguely perhaps, but unavoidably—in handwriting or typescript or print. If they are asked to think of the word 'nevertheless' for two minutes, 120 seconds, without ever allowing any letters at all to enter their imaginations, they cannot comply. A person from a completely oral background of course has no such problem. He or she will think only of the real word, a sequence of sounds, 'ne-ver-the-less'. For the real word 'nevertheless', the sounded word, cannot ever be present all at once, as written words deceptively seem to be. Sound exists only when it is going out of existence. By the time I get to the 'the-less', the 'ne-ver' is gone. To the extent that it makes all of a word appear present at once, writing falsifies. Recalling sounded words is like recalling a bar of music, a melody, a sequence in time. A word is an event, a happening, not a thing, as letters make it appear to be. So is thought: 'This is paper' is an occurrence, an event in time. We grasp truth articulately only in events. Articulated truth has no permanence. Full truth is deeper than articulation. We find it hard to recognize this obvious truth, so deeply has the fixity of the written word taken possession of our consciousness.

The oral world as such distresses literates because sound is evan-escent. Typically, literates want words and thoughts pinned down—though it is impossible to 'pin down' an event. The mind trained in an oral culture does not feel the literate's distress: it can operate with exquisite skill in the world of sounds, events, evanescences. How does it manage? Basically, in its noetic operations it uses for-mulaic structures and procedures that stick in the mind to comple-ment and counteract the evanescent: proverbs and other fixed sayings, epithets, that is, standard, expected qualifiers (the *sturdy* oak, the *brave* warrior, *wise* Nestor, *clever* Odysseus), numerical sets (the three Graces, the seven deadly sins, the five senses, and so on), balance, rhythms of all sorts ('Blessed are the poor in spirit, for theirs is the kingdom of heaven')—anything to make it easy to call back what Homer recognized were 'winged words'. Primary oral culture also keeps its thinking close to the human life world, personalizing things and issues, and storing knowledge in stories. Categories are unstable mnemonically. Stories you can remember. In its typical mindset, the oral sensibility is out to hold things to-gether, to make and retain agglomerates, not to analyse (which means to take things apart)—although, since all thought is to some degree analytic, it does analyse to a degree. Pressed by the need to manage an always fugitive noetic universe, the oral world is basic-ally conservative. Exploratory thinking is not unknown, but it is relatively rare, a luxury orality can little afford, for energies must be husbanded to keep on constant call the evanescent knowledge that the ages have so laboriously accumulated. Everybody, or almost everybody, must repeat and repeat and repeat the truths that have come down from the ancestors. Otherwise these truths will escape, and culture will be back on square one, where it started before the ancestors got the truths from their ancestors.

I have discussed these formulaic and narrative strategies in *Orality and Literacy* (1982). In 1985, John Miles Foley's new *Oral-Formulaic Theory and Research* shows, as nothing has ever done before, how universal such strategies are across the globe and across the centuries. Foley provides summaries of over 1,800 books and articles covering 90 different language areas.

Our literate world of visually processed sounds has been totally unfamiliar to most human beings, who always belonged, and often still belong to this oral world. *Homo sapiens* has been around for some 30,000 years, to take a conservative figure. The oldest script, Mesopotamian cuneiform, is less than 6,000 years old (the alphabet less than 4,000). Of all the tens of thousands of languages spoken in the course of human history only a tiny fraction—Edmonson (1971: 323) calculates about 106—have ever been committed to writing to a degree sufficient to have produced a literature, and most have never been written at all. Of the 4,000 or so languages spoken today, only around 78 have a literature (Edmonson 1971: 332). For some of the others linguists have devised more or less adequate ways of writing them, with results that appear in linguistics publications and convention papers that have no noteworthy effect at all on the actual users of the language. Dr C. Andrew Hofling has recently completed a linguistic study of discourse in the Itza Mayan language which transcribes the language in the Roman alphabet. This transcription is essential for linguistic studies, but it is useless, inconsequential, for the Itza Maya themselves. With only some 500 speakers, the language has no effective way of developing a literate culture. Most languages in the world today exist in comparable conditions. Those who think of the text as the paradigm of all discourse need to face the fact that only the tiniest fraction of languages have ever been written or ever will be. Most have disappeared or are fast disappearing, untouched by textuality. Hardcore textualism is snobbery, often hardly disguised.

Only in recent centuries have human beings generally had the idea that a language *could* be written, and even today many peoples do not believe their language can be written. In Dayton, Ohio, on 25 February 1983, I saw a videotape of a Methodist missionary and linguist who had worked out an alphabetization of a previously unwritten language in the South Pacific and witnessed her difficulty in convincing the speakers of the language that she could write down *their* utterances. They believed that only the languages they knew as written, such as English or French, *could* be written.

All this is not to deny that spoken languages are all amenable to conversion into writing (always with only partial success or accuracy) or that, given the human condition and the advantages conferred by writing, the invention of writing, and even of alphabetic writing, was sure to occur somewhere in the evolution of culture and consciousness. But to say that language *is* writing is, at best, uninformed. It provides egregious evidence of the unreflective chirographic and/or typographic squint that haunts us all.

II

Writing was an intrusion, though an invaluable intrusion, into the early human lifeworld, much as computers are today. It has lately become fashionable in some linguistic circles to refer to Plato's condemnation of writing in the *Phaedrus* and the Seventh Letter. What is seldom if ever noticed, however, is that Plato's objections against writing are essentially the very same objections commonly urged today against computers by those who object to them (Ong 1982: 79–81). Writing, Plato has Socrates say in the *Phaedrus*, is inhuman, pretending to establish outside the mind what in reality can only be in the mind. Writing is simply a thing, something to be manipulated, something inhuman, artificial, a manufactured product. We recognize here the same complaint that is made against computers: they are artificial contrivances, foreign to human life.

Secondly, Plato's Socrates complains, a written text is basically unresponsive. If you ask a person to explain his or her statement, you can get at least an attempt at explanation: if you ask a text, you get nothing except the same, often stupid words which called for your question in the first place. In the modern critique of the computer, the same objection is put, 'Garbage in, garbage out'. So deeply are we into literacy that we fail commonly to recognize that this objection applies every bit as much to books as to computers. If a book states an untruth, ten thousand printed refutations will do nothing to the printed text: the untruth is there for ever. This is why books have been burnt. Texts are essentially contumacious.

Thirdly, Plato's Socrates urges, writing destroys memory. Those who use writing will become forgetful, relying on an external source for what they lack in internal resources. Writing weakens the mind.

Today, some parents and others fear that pocket calculators provide an external resource for what ought to be the internal resource of memorized multiplication tables. Presumably, constant repetition of multiplication tables might produce more and more Albert Einsteins. Calculators weaken the mind, relieve it of the setting-up exercises that keep it strong and make it grow. (Significantly, the fact that the computer manages multiplication and other computation so much more effectively than human beings do, shows how little the multiplication tables have to do with real thinking.)

Fourthly, in keeping with the agonistic mentality of oral cultures, their tendency to view everything in terms of interpersonal struggle, Plato's Socrates also holds it against writing that the written word cannot defend itself as the natural spoken word can: real speech and thought always exist essentially in the context of struggle. Writing is passive, out of it, in an unreal, unnatural world. So, it seems, are computers: if you punch the keys they will not fight back on their own, but only in the way they have been programmed to do.

Those who are disturbed about Plato's misgivings about writing will be even more disturbed to find that print created similar misgivings when it was first introduced. Hieronimo Squarciafico, who in fact promoted the printing of the Latin classics, also argued in 1477 that already 'abundance of books makes men less studious' (Ong 1982: 80). Even more than writing does, print destroys memory and enfeebles the mind by relieving it of too much work (the pocket calculator complaint once more), downgrading the wise man and wise woman in favour of the pocket compendium.

One weakness in Plato's position is that he put these misgivings about writing into writing, just as one weakness in antiprint positions is that their proponents put their objections into print, and one weakness in anti-computer positions is that they are articulated in articles or books printed from tapes composed on computer terminals. The law at work here is: once the word is technologized, there is no really effective way to criticize its condition without the aid of the technology you are criticizing. The complaints about these three inventions are all the same because writing and print and the computer are all ways of technologizing the word.

The new technology of writing, it is now clear, was operating in Plato's lifeworld in ways far too convoluted for even Plato to understand. The technology of writing was not merely useful to Plato for broadcasting his critique of writing, but it also had been responsible for bringing the critique into existence. Although there was no way for Plato to be explicitly aware of the fact, his philosophically analytic thought, including his analysis of the effects of writing, was possible only because of the effects that writing was having on mental processes. We know that totally oral peoples, intelligent and wise though they often are, are incapable of the protracted, intensive linear analysis that we have from Plato's Socrates. Even when he talks, Plato's Socrates is using thought forms brought into being by writing. In fact, as Eric Havelock has beautifully shown in his *Preface to Plato* (1963), Plato's entire epistemology was unwittingly a programmed rejection of the archaic preliterate world of thought and discourse. This world was oral, mobile, warm, personally interactive (you needed live people to produce spoken words). It was the world represented by the poets, whom Plato would not allow in his Republic, because, although Plato could not formulate it this way, their thought processes and modes of expression were disruptive of the cool, analytic processes generated by writing.

The Platonic ideas are not oral, not sounded, not mobile, not warm, not personally interactive. They are silent, immobile, in themselves devoid of all warmth, impersonal and isolated, not part of the human lifeworld at all but utterly above and beyond it, paradigmatic abstractions. Plato's term *idea*, form, is in fact visually based, coming from the same root as the Latin *videre*, meaning to see, and such English derivatives as *vision, visible,* or *video*. In the older Greek form, a digamma had preceded the iota: *videa* or *widea*. Platonic form was form conceived of by analogy precisely with visible form. Despite his touting of *logos* and speech, the Platonic ideas in effect modelled intelligence not so much on hearing as on seeing. The visual model favoured clarity, but also shallowness. 'I see what you say' lacks the depth of 'I hear what you say.' Plato of course was not at all fully aware of the unconscious forces at work in his psyche to produce his literate reaction, or overreaction, to a lingering, and by his time retardant, orality. But he unconsciously adjusted to the threat of shallowness in his 'idea' philosophy by giving his thought what is often called a poetic cast and by avowing that the depths of truth not only escape writing but also even oral articulation.

III

In downgrading writing, Plato was thinking of writing as an external, alien technology, as many people today think of the computer. Because we have by today so deeply interiorized writing, made it so much a part of ourselves, as Plato's age had not yet made it fully a part of itself, we find it difficult to consider writing to be a technology as we commonly assume printing and the computer to be. Yet writing (and especially alphabetic writing) is a technology, calling for the use of tools and other equipment, styli or brushes or pens, carefully prepared surfaces such as paper, animal skins, strips of wood, as well as inks or paints, and much more. Writing technologies have differed in different parts of the world. In their own indigenous technologies of writing, East Asia—China, Korea, and Japan—typically used not pens but brushes, not liquid ink in inkhorns or inkwells, but ink blocks, on which the wet brush was rubbed as in making water-colour paintings, in this sense 'painting' rather than 'writing' (etymologically, 'scratching') their texts.

In *From Memory to Written Record: England 1066–1307*, M. T. Clanchy (1979) has an entire chapter entitled 'The Technology of Writing'. He explains how in the West through the Middle Ages and earlier almost all those devoted to writing regularly used the services of a scribe because the physical labour writing involved—scraping and polishing the animal skin or parchment, whitening it with chalk, resharpening goose-quill pens with what we still call a penknife, mixing ink, and all the rest—interfered with thought and composition. Chaucer's 'Wordes unto Adam, His Owne Scriveyn' humorously expressed the author's resentment at having to 'rubbe and scrape' to correct his scribe Adam's own carelessness in plying his craft. Today's ballpoint pens, not to mention our typewriters and word processors or the paper we use, are high-technology products, but we seldom advert to the fact because the technology is concentrated in the factories that produce such things, rather than at the point of production of the text itself, where the technology is concentrated in a manuscript culture.

Although we take writing so much for granted as to forget that it is a technology, writing is in a way the most drastic of the three technologies of the word. It initiated what printing and electronics only continued, the physical reduction of dynamic sound to quiescent space, the separation of the word from the living present, where alone real, spoken words exist.

IV

Once reduced to space, words are frozen and in a sense dead. Yet there is a paradox in the fact that the deadness of the written or printed text, its removal from the living human lifeworld, its rigid visual fixity, assures its endurance and its potential for being resurrected into limitless living contexts by a limitless number of living readers. The dead, thing-like text has potentials far outdistancing those of the simply spoken word. The complementary paradox, however, is that the written text, for all its permanence, means nothing, is not even a text, except in relationship to the spoken word. For a text to be intelligible, to deliver its message, it must be reconverted into sound, directly or indirectly, either really in the external world or in the auditory imagination. All verbal expression, whether put into writing, print, or the computer, is ineluctably bound to sound forever.

Nevertheless, by contrast with natural, oral speech, writing is completely artificial. There is no way to write 'naturally'. Oral speech is fully natural to human beings in the sense that every human being in every culture who is not physiologically or psychologically impaired learns to talk. Moreover, while talk implements conscious life, its use wells up naturally into consciousness out of unconscious or subconscious depths, though of course with the conscious as well as unconscious co-operation of society. Despite the fact that they govern articulation and thought processes themselves, grammar rules or structures normally originate, live, and function far below the level at which articulation functions. You can know how to use the grammatical rules or structures and even how to set up new rules or structures that function clearly and effectively without being able to state what they are. Of all the hundreds of thousands of grammar rules or structures that have been at work in all the tens of thousands of languages and dialects of humankind, only the tiniest fraction have ever been articulated at all.

Writing or script differs as such from speech in that it is not inevitably learned by all psychologically or physiologically unimpaired persons, even those living in highly literate cultures. Moreover, the use of writing or script does not inevitably well up out of the unconscious without the aid of stated rules. The process of putting spoken language into writing is governed by consciously contrived, articulated procedures: for example, a certain pictogram will be consciously determined to stand for a certain specified word or concept, or *a* will be consciously ruled to represent a certain phoneme, *b* another, and so on. (This is not at all to deny that the writer-reader situation created by writing is deeply involved with unconscious processes which are at work in composing written texts once one has learned the explicit, consciously controlled rules for transposing sound into a visual code.)

To say writing is artificial is not to condemn it but to praise it. Like other artificial creations and indeed more than any other, writing is utterly invaluable and indeed essential for the realization of fuller, interior, human potentials. Technologies are not mere exterior aids but also interior transformations of consciousness, and never more than when they affect the word. Such transformations of consciousness can be uplifting, at the same time that they are in a sense alienating. By distancing thought, alienating it from its original habitat in sounded words, writing raises consciousness. Alienation from a natural milieu can be good for us and indeed is in many ways essential for fuller human life. To live and to understand fully, we need not only proximity but also distance. This writing provides for, thereby accelerating the evolution of consciousness as nothing else before it does.

Technologies are artificial, but—paradox again—artificiality is natural to human beings. Technology, properly interiorized, does not degrade human life but on the contrary enhances it. The modern orchestra, for example, is a result of high technology. A clarinet is an instrument, which is to say a tool. A piano is an intricate, hand-powered machine. An organ is a huge machine, with sources of power—pumps, bellows, electric generators, motors—in motion before the organ is touched by its operator. Antiquity had no orchestras such as ours because it was unable to make any kind of instrument, musical or other, with the precision tooling even of a clarinet. Its maximum experience of precision was at the level of a good pair of scissors. Modern precision tooling has its roots in the late Middle Ages and its first major achievement was printing from movable alphabetic type.

A modern orchestra is the product of precision-tooled technology. Beethoven's scores consist of almost innumerable, precise directions to highly-trained technicians, specifying exactly how they are to use their individual tools. *Legato*: do not take your finger off one piano key until you have hit the next. *Staccato*: hit the key and take your finger off immediately. And so on for thousands of actions which musicians must practise until mechanically perfect. To be a first-rate musician, a *sine qua non* is to be a superb technician. There is no substitute for mechanical mastery of the tools.

As musicologists well know, it is pointless to object to electronic compositions, as non-musicologists sometimes do, on the grounds that the sounds come out of a mechanical contrivance. What do you think the sounds of a piano come out of, not to mention an organ? Or the sounds of a clarinet or bassoon or even a whistle? These things are all mechanical contrivances. The fact is that by using the mechanical contrivance a clarinettist or pianist or an organist can express something poignantly human that cannot be expressed without the mechanical contrivance. To achieve such expression effectively, of course, the musician has to have interiorized the technology, made the tool or machine a second nature, a psychological part of himself or herself. Art imitates nature. Art follows nature, and joins itself to nature. Art is second nature. But it is not nature. *Natura* in Latin, like *physis* in Greek, means birth. We are not born with art but add it to ourselves. Mastering a musical tool, making it one's own, calls for years of mechanical 'practice', learning how we can make the tool do mechanically all that it can do. Little boys and girls know how boring it can be. Yet such shaping of the tool to one's self, learning a technological skill, is hardly dehumanizing. The use of a technology can enrich the human psyche, enlarge human spirit, set it free, intensify its interior life.

I instance the modern orchestra here to make the point that writing is an even more deeply interiorized technology than the performance of instrumental music is. To understand what writing is, which means to understand it in relation to its past, to orality, one must honestly face the fact that it is a technology.

V

Writing, in the strict sense of the word, as has already been seen, was a very late development in human history. The first script, or true writing, that we know was developed among the Sumerians in Mesopotamia only around the year 3500 BC, less than 6,000 years ago. The alphabet, which was invented only once, so that every alphabet in the world derives directly or indirectly from the original Semitic alphabet, came into existence only around 1500 BC.

Speech is ancient, archaic. Writing is brand-new. Can one make out a case for some sort of archaic writing earlier than 6,000 years ago? It is of course possible to count as 'writing' any semiotic mark, that is, any visible or sensible mark which an individual makes and assigns a meaning to—a simple scratch on a rock or a notch on a stick, for example. If this is what is meant by writing, the antiquity of writing is perhaps comparable to the antiquity of speech. However, investigations of writing which take 'writing' to mean any visible or sensible mark with an assigned meaning merge writing with purely biological behaviour. When does a footprint or a deposit of faeces or urine (used by many species of animals for communication) become 'writing'? Using the term 'writing' in this extended sense to include any semiotic marking trivializes its meaning. The critical and unique breakthrough into new kinds of noetic operations and new worlds of knowledge was achieved within human consciousness not when simple semiotic marking was devised but when what we ordinarily mean by writing was developed, that is, when a coded system of visible marks was invented whereby a writer could determine, in effect without limit, the exact words and sequence of words that a reader would generate from a given text. This is what we regularly mean today by writing or script. We have to say 'in effect . . . the exact words' because no form, even of the alphabet, will always eliminate all ambiguities. The notation 'read' on a document may be the imperative (rhyming with 'bead') and mean 'read this' or it may be the past participle (rhyming with 'head') and mean 'this has been read'. But a true writing system will reduce ambiguities to a negligible minimum and make those that occur readily clarifiable.

Of course, writing is not suddenly 'invented' but grows out of orality by stages. Hence it cannot be understood in depth without circumstantial familiarity with the primary orality which is its seedbed. Discussions of writing which ignore its roots in orality and restrict themselves to alphabetic printed texts from the age of Romanticism on can produce effects which are interesting often because they are unavoidably distorted.

All writing systems do not have the same psychic or even neurophysiological structures or effects. Most studies investigating psychic, intellectual, and cultural contrasts between oral and writing cultures have looked only to contrasts between orality and alphabetic writing. The effects of other writing systems have just begun to be explored. For example, recent research (Tzeng and Wang 1983) has shown that readers of Chinese script use the right cerebral hemisphere significantly more than do readers of alphabetic script, which is geared more to the analytic left hemisphere. Such studies need to be developed still more.

Writing, in the ordinary sense of a coded system of visible marks enabling a writer to determine, in effect without limit, the exact words and sequence of words that a reader will generate from a given text, is the most momentous of all human technological inventions. It is not a mere appendage or accessory to oral speech. Because it moves speech drastically from the oral-aural or voice-and-ear world to a new sensory world, that of vision, writing transforms speech and thought as well. Notches on sticks and other *aides-mémoire* can lead up to writing, but they do not restructure the human lifeworld as true writing does. And no other writing system restructures the human lifeworld so drastically as alphabetic writing. Or so democratically, for the alphabet is relatively easy to learn. By contrast, Chinese character writing, though more aesthetically and semantically rich than alphabetic writing can ever hope to be, is élitist, despite heroic efforts to democratize its use. Its total mastery demands more time than most people can afford. As is well known, the People's Republic of China is undertaking to teach all its populace Mandarin, the largest of the many Chinese languages (referred to as 'dialects' customarily but misleadingly, for they are mutually incomprehensible when spoken). If and when everyone can speak Mandarin, it is quite certain, to my mind, that the alphabet will be introduced—with incalculable losses to literature but massive operational gains elsewhere.

VI

In treating of the effects of writing one has to guard against reductionism. All changes in social and noetic structures that can be identified after writing is introduced are not due simply to writing. Writing itself has social causes. It grows, for example, first in urban environments for use in recording ownership and related uses. Throughout its history, writing interacts massively with all sorts of social structures and practices, so that it by no means follows exactly the same development in all cultures (see Graff 1981). Although certain general cross-cultural patterns are identifiable, in various transitional cultures there are various kinds of interfaces between literacy and orality and various kinds and amounts of oral residue (Goody and Watt 1968, Ong 1982, and the many references there).

But if there is no warrant for reductionism, there is more than ample warrant for relationism. Once writing is introduced into a culture and grows to more than marginal status, it interacts with noetic and social structures and practices often in a bewildering variety of ways, as, for example, Brian Stock has shown in great detail for parts of Western Europe in the eleventh and twelfth centuries. Sooner or later, and often very quickly, literacy affects marketing and manufacturing, agriculture and stock-raising and the whole of economic life, political structures and activities, religious life and thought, family structures, social mobility, modes of transportation (a literate communication system laid the straight Roman roads and made the ancient Roman Empire, as Innis long ago pointed out), and so on *ad infinitum*. Even informal person-to-person conversations between literates are not structured like those among persons in a primary oral culture. Simple queries for information acquire a new status, for oral cultures typically use words less for information and more for operational, interpersonal purposes than do chirographic and typographic cultures. Writing is only one of the various developments making for the transformation of consciousness and of society, but once writing takes over, it appears to be the most crucial development of all. Almost everything in the noetic and social structures of a society where writing has been widely interiorized relates in one way or another to writing, although just how a particular phenomenon does so has to be examined carefully in any given case in any given culture.

VII

One of the most generalizable effects of writing is separation. Separation is also one of the most telling effects of writing and hence can serve here to give some final form to this discussion. Writing is diaeretic. It divides and distances, and it divides and distances all sorts of things in all sorts of ways. Distancing or 'distanciation' is one of the effects of writing commonly discussed by those coming from the Husserlian and Heideggerian traditions, such as Paul Ricoeur (1981), but their discussions are highly specialized and abstractly schematic, paying little if any attention to the actual history of writing, its growth out of orality, or to the sociopsychological complexities this history presents us with—that is, to the sort of things earlier detailed here. Their phenomenology is fundamentally synchronic, not diachronic. And without a diachronic phenomenology, our present situation does not show its true contours for we do not become aware of how matters stood before writing, and to that extent, as earlier stated, are relatively unaware of what writing truly is.

Many of the phenomena here associated with separation or division or distancing could also be discussed under various other headings, some of them less abstract headings than separation or division, but few other headings would be so handily inclusive. My observations here on separation or distancing will be condensed and, if only for that reason, should serve, I hope, to open discussion and to suggest further study. Here, then, are some of the ways in which writing separates or divides. Writing ties together so many things in so many interrelations that some of the itemizations here inevitably overlap.

1. Writing separates the known from the knower. It promotes 'objectivity'. Any writing system does this, but the alphabet does so most of all, since it most thoroughly dissolves all sounds into spatial equivalents. Havelock (1976) has shown how the ancient Greeks' invention of the first fully vocalic alphabet, the most radical of all writing systems, gave them their intellectual ascendancy by providing access to the thorough intellectual 'objectivity' that led to modern science, and modern forms of thought generally, although the science of the ancient Greeks remained far more rhetorically structured and far more embedded in the human lifeworld than our science is today.

Of course, language in its original oral state already begins the separation of known from knower. Simple naming is the most archaic and still the basic operation in this separation: when a small child looking at a picture-book with mother delightedly calls out 'Tree!' he or she puts the object 'out there' as different from self and mother and from other diversely named objects as well. The separated object can be both distanced and shared with mother simultaneously. It is great fun. But, involved in the real time of the interpersonal sound world, oral naming alone cannot achieve the distancing brought into being by writing, which is a time-obviating and otherwise radically decontextualizing mechanism.

Enhanced separation of the known from the knower is probably the most fundamental value of writing, from its beginnings to the present. Between knower and known writing interposes a visible and tangible object, the text. The objectivity of the text helps impose objectivity on what the text refers to (see Olson). Eventually writing will create a state of mind in which knowledge itself can be thought of as an object, distinct from the knower. This state of mind, however, is most fully realized only when print intensifies the object-like character of the text.

However, whatever its intimate effects on knowledge, the physical text is not itself knowledge, for knowledge, verbalized or other, can exist only in a knowing subject. In place of knowledge once possessed and formulated verbally by a living person, texts substitute coded marks outside any knower which a knowing subject possessed of the code can use to generate knowledge in himself or herself. Knowledge itself is not object-like: it cannot be transferred from one person to another physically even in oral communication, face-to-face, or *a fortiori* in writing. I can only perform actions— produce words—which enable you to generate the knowledge in yourself. The concept of 'medium' or 'media' applied to human communication uses an analogy which is useful but nevertheless so gross, and so inconspicuously gross, that it regularly falsifies what human communication is. I myself try to avoid the term now, though I have used it in earlier books and articles. 'Medium' applies properly to manual or machine transferral of pattern, not to human communication. Since knowledge cannot be physically transferred verbally from one human person to another but must always be created by the hearer or reader within his or her own consciousness, interpretation is always in play when one listens or when one reads.

2. Whereas oral cultures tend to merge interpretation of data with the data themselves, writing separates interpretation from data. Asked to repeat exactly what they have just said, persons from a primary oral culture will often given an interpretation of what they originally said, insisting and clearly believing that the interpretation is exactly what they said in the first place (Olson, citing Ruth Finnegan). They have difficulty in grasping what literates mean by word-for-word repetition. The text provides a new

scenario. The text is a visual given, a datum, separate from any utterer or hearer or reader. What one says (or writes) about the text is something else, distinct from the text-object and what it as such represents. This is not to deny that any understanding of a text always involves interpretation: for what the object-like text represents is not an object, but words. It is simply to state that the status of interpretation becomes different with writing.

3. Writing distances the word from sound, reducing oral-aural evanescence to the seeming quiescence of visual space. But this distancing is not total or permanent, for every reading of a text consists of restoring it, directly or indirectly, to sound, vocally or in the imagination.

4. Whereas in oral communication the source (speaker) and the recipient (hearer) are necessarily present to one another, writing distances the source of the communication (the writer) from the recipient (the reader), both in time and in space. It is as easy to read a book by a person long dead or by a person thousands of miles away as it is to read one by a friend sitting at your elbow. Oral communication provides no comparable condition until the invention of sound recordings, which, however, depend on writing for their existence and, despite their aura of immediacy, distance speaker and hearer even more than writing does, interposing between the two mechanisms far more complicated than those of writing and print, and abolishing all direct relationship to lived time.

5. Writing distances the word from the plenum of existence. In their original, spoken condition, words are always part of a context that is predominantly non-verbal, a modification of a field of personal relationships and object-relationships. The immediate context of spoken words is never simply other words. The immediate context of textualized words is simply other words.

6. By distancing the word from the plenum of existence, from a holistic context made up mostly of non-verbal elements, writing enforces verbal precision of a sort unavailable in oral cultures. Context always controls the meaning of a word. In oral utterance, the context always includes much more than words, so that less of the total, precise meaning conveyed by words need rest in the words themselves. Thus in a primary oral culture, where all verbalization is oral, utterances are always given their greater precision by nonverbal elements, which form the infrastructure of the oral utterance, giving it its fuller, situational meaning. Not so much

depends on the words themselves. In a text, the entire immediate context of every word is only other words, and words alone must help other words convey whatever meaning is called for. Hence texts force words to bear more weight, to develop more and more precisely 'defined'—that is 'bordered' or contrastive meanings. Eventually, words used in texts come to be defined in dictionaries, which present the meaning of words in terms of other words. Oral cultures present the meaning of words by using them (Goody 1968). Oral people are generally altogether uninterested in defining words by other words (Ong 1982: 53–4, citing Luria 1976). What the word 'tree' means is determined by putting the word in non-verbal context, as in pointing to a tree, not by saying in words what 'tree' means.

7. Writing separates past from present. Primary oral cultures tend to use the past to explain the present, dropping from memory what does not serve this purpose in one way or another, thus homogenizing the past with the present, or approximating past to present. To use Jack Goody's term, their relationship with the past is homeostatic. By freezing verbalization, writing creates a distanced past which is full of puzzles because it can refer to states of affairs no longer effectively imaginable or can use words no longer immediately meaningful to any living persons.

8. Writing separates 'administration'—civil, religious, commercial, and other—from other types of social activities. 'Administration' is unknown in oral cultures, where leaders interact non-abstractly with the rest of society in tight-knit, often rhetorically controlled, configurations. 'Administration' can have two senses: (1) a distinct group able to oversee and manage, in a more or less abstractly structured fashion, complex social wholes or activities or (2) the work such a group actually does. In both senses administration comes into being with the development of written documentation and scribal expertise. At first, in more marginally textualized society, administrators relied on scribes for exploitation of the possibilities of textuality but, with wider and deeper textualization, eventually found it advantageous to be able to read and write themselves (Stock 1983; Cressy, Laqueur, and Stevens in Resnick 1983).

9. Writing makes it possible to separate logic (thought structure of discourse) from rhetoric (socially effective discourse). The invention of logic, it seems, is tied not to any kind of writing system

but to the completely vocalic phonetic alphabet and the intensive analytic activity which such an alphabet demands of its inventors and subsequently encourages in all sorts of noetic fields. All formal logic in the world, down to that used for computers, stems from the ancient Greeks (the later development of some formal logic in India, which may have been an independent development, came only after Greek logic had effectively taken over and of course after India had use of the alphabet).

10. Writing separates academic learning (*mathēsis* and *mathēma*) from wisdom (*sophia*), making possible the conveyance of highly organized abstract thought structures independently of their actual use or of their integration into the human lifeworld. Wisdom regards not abstractions but holistic situations and operations in the density of the real human lifeworld. Learning by apprenticeship, with which academic learning contrasts, had kept even specialized knowledge integrated into this lifeworld and had helped to keep wisdom as the noetic as well as the practical ideal. When cultures first assimilate writing, however, they tend to put wise sayings into texts. New technologies of the word always reinforce earlier conditions of utterances but at the same time transform them. But wise sayings in texts are denatured: they do not function the way they function in oral cultures. Oral cultures do not recite lists of decontextualized wise sayings, such as are found in biblical wisdom literature, but, in fact, quite commonly and even typically use such sayings separately as parrying devices in real-life agonistic oral exchange. Once wise sayings are written down, oral culture is weakening, though its demise may take many hundreds of years. Today Ibo entrepreneurs in Onitsha in Nigeria are printing and selling collections of proverbs to marginally oral people who are unaware of the fuller implications of literacy, much as Erasmus was doing for residually oral Europeans almost five hundred years ago.

11. Writing can divide society by giving rise to a special kind of diglossia, splitting verbal communication between a 'high' language completely controlled by writing even though also widely spoken (Learned Latin in the European Middle Ages) and a 'low' language or 'low' languages controlled by speech to the exclusion of writing. Besides Learned Latin, the other high languages created and sustained by writing to produce similar diglossia have been Sanskrit, Classical Arabic, Rabbinical Hebrew (all alphabetically written) and Classical Chinese (written, but not in the alphabet). In all these

cases the high language has been not only a written language but also a sex-linked language, no longer a mother tongue, used only by males (with exceptions so few as to be negligible). As social structures changed with the advance of technologies and women worked their way out of the massive responsibilities of pre-technological household management (which often included highly skilled crafts and even major manufacturing activities) and into academic education, the diglossia was reduced and gradually eliminated. As women entered academia, some did learn the high languages, but only when these were on the wane and no longer used as languages of instruction or of normal academic discourse. Of the tens of thousands of books written in Learned Latin through the eighteenth century and beyond, virtually none are by women. Instead, women helped put the low, vernacular languages in competition with the high language. Eventually one or another dialect of various low languages was taken over by writing and replaced the original high language. This has happened to all the high languages just mentioned—which are in fact the major high languages of the world—with the partial exception of Classical Arabic in the still linguistically fluid Arabic-speaking world.

12. Writing differentiates grapholects, those 'low'-language dialects which are taken over by writing and erected into national languages, from other dialects, making the grapholect a dialect of a completely different order of magnitude and effectiveness from the dialects that remain oral. The grapholect which we know as standard English has an active or recuperable vocabulary of perhaps a million and a half words, as compared with the relatively few thousand words available in dialects without written resources (see, for example, Laughlin 1975 on Tzotzil). For this exponential development, the lexicon of a grapholect requires print as well as writing, for dictionaries are print products. (Imagine producing multiple copies of *Webster's Third International Dictionary* or of the *Oxford English Dictionary* by hand.)

13. Writing divides or distances more evidently and effectively as its form becomes more abstract, which is to say more removed from the sound world into the space world of sight. 'Abstract' in fact means removed, distanced, from *abstrahere*, to draw out or to draw away from. The alphabet in its various forms is the most abstract writing form. We have already noted that Tzeng and Wang (1983) have reported—though more work remains to be done here

—how writing and reading Chinese characters involve the right cerebral hemisphere of the brain more than do writing and reading the alphabet, which involve the left hemisphere more. The right hemisphere normally implements totalizing, intuitive, less abstractive or less analytic processes; the left hemisphere is more analytic—and more involved in the alphabet. As has been seen, formal logic, modern science, and ultimately the computer have their historical roots in the fully vocalic alphabet, the most analytic of the writing systems, dissolving all sound as such into spatial equivalents, in principle, if never completely in fact. (The alphabet, it should be recalled, was invented only once: all alphabets in the world—Greek, Roman, Glagolitic, Cyrillic, Arabic, Sanskrit, Korean, etc.—derive in one way or another, directly or indirectly, from the ancient Semitic alphabet, which, however, in contrast to Greek, did not and still does not have letters for vowels.)

14. Perhaps the most momentous of all its diaeretic effects in the deep history of thought is the effect of writing when it separates being from time. This separation has been detailed in a recent major monograph by Eric Havelock (1983), 'The Linguistic Task of the Presocratics, Part One: Ionian Science in Search of an Abstract Vocabulary'. We know that all philosophy depends on writing because all elaborate, linear, so-called 'logical' explanation depends on writing. Oral persons can be wise, as wise as anyone, and they can of course give some explanation for things. But the elaborate, intricate, seemingly endless but exact cause-effect sequences required by what we call philosophy and by extended scientific thinking are unknown among oral peoples, including the early Greeks before their development of the first vocalic alphabet. Havelock's newly seminal work, however, goes beyond showing that elaborate explanatory thinking depends upon writing and the revisionary, back-tracking operations made possible by such a time-obviating mechanism. His new monograph shows more precisely that the development of the content, the subject-matter of metaphysics itself, with its concentration on being as being, depended internally upon the elaboration of writing. Havelock's work is based upon extraordinarily careful analysis of pre-Socratic texts and upon cautious reconstruction of antecedents of the texts. Here I can only attempt to suggest in a quite sweeping, but I believe accurate way what Havelock's point comes to as related to the line of thought I have been pursuing.

Oral speech and thought narrativizes experience and the environment, whereas philosophy, which comes into being slowly after writing, is radically anti-narrative. Plato did not want story-telling poets in his republic. The philosophical enterprise required the coinage of a large number of abstract nouns. Havelock (1983: 20) cites some which around the end of the fifth century BC had become common tender for dealing with the cosmic environment: matter (*hulē*), dimension (*megethos*), space (*chōra*), body (*sōma*), void (*kenon*), motion (*kinēsis* or *phora*), change (*alloiōsis, metabolē*), rest (*stasis*). Besides such nouns, 'the conceptual task also required the elimination of verbs of doing and acting and happening . . . in favor of a syntax which states permanent relationships between conceptual terms systematically' (p. 14). In this new noetic economy, Heraclitus suggests (p. 25) that 'is' (*esti*) should replace the use of all other verbs and even of the past and future of the verb 'to be' (*einai*). Parmenides brings this reorganization of thought to completion: the imagistic, narrativistic Homeric references to the world are replaced 'by the thought world of conceptual science' (pp.28–9). In brief, the Homeric verb *kinein*, which refers not so much to our concept of 'motion' as to the earlier concept of 'commotion' (the disturbance inherent in any kind of real action, not a disembodied abstraction such as *kinēsis*), yields to *einai*, 'to be', which is not commotion at all (p. 38). Becoming becomes being. The mobile oral world has been supplanted by the quiescent text, and Plato's immutable ideas have been provided with their action-free, seemingly timeless chirographic launching pad.

One is struck by similarities between the ancient Greek situation reported by Havelock and that which Luria found among illiterates as compared to literates among the folk he studied in the southwestern Soviet Union (reported in Ong 1982: 49–57). Asked, 'What is a tree? Define a tree,' the illiterate peasant replies, 'Why should I? Everyone knows what a tree is.' To learn what a thing *is* one does not use definitions. To grasp an object's essence, one does not talk about the object, but, as has earlier been noted here, one *points* to the object physically or metaphorically. One deals with existing beings as such indexically, not verbally. Words in an oral culture are used typically not to set up static definitions but to discourse actively on the way a thing acts or behaves or operates in the human lifeworld. Words in oral cultures paradigmatically go with action and with things that act. As writing is interiorized, verbalization migrates from a predominantly action frame to a predominantly 'being' frame: the verb *to be* becomes more urgent than it had ever been in an oral culture. The quest is on to find Aristotle's *to ti ēn einai*, that is, 'what it is to be' or 'what being is'.

In these perspectives metaphysics is seen to be indebted to writing not only for the kinds of protracted analytic explanations with which it and all science works, but also for identifying its own special quarry, 'being' itself, which it has always pursued. Writing in the sense I have tried to explain here separates being from time and *a longe* sets up Heidegger's project of rejoining the two. But Heidegger's *Sein und Zeit* is written in the alphabet in a far-gone print culture, and whether it has fully achieved what it set out to do is in the minds of many open to question.

VIII

Print and electronics continue with new intensification and radical transformations the diaeretic programme initially set in motion by writing. They separate knower from known more spectacularly than writing does. Between the knower and the known print interposes elaborate mechanical contrivances and operations of a different order of complexity than writing. The computer achieves the ultimate (thus far) in separation of the knower and the known (the subject of discourse): between the two it interposes limitlessly complex structures of mechanically articulated 'bits' of information, each consisting of the ultimate in divisive patterning, the dichotomy or binary division, which translates into 'yes–no' or 'is–isn't'. Putting the simplest statement of, say, a dozen words on to a page in a word processor involves operations inside the machine, totally remote from the human lifeworld, which are thousands, perhaps millions, of times more complex than writing or even letterpress printing, though unimaginably less complex than the activities of the human cerebrum.

The computer shows its separative power not merely in distancing known from knower more drastically than writing or print. It shows its separative drive also within its own history as the digital computer today displaces more and more the analogue computer. By comparison with the digital computer, the analogue computer is holistic (as oral cultures are), whereas the digital computer is essentially analytic or separative.

An analogue computer measures by providing a model or analogue for what it is measuring. Thus a thermometer may be considered an analogue computer: to measure heat, it takes as an analogue for heat the height of mercury in a very slender tube. An analogue computer is holistic in the sense that it is unbroken or 'smooth'. As in the increase of heat there are no sudden jumps, no breaks (in rising from 38° centigrade, heat does not suddenly jump to 39° and then suddenly to 40° but passes through all the innumerable, because non-disjunct, intermediate stages between 38° and 40°), so there are no sudden jumps in the rising or falling of mercury in the tube (it does not rise by jumping abruptly from millimeter to millimeter but passes through all the intermediate stages, innumerable because non-disjunct). The scale on the thermometer breaks up into discrete parts an action which is not discrete. Analogue computers give quick results, but the results can be inaccurate, for such things as variations in transmission of heat through the glass of the thermometer tube can produce less than an exact match between the movement of the mercury and the temperature. Analogue computers are considered accurate if they are within 0.1 per cent of the correct value (Sanders 1983: 109), which is very low accuracy compared to digital operations.

A digital computer, on the other hand, counts in terms of its own built-in units. The abacus is a simple digital computer, counting whatever it is being used for in terms of invariable units structured into the abacus itself. Corresponding units must be imputed to whatever the digital computer is measuring: temperature will be considered as jumping, for example, from 40° to 41° centigrade, or from 40.0° to 40.5° to 41°, or from 40.0° to 40.0001° to 40.0002°, and so on—but, however small the units decided upon, always abruptly from one unit to the next. If the units are made small enough—say billionths of a degree centigrade—the effect is equivalently 'smooth' or totalizing, approximating more and more that of an analogue computer. The only limit to refinement in a digital computer is a matter of how precisely the hardware is designed and of how much work the programmer is willing to put in to divide the field outside the computer into smaller and smaller units. If this work is done assiduously enough, digital computers can be far more accurate than analogue computers. But division of the field always remains their mode of operation, even though, paradoxically, as they divide the field into smaller and smaller units they seem to be moving in effect to a non-divided field—the bits are too small for any one of them to make any effective difference. Nevertheless, the digital field is never really 'smooth', is always fragmented.

Today the digital computer has largely replaced the analogue, although some analogue computers and mixed-system analogue-and-digital computers are still in operation. There will always be use for analogue operations, it seems, but purely analogue computers appear to be on the way out. From friends in computer programming I have recently learned that, so far as they can find, simple analogue computers are no longer even being manufactured. Division has carried the day, even though it has become so intricate that it appears to be approximating non-division. Extremes meet—but in this case not quite. Separativeness, inherent in writing and print, has been finalized in the computer world.

In the case of the computer we are clearly dealing with physical separation of knower and known. But in the case of writing as well, it is the physical separation, the interposition of the text, created by a technology, that makes possible the psychological separation between the self and the object of its knowledge. Moreover, as is evident in computer programming, new tracks for thought are imposed by the new technologies. And the software of the computer vigorously interposes even another consciousness or other consciousnesses—the programmer or programmers—between the knower and the known.

XI

As the digital computer can be to a degree, so writing is self-corrective to a degree. It has in itself the cure for the chirographic squint commonly afflicting cultures that have deeply interiorized writing. Because it so radically separates knower from known, writing can distance us from writing itself. Writing has enabled us to identify the orality that was antecedent to it and to see how radically it differs from that orality. Writing has the power to liberate us more and more from the chirographic bias and confusion it creates, though complete liberation remains impossible. For all states of the word—oral, chirographic, typographic, electronic—impose their own confusions, which cannot be radically eliminated but only controlled by reflection.

In the noetic world, separation ultimately brings reconstituted unity. This is true of naming at the oral stage. Calling an object a 'tree', as has been seen, puts the object 'out there', as different from the knower. In place of empathetic identification, the name sets up a relatively clear subject–object relationship. But this very relationship makes for a new kind of intimacy. Now, in certain ways, the knower can deal with the tree better on its own terms, rather than on terms unreflectively imposed by the knower. He or she can better appreciate what the tree is on its own as distinct from the knower—although of course distinctness from the knower is never totally realized. With the use of names, the inarticulate identification of the infant with the surrounding world is replaced by verbally implemented distancing. The new distancing submerges the original empathetic identification in a flood of new awarenesses but does not entirely do away with it. And indeed, as distancing increases beyond those ranges made available by oral naming through the vaster distances opened by writing and print—and now electronics—the original empathetic identification becomes more and more recuperable at the level of conscious reflectivity. That is to say, with writing and its sequels, empathetic identification can be attended to as we are attending to it now, and as oral folk could not attend to it. Of course, the original innocence of the pristine empathetic identification can never be repossessed directly. Civilization entails such discomforts, for that is what they are. (Freud's title should be translated 'Civilization and its Discomforts' (*Unbehagen*), not 'Discontents'.) Human knowledge demands both proximity and distance, and these two are related to one another dialectically. Proximity perceptions feed distancing analyses, and vice versa, creating a more manageable intimacy.

As a time-obviating, context-free mechanism, writing separates the known from the knower more definitely than the original orally grounded manœuvre of naming does, but it also unites the knower and the known more consciously and more articulately. Writing is a consciousness-raising and humanizing technology. So is print, even more, and, in its own way, so is the computer. But that is another story, which has yet to be told or written or printed or processed in the course of this series. ✓

REFERENCES

Clanchy, M. T. 1979: *From Memory to Written Record: England 1066–1307*. Cambridge, Mass.: Harvard University Press. London: Edward Arnold.

Edmonson, M. S. 1971: *Lore: An Introduction to the Science of Folklore and Literature*. New York: Holt, Rinehart, and Winston.

Foley, J. M. 1985: *Oral-Formulaic Theory and Research: An Introduction and Annotated Bibliography*. New York and London: Garland Publishing Co.

Goody, J. and I. Watt 1968: 'The Consequences of Literacy', in J. Goody (ed.), *Literacy in Traditional Societies*, 27–84. Cambridge: Cambridge University Press.

Graff, H. J. (ed.) 1981: *Literacy and Social Development in the West: A Reader*, Cambridge Studies in Oral and Literate Culture, 3. Cambridge and New York: Cambridge University Press.

Hauf, J. 1984: 'Communications and Development: Some Strategies for Use in Primary Oral Cultures'. Paper delivered at the Tenth Annual Third World Conference, Chicago, Ill., 28–31 Mar. Manuscript from the author.

Havelock, E. A. 1963: *Preface to Plato*. Cambridge, Mass.: Belknap Press of Harvard University Press.

—— 1976: *Origins of Western Literacy*. Toronto: Ontario Institute for the Study of Education.

—— 1983: 'The Linguistic Task of the Presocratics, Part One: Ionian Science in Search of an Abstract Vocabulary', in K. Robb (ed.), *Language and Thought in Early Greek Philosophy*, 7–82. La Salle, Ill.: Hegeler Institute, Monist Library of Philosophy.

Hofling, C. A. 1983: Itza Maya Morphosyntax from a Discourse Perspective. Ph.D. Washington University, St Louis, Mo. Ann Arbor: University Microfilms International, DA 8310930.

Hoskin, K. W. (n.d.): 'The History of Education and the History of Writing'. Review article, manuscript from the author.

Innis, H. 1950: *Empire and Communications*. London: Oxford University Press.

Laughlin, R. W. 1975: *The Great Tzotzil Dictionary of San Lorenzo Zinacatan*. Washington, DC: Smithsonian Institution Press.

Luria, A. R. 1976: *Cognitive Development: Its Cultural and Social Foundations*, trans. M. Lopez-Morillas and L. Solataroff; ed. M. Cole. Cambridge, Mass.: Harvard University Press.

Olson, D. R. (n.d.): *The World on Paper*. Book in preparation, draft-manuscript from the author.

Ong, W. J. 1967: *The Presence of the Word*, New Haven: Yale University Press.

—— 1982: *Orality and Literacy*. London: Methuen.

Resnick, D. (ed.) 1983: *Literacy in Historical Perspective*. Washington, DC: Library of Congress.

Ricoeur, P. 1981: *Hermeneutics and the Human Sciences*, trans. and ed. J. B. Thompson. Cambridge and New York: Cambridge University Press.

Sanders, D. H. 1983: *Computers Today*. New York: McGraw-Hill.

Stock. B. 1983: *The Implications of Literacy: Written Language and Models of Interpretation in the Eleventh and Twelfth Centuries*. Princeton, NJ: Princeton University Press.

Tzeng, O. J. L. and W. S.-Y. Wang 1983: 'The First Two R's', in *American Scientist*, 71: 452–6.

FORMS OF WRITING IN THE ANCIENT MEDITERRANEAN WORLD

ANNA MORPURGO DAVIES ✓

In the study of writing everything is problematic. I start by rehearsing some of the things which we do not know before I come to my more specific theme. First we do not know how to define writing. The problem is pressing: in 1980 one of the main authorities on ancient writing, I. J. Gelb, found it necessary to reconsider the definition of writing which he had supported since 1952 (Gelb 1963: 12); among his reasons for reconsidering the problem he listed the findings by Marschack (1972) and Schmandt-Besserat's (1977, 1979) about prehistoric systems of reckoning and perhaps writing which may go back as far as the palaeolithic period. It is difficult to predict whether Gelb's new definition: 'writing in its broadest sense is a recording system or device by means of conventional markings or shapes or color of objects, achieved by the motor action of the hand of an individual and received visually by another' (Gelb 1980: 22) will gain general acceptance. In practical terms, the philologist or linguist finds it often difficult to answer the questions posed by archaeologists or anthropologists: are these scratches or signs a form of writing? Any clear-cut criterion for decision hits against marginal cases. We may agree to suspend judgement and to start any inquiry by including only those forms of writing which are traditionally acknowledged as such; Gelb would label them as full writing or phonography and argue that their distinctive features are a close correlation with oral language, and the sequential order. This instantly leads us to problems of classification. Traditionally, 'natural' writing has been classified into pictographic (the signs are pictorial images of objects or events), logographic (the signs correspond to words), syllabic (the signs correspond to syllables), and alphabetic (the signs correspond to phonetic or phonemic segments).[1] Is this correct? The partition is oddly reminiscent of the nineteenth-century classification of languages into isolating, agglutinative, and inflected, a classification which we partly retain but which the specialist considers with deep misgivings.[2] The comparison is particularly worrying when we look at the standard way of dealing with the question of origins. The traditional view is that writing starts in a pictographic form; it then develops first into logographic and then into syllabic writing; eventually the alphabet is created. Having thus reached perfection creativity stops; the alphabet, we are told, was created only once; after that it was borrowed. Here too we are forcefully reminded of the nineteenth-century attitude to languages. For a long period it was assumed that there was a 'perfect' language family—needless to say our own—and a number of 'imperfect' families, classified, as we have seen, into two main groups, agglutinative and isolating. The connection between the various types was seen in different manners: one version of the theory assumed regular progress from isolating to agglutinative to inflectional.[3] An ill-defined idea of perfection plays a part in both theories, and both in the case of scripts and in the case of languages the classification and the presumed development are somewhat too tidy for comfort.

Another point for dispute concerns the connection between writing and language; traditionally, writing has been interpreted as secondary with reference to spoken language—an imperfect attempt to render speech. If so, communication in writing would in effect be communication in speech made through a replacement medium: in the same way a system of flash lights conventionally started and stopped can render the letters of the alphabet and is in essence writing done through a replacement medium. More recently, writing has been considered as an independent communicative code, a semiotic system with a status parallel to that of other systems (Cardona 1981: 21 ff.). Alternatively—and more helpfully—writing can be seen as a form of linguistic behaviour with similar status to that of speech; language is expressed either through writing or through speech—which may explain why we find written sequences which are never matched by verbal expressions, and vice versa (Vachek 1973: 14 ff.; McIntosh 1956, etc.). This does not exclude, of course, the existence of infinitely important links between speech and writing, but draws attention to the fact that they have to be separately identified and established for each script, each language, each period, and each society. At one extreme we have the so-called dead languages which, in some instances at least, are languages no longer spoken but still written: here writing is obviously independent of speech.[4] At the other extreme we have oral languages, that is languages which are spoken but not written. In the middle there is an infinite gamut of possibilities.

Further worries arise apropos of the impact of writing on society, and, in particular, of the impact of specific forms of writing on society. The distinction between oral and literate or semi-literate societies has been discussed at length in recent years. Should we recognize a great dividing line between oral and literate societies and does literacy impinge, as has been argued, both on cultural patterns and on cognitive processes? The question is far from settled but the 'autonomous' view of literacy which underlies these claims (Goody and Watt 1963; Greenfield 1972, etc.) has recently been attacked from different quarters (for example Basso 1980, Scribner and Cole 1981, Tannen 1982*a*, Romaine 1984: 196 ff., Street 1984 with further literature). Whatever the final conclusion, it is necessary to distinguish between different types and grades of literacy and orality and different uses made of literacy by different societies. In this context the claims originally made for example by Goody and Watt (1963), partly in the steps of Havelock, for a special position of the alphabet as a type of writing which leads to forms of literacy more capable than any other of impressing their seal on the intellectual and social character of the community, acquire greater importance and call for further reappraisal. Goody has withdrawn part of his early statements,[5] but Havelock has not ceased to emphasize the importance of the alphabet as a major Greek breakthrough; for him real literacy starts in Greece only round the end of the fifth century BC but from that period onwards we witness the start of an intellectual revolution where the new technology leads to the creation of new moral laws and a new scholarly, scientific, and philosophical approach.[6] Yet the real nature of the point being made is ambiguous. A possible interpretation is that the spreading of literacy brings about a dramatic change in culture, and, according to some, in cognitive powers: on the other hand the spreading of literacy is seen as necessarily associated with the alphabet because all other forms of writing are too unmanageable;[7] consequently the alphabet counts as the real begeter of the new non-oral culture. A different, more extreme view (which seems to have found some acceptance—conscious or unconscious) is that the very nature of the alphabet favours a specific type of analytic thinking which is indeed the mark of a new culture. In either case the alphabet is given a special status which marks it off from all other forms of writing. Thus, strangely enough, these modern views of literacy return to—or are based on—the nineteenth-century assumptions about the alphabet as the perfect repository of all wisdom.

So much for some of what is discussed: it is probably true, as has been argued, that both the history and the ethnography of writing must still be written. At present we can only ask general questions and look at details. Anyone interested in the Mediterranean area between the second and the first millennium BC is necessarily concerned with the relationship (differences and similarities) between the various types of writing available in what obviously was a melting pot of both languages and scripts. It is only, I suggest, if we make some headway in the discussion of these more limited problems that we can then consider the wider questions I mentioned above. Part at least of the views proposed is based on historical evidence discussed in turn by for example Havelock and Goody (see also Street 1984: 49 ff.); a return to the historical approach is not untimely.

Any attempt at comparing two or more forms of writing can be done, as it were, from the inside or from the outside: we may be concerned with the code or with the use of the code, the users, and their reactions or attitudes to it. In the first mode we shall compare, for instance, a syllabic writing system with an alphabetic writing system and try to define differences and similarities; it may prove necessary to do this while keeping in mind not only the nature of the writing systems to be analysed but also the nature of the linguistic systems concerned.[8] In the second mode we shall enquire about the purposes for which each script is used and about the individuals who use it. Here we shall distinguish for example between scripts which are in use merely as reckoning or list-making devices and scripts with a wider range of uses; we shall also want to know for each script how many people were literate in it at any given moment, what grade of literacy they had, and what proportion they were of the community which used the script. Turning to the reactions and attitudes to writing we may ask whether users react for instance to syllabic writing in the same way in which they react to alphabetic writing; it may then be useful to see how in given communities the general attitudes to language compare with the general attitudes to writing: do people trust more the written word or the spoken word? Do they attribute magical power to spoken formulae or to written words? What is taken to guarantee immortality, the spoken or the written word, and so on? Work which needs to be done for a number of periods and areas but has rarely been done concerns the terminologies of writing and speaking. How far do they overlap at any given period and in any given area? Is the constant confusion between letter and sound, writing and saying, written and spoken word, which characterizes our language, only characteristic of fully literate and alphabetic cultures or is it also shared by other non-alphabetic cultures?

Finally, and at a higher level of generality, we shall want to know what difference it makes to any given society to have for example 1 per cent literate members versus 5 per cent or 10 per cent or 20 per cent or even 60 per cent.[9] The extent of literacy may be linked with the prestige of literacy. Do people acquire prestige because they can write or do they not? And vice versa do people lose prestige because they cannot write? In our society it is possible to write sentimental novels of the Mills and Boon type where a whole highly dramatic plot is built on the fact that a successful business man is illiterate and does not have the courage to reveal it to the world (Meadmore 1980); in seventh-century BC Assyria it was possible for Ashurbanipal, a great king, to boast (admittedly wrongly) that he was the first king who had ever learned to read and write (Driver 1976: 72 f., 238; Kraus 1973: 19). Obviously, until then at least, one did not lose face by being illiterate.

An analysis of these problems is well beyond the scope of my discussion—and in a number of instances the evidence is not available. In what follows I shall address myself to the more specific question of the difference between alphabetic and pre-alphabetic writing, with special reference to five forms of script all used roughly speaking in the Mediterranean area between the second and first millennia BC.[10] My choice of evidence is determined to a large extent by a firm wish to use firsthand material and to keep linguistic, geographical, chronological, and sociological differences to the minimum.

The oldest script I shall consider is the mixed logographic and syllabic form of cuneiform used in Anatolia (modern Turkey) to write Hittite, an Indo-European language directly or indirectly attested during most of the second millennium BC. Cuneiform writing was first developed for Sumerian, a Near Eastern language with no known cognates.[11] As a result of cultural and to some extent political symbiosis the script was borrowed by the Semitic population of the area and adapted to write their langauge, Akkadian. In their turn the Hittites first borrowed it from Akkadian through a North Syrian scribal school in the eighteenth or seventeenth century BC. They introduced some simplifications and modifications but the full system consists of almost 300 signs of which more than 100 may indicate different syllables; the others are purely logographic, that is they indicate words. The syllabic signs are of the type *a* (vowel only), *na* (consonant + vowel), *an* (vowel + consonant), and, more rarely, *kan* (consonant + vowel + consonant).[12]

At the same time as the latest phases of Hittite writing we have in Crete, the island in the southern part of the Aegean, in the Peloponnese, and in continental Greece, the so-called Linear B, a script used to write an old form of Greek between *c*.1400 and 1200 BC. The script is syllabic with some 90 signs, mostly of the type *a* (vowel) or *na* (consonant + vowel); there are some 160 logograms but they play a limited role in our texts. The script is certainly borrowed from an older Cretan script, possibly developed for a local language, and we have the impression, no more than that, that a great deal of adaptation was necessary to make the script viable for Greek.[13]

The third script, the so-called Hieroglyphic Hittite or Luwian (in both cases a misnomer), brings us back to Anatolia; the first monuments (mostly seals, stelae, rock inscriptions) are far from comprehensible and belong to the second part of the second millennium BC. Towards the end of this period and above all in the first three hundred years of the first millennium the script is in more frequent use as the official script of a series of small city states which survived the end of the Hittite Empire in Syria and southern Anatolia. The language of these later texts belongs to the Luwian subgroup of Anatolian and is very similar to Cuneiform Luwian, an Indo-European language closely related to Hittite, written in the Hittite cuneiform script and attested in the second millennium BC. The important point, however, is that the so-called Hieroglyphic script was devised for either Luwian or Hittite. We still do not know what made this invention necessary, since the Cuneiform script, which was used both for Hittite and for Luwian, was in existence at the time—with a far wider diffusion; it is possible that Hieroglyphic

was devised for monumental purposes. The signs are either syllabic
or logographic; some 500 have been counted but the syllabic signs in
regular and frequent use are no more than 70 and mostly are of the
type *a* (vowel) or *na* (consonant + vowel). Of the logographic signs
some are very rare.[14]

The fourth script is Syllabic Cyprian, used in Cyprus during most
of the first millennium BC (until the fourth–third century BC) to
write the local Greek dialect. The script itself was adapted from an
earlier second-millennium script used in Cyprus, still undeciphered,
conventionally called Cypro-Minoan, and distantly related to the
ancestors of Linear B. Its later descendant, Syllabic Cyprian, has
some 56 signs all of which are syllabic (of the *a*, *na* type). There are
no logographic signs (except for the numerals).[15]

The fifth script needs no introduction: it is the Greek alphabet
for which we have definite evidence in the Greek islands, the Greek
colonies, and the Greek mainland from the mid-eighth century BC
to present days; it is the ancestor of our own alphabet. Letter shapes,
letter values, letter ordering, and letter names are derived from
forms of writing used for Semitic languages (probably Phoenician).
We are back again to an Indo-European language which borrows a
script used for Semitic. The traditional view is that the Greeks borrowed an alphabet where each sign represented a consonant but the
vowels were ignored: their great contribution consisted in adapting
some of the old signs or devising new signs for the vowels; a less
traditional view is that we ought to understand the so-called Semitic
alphabets as syllabaries where each sign indicated a consonant
followed by a potential vowel and we ought to attribute to the
Greeks the discovery of the alphabetic principle according to which
different signs are used in correspondence to different segments, be
they vowels or consonants.[16]

The five scripts and, so to speak, their accompanying circumstances have notable similarities: chronologically and geo-
graphically they are not too distant from each other. Moreover,
they are all used for Indo-European languages, and they can be
grouped in pairs or triplets used for the same language or closely
related languages. Yet, the scripts are also very different; we may
group them into two or three of the traditional typological classes
(logographic-syllabic, syllabic, and alphabetic) but we should
remember that the four non-alphabetic scripts show considerable
divergencies. Genetically, the differences are still greater. Only one

script, Hieroglyphic Luwian, was originally devised for the language for which we see it used or for a closely related language; the other scripts were variously borrowed or adapted, and sometimes had remote origins both in time and space. The material support of the four scripts differs too (the importance of this should not be underrated): the bulk of the cuneiform Hittite texts is found on highly refined clay tablets (though other materials were used too); Linear B is found on rough clay tablets and pots; Hieroglyphic Luwian on rock and stone monuments but also on seals, lead strips, and possibly on wood; Syllabic Cyprian on stone, metal, and occasionally pots; the Greek alphabet on stone, wood, metal, papyrus, leather, waxed tablets, etc. Historically and sociologically the background is obviously difficult to define; Cuneiform Hittite in its *floruit* period belongs to the archives of an important Empire and is mainly used for religious, administrative, legal, and literary texts. Linear B also belongs to royal archives in various parts of Greece but what we have is of a purely administrative nature. Hieroglyphic Luwian is largely found in monumental texts set up by kings or men in power but is also attested in a few private letters by merchants and in a few economic documents. Syllabic Cyprian was mostly used for public inscriptions, but is also found in private documents (dedications, graffiti, etc.). The Greek alphabet, after its first beginnings, is less limited in usage than any of the other four scripts—not least because we know more about it. It has often been noticed that even in early Greece writing was not an esoteric craft, since some of our earliest texts are casual graffiti (Jeffery 1961: 62; 1982: 831 f.).[17]

If we take these five scripts as our testing ground what can we learn about the questions I asked above? Do we want to imagine the development of writing as a continuous striving towards the segmental representation of speech, that is towards the alphabet? Do we believe that as soon as the possibility of alphabetic writing looms on the horizon no one can resist it? If that were so, the fact could be used to support the view that writing in its proper manifestation is entirely dependent on speech. The point must be clarified. On this assumption the ideal form of script is the phonetic alphabet: in theory anything written in a narrow phonetic transcription can be read correctly by anyone who knows the symbols, whatever his linguistic knowledge; speech is not perfectly represented but a valiant attempt is made at doing so. Should we then understand the various forms of writing as successive attempts at the creation (or discovery) of the phonetic alphabet? Of the ancient scripts which we know the Greek alphabet is perhaps the one which comes closest to the phonetic alphabet, though it falls well short of it; if it is in fact the case that everything yields to the Greek alphabet and that the alphabetic principle automatically takes over as soon as it appears on the scene, this can be used as an argument for a real dependence of writing on speech.

Of these questions some are unanswerable. The first question I propose to consider with the help of the scripts I mentioned concerns the way in which logographic-syllabic scripts innovate before the appearance of the alphabet or in a period when the alphabet is present or approaching. Of our scripts the only one which survived is the alphabet and it is the closest to the ideal phonetic alphabet: an argument in favour of the original hypothesis. On the other hand a close look at the development of the other scripts may lead to different conclusions. Together with the cuneiform script the Hittites acquired one of the most remarkable features of their writing, namely the use of Sumerograms for a large number of words; to these they added Akkadograms in large number. A look at a text will not at first sight show anything odd; regular cuneiform signs appear all through, but reading will reveal a number of words not written in Hittite: some are Sumerian word signs, some Akkadian word-signs. We can look at the starting passage from the Apology of Hattusilis III, a thirteenth-century BC king (Otten 1981: 4 ff.). I print first the transliteration (with the Sumerograms in Roman capitals, the Akkadograms in Italic capitals, and the Hittite forms in italics) and then a literal translation.

1   *UM-MA* ᵐ*Ta-ba-ar-na* ᵐ*Ḫa-at-tu-ši-li* LUGAL.GAL LUGAL KUR ᵁ[(ᴿᵁ*Ḫa-*)]*at-ti*
2   DUMU ᵐ*Mur-ši-li* LUGAL.GAL LUGAL KUR ᵁᴿᵁ*Ḫa-at-ti*
3   DUMU.DUMU-*ŠÚ ŠA* ᵐ*Šu-up-pí-lu-li-u-ma* LUGAL.GAL LUGAL KUR ᵁᴿᵁ*Ḫa-at-ti*
4   *ŠÀ*.BAL *ŠA* ᵐ*Ḫa-at-tu-si-li* LUGAL ᵁᴿᵁ*Ku-uš-šar*
5   *ŠA* ᴰ*IŠTAR pa-ra-a ḫa-an-da-an-da-tar me-ma-aḫ-ḫi*
6   *na-at* DUMU.NAM.LÚ.ULÙᴸᵁ-*aš iš-ta-ma-aš-du* . . .

1 'Thus (spoke) the Tabarna Hattusili, Great King, King of the land of Hatti,

2	son of Mursili, Great King, King of the land of Hatti,
3	his grandson of Suppiluliuma, Great King, King of the land of Hatti,
4	descendant of Hattusili, King of Kussar:
5	"I shall say of the power of (the goddess) Istar,
6	and let everyone hear of it . . ."'

A literal rendering of the text which made use of English for the Hittite words, of Latin (in capitals) for the Sumerograms, and of French (in italics) for the Akkadograms, would read as follows:

1	'*De cette façon* the Tabarna Hattusili (spoke), MAGNUS REX, REX REGIONIS Hatti,
2	FILIUS of Mursili, MAGNUS REX, REX REGIONIS Hatti,
3	NEPOS *à lui de* Suppiluliuma, MAGNUS REX, REX REGIONIS Hatti,
4	PROGNATUS *de Hattusili*, REX of Kussar:
5	"*De Istar* I shall say the power,
6	and let OMNES-s hear of it"'.

It is certain that the Sumerograms (a modern conventional term) were read aloud as Hittite words; probably the same happened to the Akkadograms.[18] In effect these signs or sequences of signs had the same functions which the Arabic numbers or the odd abbreviations like the ampersand have in our texts. But why did the Hittite scribes make their task so difficult? Is it all to be explained with the origin of the script and the conservative nature of writing systems? The Akkadians acquired from the Sumerians a number of word-signs and the Hittites acquired from the Akkadians both these and Akkadian word-signs; it is only natural inertia which preserved them even when they were oddities no longer understood? This view is demonstrably erroneous. Recent work has shown that in some instances the early Hittite texts regularly use Hittite syllabic spelling where the late texts use Sumerograms or Akkadograms. Thus the word for 'back, behind', Hittite *appan* is written *a-ap-pa-an* in the older texts but EGIR or EGIR-(*pa-*)*an* (the Sumerian EGIR means 'behind') in the later texts (Friedrich and Kammenhuber 1975– : 149); the word for 'not', Hittite *natta*, is written *na-at-ta* in the early texts, but in the late texts the Akkadian *UL* or *Ú.UL* is used (Houwink Ten Cate 1970: 46–9). Here the language did not change, but the spelling did, and the new spelling, the result of a deliberate innovation, is *less* close to speech than the old one.[19]

Let us now turn to Hieroglyphic Luwian. We ought to remember that the script was developed for the Hittite or Luwian languages, and that it was certainly developed and used by scribes who knew cuneiform. Yet, while Cuneiform has signs for syllables of the type *a*, *na*, *an*, and (more rarely) *kan*, Hieroglyphic Luwian has only signs of the *a* and *na* type, which makes it far more difficult to represent the closed syllables ([consonant +]vowel + consonant) which certainly existed in the language. In Cuneiform a sequence like *annan* would be written (*a*)-*an-na-an*, but in Hieroglyphic it could only be written *a-na-na*; the same spelling would also have to be used if the word ended in -*a* and not in -*n*. Yet to have signs of the *an* type leads to a system with a larger number of signs; the scribes happily gave up the possibility of bringing their script closer to speech in order to keep the number of signs down. Even more striking, however, is the way in which Hieroglyphic Luwian developed. An old view is that in the later texts the script had developed or was developing into a semi-alphabet: signs of the *na* type had effectively come to have an *n* value.[20] We now know more and realize that this is wishful thinking; in the late stages the script became more and more syllabic (Morpurgo Davies and Hawkins 1978: 781 f.). Consider for instance the two signs nos. 376 and 377 Laroche which probably originated as pictorial representations (a pointing finger or an arrow) of the demonstrative 'this' (Luwian *za-*). In the second millennium there was only one sign which had the value *za/i* (↑). In the first millennium we have two signs: no. 377 *za* (⚟) and no. 376 *zi* (↑). We can probably understand how the two signs were developed: *za* arose from a ligature of the earlier *za/i* sign with no. 450 Laroche *à* (⚟); the older sign shape is then reserved for *zi*. A similar development is attested for another couple of signs.

In other words, starting with signs of the *za/i* type, the script could have easily turned into an alphabet, but in fact moved towards a regular syllabic system (Morpurgo Davies and Hawkins 1978). This interpretation is confirmed by a further example. The sign for *u* (and possibly *uwa*, no. 105 Laroche) is attested from our earliest texts; it is an ox or cow head (🐂) and the Luwian word for ox or cow is *uwi-* or *wawi-*. Hence the origin is clear. The sign for *mi* (no. 391 Laroche) is equally well known; it is formed by four parallel strokes (ıı ıı) and is also used to indicate the number 4: the Luwian word for '4' was *mauwa-* or *miw-*. In the early period the four strokes had the value *ma/i*, while in the later period the sign stands for *mi* only. At an early stage a new sign *mu* (no. 107 Laroche) was created by the simple device of adding four strokes to the cow's head: *m + u ·mu* ( ) . Here too it all works as if in the second millennium the four strokes practically had an *m* value and were then joined to *u* according to principles which are almost alphabetic; later on the new *mu* sign was taken as an unanalysable sign. In other words, in the first millennium BC when Semitic consonantal writing (an alphabet according to most scholars) was well known in the region, the script was moving away from the alphabet and was developing into a well-organized syllabary. Is this perverse tendency a peculiarity of Anatolia?

The answer is likely to be negative if we consider what happened in Greek territory. There Linear B, a syllabic script, is used for Greek in the second millennium; as we have seen, a distantly related syllabic script is also used for Greek at Cyprus. But we are now in the first millennium and Syllabic Cyprian is used in preference to, but concurrently with, the Greek alphabet. How does it compare with Linear B? There are some innovations, but none of these is alphabetic in nature; the number of signs is smaller and the syllabary has simply become a better organized syllabary with stricter rules which determine its use. The conclusion at this stage seems trivial but clear: the alphabetic principle has no magic power which influences the destiny of other forms of writing; as Cuneiform Hittite shows, in the development of writing there is no necessary tendency towards an increasingly exact phonetic rendering of speech. Other, and contradictory, types of development seem to occur. Some may well be determined by speed requirements: it is faster to write *Ú.UL* or *UL* than to write *na-at-ta*, nor is there any reason to suppose that this would have caused reading difficulties. We constantly tend to forget that the people who wrote these texts knew, far better than we do, the language they were writing in. There may be a tendency to keep the number of signs down and, at least for the period and the part of the world I am concerned with, there seems to be a general tendency towards a clarification and simplification of the writing system and of the principles on which it operates. Hieroglyphic Luwian becomes fully syllabic; Syllabic Cyprian, if contrasted with Linear B, has abolished all logograms, and clarified some of the conventions, that is it has become the perfect syllabary. This too is something which would deserve further study: a writing system which is typologically consistent is no easier to use than one that is not, nor I suspect is it less prone to ambiguous writings. If so, what prompts this movement towards typological consistency? Did the pedagogical needs of the writing schools have any part in it?[21]

So much for the thesis that once the shift from pictographic to non-pictographic has been accomplished scripts inevitably tend towards the alphabet. My next objective is to consider whether the development or the interiorization of the alphabet (to use Professor Ong's expression) is in fact responsible, as has sometimes been argued, for a complete change in the modes of thought of the users. I cannot obviously tackle the question in full here. Is it true that Plato could not have discussed moral justice as he did, had he not belonged to a society which was both literate and 'alphabetic'? I prefer to leave aside this problem—to my mind insoluble—and turn to a humbler sort of question. I shall discuss two different types of evidence in turn. I start with something which is for us entirely trivial: though we are fully aware of the possibility of forging documents we still tend to assume that proof of the validity of some statements is best found in the written text. There are moments in one's life when birth certificates must be produced; less solemn occasions when passports must be shown. Both in private and in public life we trust written more than verbal communication (or so we say). On a recent occasion the British Prime Minister is reported to have said in Parliament: 'The NCB has made its position clear in writing. I believe this is the best basis on which to enter into negotiations—to make it clear in writing' (Speech of 24 January 1985 reported in *The Times* of 25 January 1985: 4). We are fully entitled to think that this attitude is the product of literacy. If we now turn to ancient Greece we may draw attention to at least one example of a similar attitude. The historian Thucydides (vii. 8. 2) reports that in 414 BC the Athenian General Nicias, who was worried about the position of his army in Sicily, composed a written message to send to Athens; we are told that he did not send a verbal message since he was afraid that his messengers would not report the full truth either because they were not good at speaking or because they did not have sufficient memory or because they wanted to please the crowds. Nicias' decision to write was obviously a new step; hence Thucydides' explanation of his motives. According to scholars interested in the techniques of communication in Greece, this passage reveals how deep was the technological transformation which was happening in Athenian society as the result of literacy (Longo 1981: 82). The interpretation is no doubt correct, and reveals that Thucydides at least, and probably Nicias, if the story is true, shared our feelings about the greater reliability of the written text; let us not forget, incidentally, that Nicias was certainly capable of writing and would probably have written the letter himself. Yet the attitude which prompted Nicias' decision is not peculiar to Greek literacy. Let us now look at another letter written almost one thousand years earlier. It is in Hittite, written in cuneiform, and was sent by an Anatolian king to Amenophis III of Egypt in the early fourteenth century BC in connection with the possibility of a royal marriage (VBoT 2; Rost 1956: 328 f.). It reads, 'I do not trust Kalbaya. He said it as a word, but it is not put down on a tablet. If you really wanted my daughter, would I not give her to you? (Of course) I shall give her to you. Send back in a hurry Kalbaya together with my messenger. And write me back this thing/word on a tablet.' The odds are that the king, who dictated this message to his scribe, was illiterate (as was the normal pattern);[22] nevertheless he was interested in a written commitment: words are words and he wanted it in writing. From this point of view syllabic literacy by proxy (because this was the position of the Anatolian king) and alphabetic direct literacy (the position of the Greek general and that of Mrs Thatcher, the British Prime Minister) do not differ.

I turn now to my second type of evidence. If we take for granted that there is a connection, of whatever nature, between writing and language we might a priori expect that knowledge of a particular form of writing is likely to influence an individual's perception of linguistic phenomena. This is no doubt true in the modern world. There are linguistic concepts, such as that of word, which most speakers of English assume are entirely clear, and yet cause desperate problems to linguists.[23] The layman does not worry since he 'knows' what a word is: a word is something which, when written, appears between two empty spaces, and he has learned at school how to divide words.[24] I want to consider whether at this level we can recognize some fundamental difference between alphabetic and for instance syllabic writers. The discussion, however, needs some introduction and a digression. It is often said—wrongly—that alphabetic texts provide more information about the language in which they are written than any other form of script. This is, or may be, true, for some phonological aspects of language, but need not be true for other aspects. An example is enough: in common with other Near-Eastern languages Cuneiform Hittite and Hieroglyphic Luwian mark some written words with special symbols (determinatives); these in practice correspond to a semantic and grammatical classification of linguistic units: we have determinatives for god, man, woman, city, country, river, flesh, leather, cloth, vessel, and so on. The Near-Eastern word lists which we have preserved and which are often trilingual (Sumerian, Akkadian, Hittite), are sometimes organized on the basis of the determinative which precedes the word. Determinatives do not always make 'concrete' distinctions. In Hieroglyphic Luwian verbs of movement (including 'go', 'come', 'bring', 'transport', and so on) tend to be marked by one of two possible determinatives, that is by one of two signs (nos. 90 and 93 Laroche) which have the shape of a foot and a reversed foot respectively: the foot is used for verbs of coming or bringing (movement towards the speaker); the reversed foot for verbs of going (movement away from the speaker). In the language the distinction is largely semantic but partly grammatical too. Are these facts not revealing both for the language and for the analysis which its speakers make of it?

Eric Havelock (1982: 8) in his description of what he calls 'the alphabetic mind' argues that 'the alphabet converted the Greek spoken tongue into an artefact, thereby separating it from the speaker and making it into a "language", that is an object available for inspection, reflection, analysis'; he then proceeds to ask: 'Was this merely a matter of creating the notion of grammar?' Whatever the answer to the question, the implication is that, if nothing else, at least the start of grammatical thought must be seen as the result of the diffusion of the alphabet. Is the claim acceptable? Once again, I shall not tackle the main question—what determined the creation of grammar in Greece—partly because this would oblige me to consider at what stage we assume grammatical thought or grammar proper started. I shall simply discuss a detail. In contrast with classical Greek texts, the syllabic texts I have described are highly informative about two notions, which, if we are to judge from the Greek developments, are essential for grammatical analysis. I refer to the notions of word and syllable.

We have far clearer ideas about what was taken to be a word in Cuneiform Hittite, Hieroglyphic Luwian, Linear B, and Syllabic Cyprian than we do for the much later period in which the Greeks wrote. The reason is that in all these syllabaries word-division is regularly marked—either with empty spaces as in Cuneiform Hittite, or with special signs used as word dividers, as in Hieroglyphic Luwian and in Linear B, or with special writing conventions, as in Syllabic Cyprian. In classical Greek inscriptions the writing is continuous: no word-division, no capitals, no accents, and no real breathings. Since, as Havelock rightly observes, there is no unambiguous Greek word for 'word', it follows that we do not know until relatively late whether the Greeks had or did not have a notion of word. For Havelock (1982: 289 f.) this first appears in the fifth century BC: 'Archaic terminology had described human language synthetically, as song, speech, utterance, saying, talk. (Neither *epos* nor *logos* originally signified the separated word)'; by contrast in Aristophanes (fifth century BC) 'one detects an increasing tendency to view language as though it were broken up into bits and pieces . . .'. The new terminology is fostered 'by new habits of seeing language as a physical thing'; in their turn these habits are largely due to the new writing technology. Yet neither Havelock nor others have noticed that some notion of word existed in Greek territory as early as the second millennium BC: Linear B scrupulously divides words. It could be objected that a question of continuity arises. Even if Linear B word-division points to some grammatical notion of word—however subconscious—in the second millennium, why cannot we assume that this was lost and was then 'rediscovered' in the fifth century under the impact of the new literacy, as suggested by Havelock? The answer here is not too difficult to find. First, we have word-division, albeit with different means, in Syllabic Cyprian in the first millennium; secondly, and far more important given the isolation of Syllabic Cyprian, word-division of sorts appears in some archaic alphabetic inscriptions (sixth–fifth centuries). There, in contrast with the later inscriptions, one or more dots are occasionally used to separate words. Does anything indicate that the Mycenaean notion of word and the alphabetic Greek notion of word are the same? This too can be supported. Mycenaean word-dividers mostly overlap with modern spacing but do not always do so. What they mark off is an accentual unit, that is either a single accented element or a sequence of accented and unaccented elements. On this criterion an English phrase like 'the dog' would count as a single word and a sequence like 'the north wind and the sun were disputing' would consist of four words, corresponding to the four main accents of 'north' 'wind', 'sun', and 'disputing'. Roughly the same division criteria, based on accent, apply to Syllabic Cyprian and to the archaic alphabetic inscriptions where words are divided. More strikingly there are passages in fourth-century authors such as Plato and Aristotle which can only make sense if Plato and Aristotle operated on the basis of a similar notion of word. Indeed that this was the dominating notion emerges from the grammatical discussions of scholars as late as Apollonius Dyscolus who wrote in the second century AD. Apollonius' discussion starts by taking for granted the accent-based notion of word, but then expresses doubts about it and wonders whether other approaches are possible. It would be perverse, I submit, to assume that the Mycenaean Greeks round 1300 BC, the first millennium Greeks of Cyprus, the sixth- and fifth-century authors of alphabetic inscriptions which mark word-division, the fourth-century philosophers, and the late grammarians, all independently rediscovered the same criteria for word-division; it would be equally perverse to argue that in spite of all this the notion of word was absent in the early fifth century and was then rediscovered by the 'alphabetic mind' of some fifth- and fourth-century authors.[25]

Similar observations may be made apropos of other notions that Havelock does not consider, those of syllable and syllabic division; here too we find a complete continuity between Mycenaean times and the much later Greek period when syllabic division was discussed (Morpurgo Davies 1986*b*). The continuity is all the more noticeable in that it goes against all the evidence we have about syllabic division in speech. Because of some facts of Greek metre, we assume that an intervocalic sequence such as -*kt*- was always split between two syllables: hence a word like *Hektōr* was formed of two syllables, *Hek*- and -*tōr*.[26] What we now find is that in Mycenaean writing a noun like *Hektōr* is treated as formed by two syllables which are *He*- and -*ktōr*, not the expected *Hek*- and -*tōr*.[27] The same applies to Syllabic Cyprian. We do not find references to syllables in the linguistic sense until the fifth century BC and the Greek alphabetic texts are normally silent about syllabic division.[28]

Yet starting with the third and possibly late fourth centuries BC it became fashionable to split words at the end of the line according to some criteria of syllabic division. In Attica at least the alphabetic texts where this is done also divide *He-ktōr* against our expectations (Threatte 1980: 64 ff.). Later on, in the first centuries of our era, the grammarians seriously discussed the problems which arose from syllabic division. In the second century AD Herodianus produced a full set of rules and concluded once again that the correct division was *He-ktōr*. Differently from his ancient predecessors, he also explained the rationale for his decisions. Syllabic division should be made according to the principles which govern the possible combinations of sounds at the beginning of a word. Greek words can begin with *kt-* but cannot end with *-k*; hence *Hek-* does not form a syllable and only one division is possible: *He-ktōr* (Hermann 1923: 126–30). Here too, we find a surprising form of continuity, as revealed by writing, in what I should like to call metalinguistic reactions, from the period of the syllabic scripts down to the period of full alphabetic literacy. Can this be by chance? We know how the late grammarians explained their decisions; did they simply produce a rationalization of the principles which they had somehow inherited? What prompted the earlier decision of the first syllabic writers of Greek?

This may seem a trivial collection of details—and one which is not relevant to the main purpose of this chapter. Yet even these details lead to more general conclusions than at first appears. The last facts I have mentioned reveal a continuity of linguistic, or perhaps folk-linguistic, reactions, which lasted in Greece for more than one millennium and survived through a violent disruption such as that which signed the end of the Mycenaean civilization and a cultural renewal such as that marked by the introduction of the alphabet and the new literacy. If it is true that the 'alphabetic mind' is fundamentally different from the pre-alphabetic mind it is striking that it is just this type of linguistic-grammatical attitudes which survives. Havelock argues that the alphabetic revolution was shattering and not merely for grammar. I want to argue that the size of the gap between the 'alphabetic mind' and the 'syllabic mind' has been overrated, largely through the fault of omission. Undoubtedly in the ancient world there are considerable differences between illiterate and literate societies and between pre-alphabetic and alphabetic societies but we cannot a priori assume that these are connected with the writing technology used or with its absence, nor can we a priori define the cultural features which in any given society are likely to be affected by a change in writing technology.[29] I have made a case for the survival of some fundamental linguistic or folk-linguistic notions in Greece through a period of loss and acquisition of literacy. It would also be possible to argue that the Near-Eastern pre-alphabetic civilizations were not as deprived of scientific and scholarly results, that is of those results which tend most obviously to be associated with literacy, as is sometimes assumed. There is a Sumerian proverb which reads: 'The scribal art is the mother of orators and the father of scholars' (Lambert 1960: 259)—it was written long before the alphabet was invented. The Sumerian concept of scholarship may well have been very different from our own, but serious scholarship—cuneiform scholarship—existed in the Near East earlier than in Greece, and is not the product of an alphabetic culture.[30]

NOTES

1. Strictly speaking pictographic writing does not belong in this list since its link with language is or may be of a different order from that of the other types.
2. A comparison between the two classifications is drawn by Cardona (1981: 21 ff. and 34 f.) who should also be consulted for background information to the problems mentioned above and below.
3. This was the view held e.g. by Max Müller in the second half of last century (cf. in general Morpurgo Davies 1975).
4. Romaine (1982: 15) points out that when modern linguists speak of the death of a language they normally refer to the loss of its spoken form—which contrasts or ought to contrast with the view supported above.
5. Cf. Goody 1968: 20 ff. (see also Goody 1977): 'in Greece it was not only the alphabet which was being introduced but writing of any kind (at least, for the first time for some 500 years)'; in other words, what matters is the introduction of literacy rather than that of a specific writing system. Part of the papers collected in Goody 1968 (e.g. Gough 1968) also point out that relatively widespread literacy is possible even with non-alphabetic scripts.
6. See Havelock 1963, 1971, 1976, 1978, and the collection of articles in Havelock 1982; a recent summary of Havelock's views can be found in Havelock 1982: 3–38.
7. That the alphabet is a more efficient writing system than any other is

normally accepted: cf. e.g. Scribner and Cole 1981: 239, but see also ibid. 240 for further references and observations about the efficiency and success of some syllabic scripts and of the syllabic system in general.

8. In recent years linguists, sociologists, anthropologists, and education-alists have done a certain amount of work about the differences between spoken and written language in the use of specific linguistic communities or even of specific individuals (cf. e.g. Greenfield 1972, O'Donnell 1974, Poole and Field 1976, and the articles collected in Tannen 1982*b*). In comparing different scripts it would obviously be useful to know whether there is a correlation between the specific features of a script and the way in which the written and spoken norms differ in the society which uses the script in question. We ought to be able to ask questions such as: are texts in for example syllabic scripts more likely than alphabetic texts to show linguistic features which are not found in the spoken language? Unfortunately this approach is unsuitable for ancient cultures which are only known through written records—even if interesting inferences can sometimes be made in this field too (in ancient Greek it is possible to identify some features which are likely to have belonged to written language only; some inferences are possible for classical Chinese (Li and Thompson 1982), etc.).

9. Street (1984: 2) refers to the somewhat ill-defined claim that a society needs a 40 per cent literacy rate for economic 'take off'; other classifi-cations of society development, such as that by Parsons 1966, in terms of different rates of literacy (in an 'advanced intermediate society' literacy is characteristic of all upper-class adult males), are also open to the objection that the 'quality' and uses of literacy are as important as its spread.

10. For some general data and references about these and other contem-porary scripts see Hawkins 1979, as well as the standard histories of writing quoted e.g. in Gelb 1963 and Cardona 1981.

11. Gelb 1960 has suggested that the script may have been originally devised for a non-Sumerian population.

12. General introduction, Friedrich 1960*b*; list of signs, Friedrich 1960*a*; brief account of the development of the script and its problems. Laroche 1978.

13. General introductions, Ventris and Chadwick 1973, Hooker 1980; detailed information about the script and further references, Duhoux 1985.

14. There is nothing 'hieroglyphic' about the script; the adjective refers to the appearance of the signs, which often are easily identifiable rep-resentations of objects, animals etc. General introductions, Laroche 1975, Meriggi 1966–75; historical data, Hawkins 1982; list of signs, Laroche 1960; new transliterations, Hawkins, Morpurgo Davies,

Neumann 1973, Hawkins 1975; development of the script, Morpurgo Davies and Hawkins 1978.

15. Introduction, texts, signs etc., Masson 1983 (cf. p. 408, no. 18g for a reference to the earliest text now available which dates from the eleventh century BC). Cf. also Mitford and Masson 1982.

16. For early Greek writing see Jeffery 1961 and 1982; for the derivation of the alphabet from a Semitic script cf. Driver 1976: pt. iii; Isserlin 1982. The view that the so-called Semitic alphabets are in fact syllabaries was proposed by Gelb (1963: 146 ff.) and is still disputed.

17. At least for the four non-alphabetic scripts the types of texts we have and the material on which they are written may be determined by chance only; writing on perishable material was easily lost, it is conceivable that specific genres were confined to specific types of material support, and the evidence is not sufficient, as in the case of the alphabet, to provide adequate references to what was lost. Lack of evidence also prevents us from answering a basic question: how many people were literate in the scripts listed? Some serious work has been done for Greece, and above all for Attica: cf. most recently Harvey 1966, Woodbury 1976 with the conclusion that the majority of adult Attic citizens in the fifth century BC had basic literacy; the position was different in Sparta (Cartledge 1978; Boring 1979); for most other regions and periods we do not know, though there is more information about Hellenized Egypt. Knowledge of writing in second millennium Anatolia was probably limited to scribes and we do not know what their number was; Laroche (1971: 193) refers to more than 91 different scribes whose name is known, but this means but little. The evidence is even more limited for Hieroglyphic Luwian and Cyprian, though it is worth pointing out that we have Cyprian graffiti in Egypt which look like the work of individuals (mercenaries, etc.) who were not professional scribes. For Linear B we know that at the same period there may have been some one hundred scribes at Knossos and some fifty scribes at Pylos (Olivier 1967, 1984), but we do not know what the size of the population was. It is useful to compare the data for other contemporary cultures; in his interesting studies of Egyptian literacy J. Baines (1983; Baines and Eyre 1983) suggests that in most periods only 1 per cent of the Egyptian population was literate.

18. Sumerograms are often accompanied by phonetic complements, i.e. by Hittite terminations: DUMU-*aš* 'son' has the Hittite nominative ending -*aš*; Akkadograms can also have Hittite phonetic complements but this is rare.

19. In modern English writing the alphabetic principle (one letter, one segment) obviously does not apply, but in a number of instances at least it could be argued that this is due to the conservative nature of

spelling which does not reflect language change. That is why I have concentrated on innovations rather than on old features.

20. Cf. the brief resumé of Bossert's views in Laroche 1960: 259.

21. A factor that we cannot test with this set of data concerns once again the extent of literacy; it would be possible to argue that when writing is limited to a small group of scribes it develops differently from when it is more widely used.

22. The same tablet contains a few sentences addressed by the writer directly to his fellow scribe: 'You, scribe, write clearly to me, and add your name (to the text). And as for the tablets which they will bring to me write them in Hittite.' Presumably neither the Anatolian nor the Egyptian king were likely to read the text by themselves.

23. Cf. the simple, but clear, discussion by Frank Palmer (1971: 41–51) which ends negatively: 'In conclusion, sadly, we have to say that the word is not a clearly definable linguistic unit.'

24. Pre-school children do not find it easy to segment speech into words, or into what we call words (Romaine 1984: 206 f.).

25. For the basic data, which cannot be given here, and for a more detailed discussion cf. Morpurgo Davies 1985 and above all 1986*a*.

26. For the main facts of Greek syllabification cf. Hermann 1923 and Allen 1973: 203–23. This is not the place to discuss Pulgram's views, which I find impossible to accept. Pulgram (e.g. 1981, with earlier references) knows that a Greek word like *Hektōr* is scanned as two long syllables but nevertheless assumes that the correct syllabic division is *He-ktōr* and the first vowel is lengthened because of metrical convention. Cf. in general Morpurgo Davies 1986*b*.

27. In Linear B we have words like *te-ko-to-ne, e-ko-to, e-ko-to-ri-jo,* i.e. *tektones, Hektōr, Hektorio-* where the signs chosen to render the *-kt-* cluster (*te-ko-to-, e-ko-to-* rather than **te-to-, *e-to-*) point to a division of the *He-ktōr* (not *Hek-tōr*) type. Similarly in Syllabic Cyprian we have forms like *ti-mo-wa-na-ko-to-se*: *Timowana-ktos* (rather than **ti-mo-wa-na-ke-to-se*: *Timowanak-tos*).

28. The word *syllabē* 'syllable' in its technical meaning first appears in the fifth century BC (possibly in Aeschylus *Septem*, 468 and certainly in Euripides fr. 578 Nauck); words and concept are well attested in the fourth century (Plato and Aristotle). Grammatical discussion of syllabic division is attested much later; the most complete account we have is by Herodianus in the second century AD (Hermann 1923: 123–32).

29. Cf. for similar observations apropros of Egypt Baines (1983).

30. Speaking not of scholarship but of poetry Havelock (1982: 166 ff.) compares the translations of two passages which contain descriptions of natural events in the *Epic of Gilgamesh* and in the *Iliad*, notices that the Greek passage is less tautological and less ritualized in style than the Akkadian passage, and suggests that the difference is due to the

writing form in which the two compositions were recorded: 'the deficiencies of cuneiform as an instrument of acoustic-visual recognition have discouraged the composer from packing into his verse the full variety of expression which such a description calls for; the alphabet on the other hand applied to a transcription of the same experience places no obstacles in the way of its complete phonetic translation' (1982: 172). The hypothesis is obviously untestable; I can simply observe that my experience of syllabic scripts does not make me feel that it would be impossible to write Homeric poetry in a syllabary, and that, as Havelock himself points out, the contrast between Gilgamesh and the Iliad is also capable of a different explanation.

REFERENCES

Allen, W. S. 1973: *Accent and Rhythm*. Cambridge: Cambridge University Press.

Baines, J. 1983: 'Literacy and Ancient Egyptian Society', in *Man* (NS), 18: 572–99.

—— and C. J. Eyre 1983: 'Four Notes on Literacy', in *Göttinger Miszellen*, 61: 65–96.

Basso, K. H. 1980: Review of Goody 1977, in *Language in Society*, 9: 72–80.

Boring, T. A. 1979: *Literacy in Ancient Sparta* (Mnemosyne: Supplement 54). Leiden: Brill.

Cardona, G. R. 1981: *Antropologia della Scrittura*. Turin: Loescher.

Cartledge, P. A. 1978: 'Literacy in the Spartan Oligarchy', in *Journal of Hellenic Studies*, 98: 25–37.

Driver, G. R. 1976: *Semitic Writing. From Pictograph to Alphabet*, rev. edn. ed. S. A. Hopkins. London: Oxford University Press for the British Academy.

Duhoux, Y. 1985: 'Mycénien et écriture grecque', in A. Morpurgo Davies and Y. Duhoux (eds.), *Linear B: A 1984 Survey*, pp. 7–74. Louvain: Cabay.

Friedrich, J. 1960a: *Hethitisches Keilschrift-Lesebuch*, vol. 2. Heidelberg: Winter.

—— 1960b: *Hethitisches Elementarbuch*, vol. 1. Heidelberg: Winter.

—— and A. Kammenhuber 1975– : *Hethitisches Wörterbuch*, 2nd edn. (in progress). Heidelberg: Winter.

Gelb, I. J. 1960: 'Sumerians and Akkadians in their Ethno-linguistic Relationship', in *Genava*, 8: 258–71.

—— 1963: *A Study of Writing*, rev. edn. Chicago: Chicago University Press. (1st edn. 1952.)

—— 1980: 'Principles of Writing Systems within the Frame of Visual Communication', in P. A. Kolers, M. E. Wrolstad, H. Bouma (eds.). *Processing of Visible Language 2*, pp. 7–24. New York: Plenum Press.

Goody, J. (ed.) 1968: *Literacy in traditional Societies.* Cambridge: Cambridge University Press.

—— 1977: *The Domestication of the Savage Mind.* Cambridge: Cambridge University Press.

—— and I. Watt 1963: 'The Consequences of Literacy', in *Comparative Studies in Society and History*, 5: 304–45, repr. in Goody (ed.) 1968: 27–68.

Gough, K. 1968: 'Implications of Literacy in Traditional China and India', in Goody (ed.) 1968: 70–84.

Greenfield, P. M. 1972: 'Oral or Written Language: the consequences for cognitive development in Africa, the United States and England', in *Language and Speech*, 15: 169–78.

Harvey, F. D. 1966: 'Literacy in the Athenian Democracy', in *Revue des études grecques*, 79: 585–635.

Havelock, E. A. 1963: *Preface to Plato.* Oxford: Basil Blackwell.

—— 1971: *Prologue to Greek Literacy.* Cincinnati: Cincinnati University Press.

—— 1976: *Origins of Western Literacy.* Toronto: Ontario Institute for the Study of Education.

—— 1978: *The Greek Concept of Justice from Its Shadow in Homer to Its Substance in Plato.* Cambridge, Mass.: Harvard University Press.

—— 1982: *The Literate Revolution in Greece and its Cultural Consequences.* Princeton, NJ: Princeton University Press.

Hawkins, J. D. 1975: 'The Negatives in Hieroglyphic Luwian', in *Anatolian Studies*, 25: 119–56.

—— 1979: 'The Origin and Dissemination of Writing in Western Asia', in P. R. S. Moorey (ed.), *The Origins of Civilization. Wolfson College Lectures 1978.* Oxford: Clarendon Press.

—— 1982: 'The Neo-Hittite States in Syria and Anatolia', in J. Boardman, I. E. S. Edwards, N. G. L. Hammond, E. Sollberger (eds.), *The Cambridge Ancient History*, 2nd edn., iii (1): 372–441. Cambridge: Cambridge University Press.

——, A. Morpurgo Davies, G. Neumann 1973: 'Hittite Hieroglyphs and Luwian: New evidence for the connection', in *Nachrichten der Akademie der Wiss. in Göttingen. Phil.-hist. Klasse*, Nr. 6.

Hermann, E. 1923: *Silbenbildung im Griechischen und in den andern indogermanischen Sprachen.* Göttingen: Vandenhoeck & Ruprecht.

Hooker, J. T. 1980: *Linear B. An Introduction.* Bristol: Bristol Classical Press.

Houwink Ten Kate, Ph. H. J. 1970: *The Records of the Early Hittite*

Empire. Istanbul: Nederlands historisch-archaeologisch Instituut in het Nabije Oosten.

Isserlin, B. S. J. 1982: 'The Earliest Alphabetic Writing', in J. Boardman, I. E. S. Edwards, N. G. L. Hammond, E. Sollberger (eds.), *The Cambridge Ancient History*, 2nd edn., iii (1): 794–818. Cambridge: Cambridge University Press.

Jeffery, L. H. 1961: *The Local Scripts of Archaic Greece*. Oxford: Clarendon Press.

—— 1982: 'Greek Alphabetic Writing', in J. Boardman, I. E. S. Edwards, N. G. L. Hammond, E. Sollberger (eds.), *The Cambridge Ancient History*, 2nd edn., iii (1): 819–33. Cambridge: Cambridge University Press.

Kraus, F. R. 1973: *Vom mesopotamischen Menschen der altbabylonischen Zeit und seiner Welt*. Amsterdam: North Holland.

Lambert, W. 1960: *Babylonian Wisdom Literature*. Oxford: Oxford University Press.

Laroche, E. 1960: *Les Hiéroglyphes hittites*. Paris: Centre nationale de la recherche scientifique.

—— 1971: *Catalogue des textes hittites*. Paris: Klincksieck.

—— 1975: 'Hieroglyphen, hethitische', in *Reallexicon der Assyriologie*, iv: 394–9. Berlin: de Gruyter.

—— 1978: 'Problèmes de l'écriture cunéiforme hittite', in *Annali della Scuola Normale di Pisa. Classe di Lettere*, iii. 8: 739–53.

Li, C. N. and S. A. Thompson 1982: 'The Gulf between Spoken and Written Language: a Case Study in Chinese', in Tanner 1982*b*: 77–88.

Longo, O. 1981: *Tecniche della comunicazione nella Grecia antica*. Naples: Liguori.

Marschack, A. 1972: *The Roots of Civilization: The Cognitive Beginnings of Man's First Art, Symbol and Notation*. New York: McGraw-Hill.

Masson, O. 1983: *Les Inscriptions chypriotes syllabiques*, enlarged 2nd edn. Paris: Boccard.

McIntosh, A. 1956: 'The Analysis of Written Middle English', in *Transactions of the Philological Society*: 26–55.

Meadmore, S. 1980: *Behind the Mask*. London: Hale (Italian trans.: *A come Amore*. Milan, 1981).

Meriggi, P. 1966–75: *Manuale di eteo geroglifico*, 4 vols. Rome: Edizioni dell'Ateneo.

Mitford, T. B. and O. Masson 1982: 'The Cypriot Syllabary', in J. Boardman and N. G. L. Hammond (eds.), *The Cambridge Ancient History*, 2nd edn., ii (3): 71–82. Cambridge: Cambridge University Press.

Morpurgo Davies, A. 1975: 'Language Classification in the Nineteenth Century', in T. Sebeok (ed.), *Current Trends in Linguistics*, 13: 607–716. The Hague: Mouton.

—— 1985: 'Mycenaean and Greek Language', in A. Morpurgo Davies and Y. Duhoux (eds.), *Linear B: A 1984 Survey*, pp. 75–125. Louvain: Cabay.

—— 1986*a*: 'Folk-linguistics and the Greek word', to appear in *Festschrift* H. M. Hoenigswald.

—— 1986*b*: 'Mycenaean and Greek Syllabification', to appear in *Tractata Mycenaea*. Proceedings of the 8th Int. Colloquium on Mycenaean Studies. Skopje.

—— and J. D. Hawkins, 1978: 'Il sistema grafico del luvio geroglifico', in *Annali della Scuola Normale di Pisa. Classe di Lettere*, iii. 8: 755–82.

O'Donnell, R. C. 1974: 'Syntactic differences between speech and writing', in *American Speech*, 49: 102–10.

Olivier, J.-P. 1967: *Les Scribes de Cnossos*. Rome: Edizioni dell' Ateneo.

—— 1984: 'Administrations at Knossos and Pylos: What differences?', in *Pylos comes alive. Industry and Administration in a Mycenaean Palace*, pp. 11–18. New York: Fordham University.

Ong, W. J. 1982: *Orality and Literacy. The Technologizing of the Word*. London and New York: Methuen.

Otten, H. 1981: *Die Apologie Hattusilis III*. Wiesbaden: Harrassowitz.

Palmer, F. 1971: *Grammar*. Harmondsworth: Penguin Books.

Parsons, T. 1966: *Societies. Evolutionary and comparative perspectives*. Englewood Cliffs: Prentice Hall.

Poole, M. E. and J. W. Field 1976: 'A Comparison of Oral and Written Code Elaboration', in *Language and Speech*, 19: 305–12.

Pulgram, E. 1981: 'Attic Shortening or Metrical Lengthening?' in *Glotta*, 59: 75–93.

Romaine, S. 1982: *Socio-historical Linguistics*. Cambridge: Cambridge University Press.

—— 1984: *The Language of Children and Adolescents*. Oxford: Blackwell.

Rost, L. 1956: 'Die ausserhalb von Boğazköy gefundenen hethitischen Briefe', in *Mitteilungen des Instituts für Orientforschung*, 4: 328–50.

Schmandt-Besserat, D. 1977: 'An Archaic Recording System and the Origin of Writing', in *Syro-Mesopotamian Studies*, 1: 1–32.

—— 1979: 'An Archaic Recording System in the Uruk-Jemdet Nasr Period', in *American Journal of Archaeology*, 83: 19–48.

Scribner, S. and M. Cole 1981: *The Psychology of Literacy*. Cambridge, Mass.: Harvard University Press.

Street, B. V. 1984: *Literacy in theory and practice*. Cambridge: Cambridge University Press.

Tannen, D. 1982*a*: 'Oral and Literate Strategies in Spoken and Written Narratives', in *Language*, 58: 1–21.

—— (ed.) 1982*b*: *Spoken and Written Language: Exploring Orality and Literacy*. Norwood: Atlex Publishing Corporation.

Threatte, L. 1980: *The Grammar of Attic Inscriptions*, i. Berlin: de Gruyter.

Vachek, J. 1973: *Written Language. General Problems and Problems of English.* The Hague: Mouton.

Ventris, M. and J. Chadwick 1973: *Documents in Mycenaean Greek*, 2nd edn. Cambridge: Cambridge University Press.

Woodbury, L. 1976: 'Aristophanes' *Frogs* and Athenian Literacy *Ran.* 52-3, 1114', in *Transactions of the American Philological Association*, 106: 349-57.

SCRIPTURE AND TRADITION
IN JUDAISM: WRITTEN AND
ORAL TORAH

GEZA VERMES

I

AFTER two chapters enquiring into the impact of writing on thought, and into the linguistic and ethno-linguistic aspects of the written word in Mediterranean antiquity, it falls to me, a historian of ancient Judaism, to consider the religious dimensions and implications of the text that has become known as Scripture or the Book, that is the Bible.

Let me begin with a light-hearted appendix to Professor Anna Davies' disquisition on the origin of the alphabet. We all know that the Greeks borrowed it from the Phoenicians. But where did the Phoenicians obtain it from? From the Jews, of course, as we are left in no doubt by Eupolemus, a Hellenistic Jewish historian, who flourished in the mid-second century BC. Moses taught them the alphabet (Eusebius: 26,1). And incidentally he also invented the Egyptian hieroglyphs according to another second-century BC Jewish writer, Artapanus (Eusebius: 27,4)! Civilization was created by the Jews. The Phoenicians and the Hellenes acquired literacy only at second hand.

But Hellenistic Jewish cultural imperialism apart, there is a serious reason why Judaism should be chosen as a paradigm to illustrate the role of the written word and its relation to oral tradition. Among the three monotheistic 'book' religions, that is, religions claiming to be based on a divine revelation subsequently recorded in script, not only is Judaism the oldest; it is also causally related to the other two, being the parent of Christianity and an essential source of Islam.

My chronological framework is post-biblical, or if you like, inter-Testamental (roughly from 200 BC to AD 200 with occasional extension of the boundaries by about 200 years each way). I shall be concerned with the connection between what is known as the Bible or written Torah (Torah means literally 'instruction'), and the so-called unwritten Torah, a postulated supplementary revelation that provided the originally verbal interpretation of the Holy Book.

However, in order to understand the genesis of the Bible as such, it may be helpful to sketch the part played by writing in ancient Israel. The theological view, conveyed by Scripture itself, is that writing started with the recording by Moses of the laws revealed to him by God on Mount Sinai. It is highly significant, yet I imagine not generally realized, that the Hebrew verb *katav*, to write, never occurs in the Book of Genesis, where the biblical account of human and Jewish prehistory is told. Its first appearance is in the Book of Exodus. This is what Eupolemus must have noted and probably explains why he portrays Moses as the inventor of the alphabet. Before Moses, only God knew how to write. He had a 'book' in which the name of Moses was inscribed (Exod. 32: 32–3), and it was the finger of God that engraved the ten commandments on the recto and verso sides of the two stone tablets (Exod. 31: 18; 32: 15). It was again God who had to write them a second time, after the outraged Moses had smashed to pieces the original copy of the Decalogue after the incident of the golden calf (Exod. 32: 19; 34: 1).

If we are to believe the Pentateuch, that is the five books of the Law of Moses, and the Book of Joshua, early scribal activity was essentially associated with the Torah, but the Bible itself refers to other written works, for instance the divorce bill (Deut. 24: 1) and the deed of purchase (Jer. 32: 10–11). The latter is described by the prophet Jeremiah apropos of his buying a plot of land from one of his relatives. Epic poetry is also attested by quotations, and since these derive from the *Book* of the Wars of the Lord (Num. 21: 14) and the *Book* of the Upright (Josh. 10: 13), we presume that they existed in writing. In the purely secular domain, we find biblical hints at the annals (1 Kings 14: 29) and letters (2 Sam. 11: 14) of Jewish kings, and still later at genealogical records (Neh. 7: 5). The Book of Daniel (1: 4) even reports that young Jews, educated in the court of Nebuchadnezzar in Babylon, learned the language and the writing of the Chaldeans, that is the Akkadian tongue and the cuneiform script.

Archaeological evidence also confirms a relatively widespread use of writing, but prior to the earliest scriptural fragments among the Dead Sea Scrolls, dating probably to the late third century BC, these have nothing to do with the Bible or with religious matters. From as early as the tenth century BC, we have an agricultural calendar on stone, found at Gezer; we possess inscribed jars of old wine and fine oil from eighth-century Samaria. An inscription from c.700 BC commemorates a major civil-engineering feat, the completion of the Siloam tunnel in Jerusalem. The essentially military Lachish ostraca, letters written on potsherds by the captain of an outpost to the commander of the city of Lachish during the Babylonian siege in the early sixth century BC, are the only surviving written documents of the pre-exilic age to reflect, though very indirectly, the Jewish faith in several pious formulae (Pritchard 1950: 320–2).

So in spite of the fundamental importance of 'the *Book* of the Law of God', that Joshua, Moses' successor (Josh. 1: 8), and the Israelite king (Deut. 17: 18), and every pious Jew (Psalm 1: 2) were to read and study always, 'day and night', neither Scripture, nor Palestinian archaeology indicates that the written word exerted much influence before the exile. On the contrary, the story of the discovery in the Jerusalem Temple, during the days of King Josiah in the late seventh century BC, of the Book of the Law (2 Kings 22: 8), the contents of which turned out to be unknown to the high priest and the religious authorities—to their utmost consternation— would suggest that Moses' famous work had been lost from sight for a long period and at least partly forgotten. Whether the account in the Second Book of the Kings is a cover story for a pious fraud, namely that the Jerusalem priests, wishing to introduce a religious reform favouring their cause, planted Deuteronomy, or something like it, in the sanctuary so that it might be found there accidentally by innocent workmen, is quite irrelevant. The real point is that, while the written Torah is depicted as enjoying ultimate authority, its direct influence from the time of Joshua to that of Josiah appears to have been dormant, with the further implication that during those centuries everything pertaining to religion, worship, law, instruction, was handed down verbally by Levitical priests.

This deduction is further confirmed by the fact that prophecy, one of the most remarkable spiritual activities during that period, was by definition an oral discipline. 'Go and *tell*!' or 'Prophesy and *say*!', are the commands addressed to Isaiah (6: 9) and Ezekiel (11: 4). Jeremiah, the most informative of the prophets, reports that the words of God were put into his *mouth* (Jer. 1: 9). It was only after many years of preaching that one day the heavenly voice enjoined him to transform his *ad hoc* oracles of doom into a single *written* message. He began therefore to dictate them to Baruch, his 'secretary', who wrote them down on a papyrus scroll (Jer. 36). The purpose was to produce a document that would convert the king, but when Jehoiakim heard Jeremiah's gloomy words, he fed the manuscript, piece by piece, into the open fire. So the prophet directed Baruch to make another copy, to which it is said much supplementary material was added (Jer. 36: 32).

In the chaos of the Babylonian invasion and the overthrow of the kingdom of Judah, which saw in its aftermath the deportation of the élite of Jerusalem to Mesopotamia, no one knows what happened to this second scroll. Nevertheless, the Jeremiah chapter provides a valuable glimpse into the actual making of a biblical book.

Many such scrolls are believed to have been produced during the four decades of Babylonian captivity in the sixth century, when not only other prophecies, but also the various versions of the Mosaic law and historical traditions were consigned to script. With the cessation of the monarchy and the destruction of the Temple seriously threatening the continuity of Judaism, the firmness and durability of the written word was thought to afford the best safeguard for the future.

Josiah's law book and Jeremiah's oracular anthology illustrate the emergence of individual compositions which were to become parts of an official collection of Holy Scriptures. But to attain this elevated status, they needed to surmount another important hurdle, that of canonization—if I may use this theological notion—that is the proclamation by a religious authority that the works in question were 'inspired', that they were endowed with a particular supernatural quality and were in consequence able to convey 'infallible' and obligatory doctrine. Historically, the process of the canonization of the Hebrew Bible took place between the fifth century and 200 BC. In other words, although, as we shall see presently, several attempts were made in the second century BC to introduce fresh titles to the list, it may be said that by the close of the third century the Palestinian canon was complete. The statement, still figuring in more than one textbook, that the Hebrew Scriptures did not acquire their final shape until the last decades of the first century AD, is mistaken. It is true that some rabbis of that epoch raised objections (Mishnah: Yadaim 3: 5) in connection with the Song of Songs (it was too erotic for them), and Ecclesiastes (a book inspiring agnosticism, they thought), but in the end, the status quo prevailed and neither work was deprived of its sacred character. How exactly the selection came about, no one knows, but it is clear that the Law of Moses was the first to be promulgated as Holy Scripture. This occurred around 400 BC, when the priest Ezra, returning from Babylonia to Jerusalem, brought with him a copy of the written Torah and, having read it publicly to the assembled Israelites, made them swear to accept and remain faithful to the divine commandments (Neh. 8).

This recognition of a text as the charter of Judaism was an event far-reaching in its consequences. Until that moment, a certain openness and elasticity had reigned, despite the likely existence of earlier forms of sacred books. To limit ourselves to the domain of law, changed political, social, or religious circumstances were catered for by a revision of the earlier rules, or even by the enactment of fresh legislation. Thus, whereas the more ancient Code of the Covenant (Exodus 20-4) is rather vague about altars and places of worship—'*Wherever* I cause my name to be invoked, I will come to you and bless you', a statute reflecting the pre-Deuteronomic plurality of Israelite temples—Deuteronomy 12: 5-7 decrees a single sanctuary in Jerusalem: 'You shall resort to the place which the Lord . . . will choose . . . to receive his name . . . There you shall . . . bring your . . . sacrifices.' More recent statutes superseded older ones without deleting them from the code. Indeed they continued to figure there (and be ignored) side by side with laws recognized as binding.

The same innovative tendency appears also in the narrative sections of the Torah. After the crystallization of more ancient traditions which may even have reached the written stage, (oral) development went on, sometimes far from consonant with the original ideas. For example, the primitive story of the faithful, God-seeking Gentile prophet Balaam (in Numbers 22-4) was distorted and rendered unrecognizable by the addition of priestly after-thoughts which describe him as a malicious adviser who caused the downfall of many Jews and was subsequently put to death by the surviving Israelites. The earlier, favourable, story was not altered; the pejorative remarks occur incidentally in separate passages; yet, as is manifest from both post-biblical Jewish and

New Testament allusions, the negative image attained a dominating position (Vermes 1973: 169–77).

Similarly, in the historical genre, the fairly objective account of the life of King David in the Second Book of Samuel includes such episodes as the illicit love-affair with Bathsheba which led to a disgraceful plot to kill her husband, Uriah, a brave and honourable officer in David's army. In the revised narrative presented centuries later by the author of the First Book of Chronicles, David becomes a saintly king busy with the organization of Temple worship and no trace of adultery or murder is to be found in his connection.

II

The pre-canonical state of the Hebrew Scriptures was marked by continuous growth (including the addition of entire new works) and permanent corrigibility. Canonization put an end to both. For reasons that elude our full grasp, Jewish religious authority decided one day that not only the two major units of Scripture, the Torah and the Prophets, were complete, but that the third, more hetero-geneous division of the Writings (starting with the Psalms and accommodating poetic and wisdom books and the historical review of the Chronicler) had also reached its full size. It would seem that one of the decisive arguments, or perhaps *the* decisive argument, for closing the canon was the conviction that holiness belonged to antiquity. If we are men—so a later rabbinic dictum asserts—then the ancients were angels; but if they were men, we are nothing but asses (Babylonian Talmud: Shabbath 112*b*). The relevance of the time factor at the final stages of the canonization process may be inferred from the fate of the last two claimants for recognition as Holy Scripture. The Wisdom of Jesus ben Sira (later surnamed Ecclesiasticus in Christian churches) which circulated under the name of its real early second-century BC author, did not quite make it. By contrast, the Book of Daniel, completed as late as the 160s BC, was admitted to the canon because it was falsely—or let us use a euphemism, pseudepigraphically—attributed to a legendary figure of the Babylonian exile and thus antedated to the sixth century BC. This was a fluke. None of the other pseudepigrapha which prolifer-ated in the last two centuries of the pre-Christian era, say the Book of Enoch, the Testaments of the Twelve Patriarchs, and so on, managed to share Daniel's good fortune.

The first obvious consequence of this new policy was to confer a uniquely privileged status on each single work as well as on the collection as a whole. Thus since its inclusion in the canon was synonymous with the acknowledgement that a book contained the 'words of God', the canonized Scriptures amounted to the sum total of the religious truth in Judaism.

Each volume or scroll of the Bible enjoyed this eminent dignity, although the Torah of Moses was rated higher than the rest. Every word of the Bible was accepted as divine, notwithstanding the fact that for hundreds of years rival types of Hebrew text coexisted, as we know today from the Dead Sea Scrolls.

In sum, canonized Holy Scripture was expected to answer every question concerning the past, the present and, yes, even the future. Here is a concrete example. The compiler of the Community Rule of the Dead Sea sect easily condensed, in around 100 BC, the essence of religious life as follows. The sectaries were to undertake 'to seek God with a whole heart and soul, and to do what is good and right before him as he commanded by the hand of Moses and all his servants, the Prophets' (Vermes 1975a: 72). As for the future, the same Dead Sea literature discloses that all the secrets of the *eschaton*, the last phase of the present epoch, were taken to have been adumbrated in the mysterious words preserved in the books of the Prophets.

III

It would be easy to imagine, given these conditions, that the nation which thought of itself as the 'people of God' or perhaps even the 'people of the Book', lived in confident security. Yet this was not so, and could not possibly have been so; for the very moment when the Bible became the Bible, the moment of canonization, carried with it an inescapable corollary: an end to adaptability and to the possibility of further development along accustomed lines. The living word of revelation, of instruction, of prohibition, of command, responding to the queries or doubts of an individual in a particular place and time and providing for his needs, lost its power of actuality and tended, potentially at least, to become a dead letter. Something new was required, a vehicle especially adapted to the circumstances. And this something, unwritten in the first instance, was Bible interpretation, designated later as the oral Torah.

As George Foot Moore writes in his classic *Judaism* (1927: i. 251), the whole revelation of God was not covered by the sacred books alone. Side by side with Scripture had always gone an unwritten tradition which had in part interpreted and applied the written Torah, and in part supplemented it.

The verbal nature of the interpretation of the written word is attested both concretely and in an institutionalized form by biblical and post-biblical Judaism. Thus the reading of the Law of Moses by Ezra was followed by an oral exposition delivered by Levites 'who gave the sense so that the people understood the reading' (Neh. 8: 7–8). Jewish tradition sees in this episode the establishment of a custom, adopted afterwards in the synagogue worship, of *reading* a passage from a Scripture scroll in Hebrew and accompanying it by an *unscripted* interpretative paraphrase in the Aramaic vernacular, the so-called Targum, so that even the uneducated could distinguish at once the Bible from its exposition (Palestinian Talmud: Megillah 74*d*).

Depending on the nature of the text, scriptural exegesis falls into two categories. If it is legal, the interpretation seeks to determine by means of clarification and supplementation the exact obligation imposed by the rule. This is called *halakhah* or way of conduct. If, on the other hand, the exegete is faced with a narrative or doctrinal passage, his aim is to derive by means of *haggadah* or explanation an appropriate moral or religious teaching (Schürer 1979: ii. 337–55). But whether it is *halakhah* or *haggadah*, Bible exegesis may serve two distinct functions. It may attempt either to expound a problematic text, or provide a religious community with a biblically based solution to a question arising not from Scripture, but from contemporary issues.

I propose to designate the first of the interpretative categories as *pure* exegesis (Vermes: 1975*b*: 62). When the expositor encountered a word or a verse, or a longer paragraph in the canonized sacred Scripture, which his audience, and perhaps even he himself, found difficult, it was his job to render the meaning plain.

He may have tumbled on a genuine textual problem. For instance, the traditional Hebrew text of Genesis 4: 8–9 reads:

Cain said to his brother Abel, and when they were in the field, Cain rose against Abel and killed him.

But what did Cain say? The words are missing. Jewish exegetes of antiquity offered various solutions. Some proposed an unadventurous and probably correct reconstruction:

Cain said to his brother Abel, Let us go out to the field

and when they arrived there, the murder took place. Others more imaginatively introduced a lengthy and complicated doctrinal debate between the two brothers concerning the principle guiding the divine government of history. It resulted in a bloody outcome, in anticipation of many a future theological argument, more common among Christians than among Jews.

A regular feature calling for exegesis is the dearth of sufficient detail in a biblical text. Many of the legal lacunae postulate a parallel unwritten Torah without which the rules cannot be put into practice. For example, one of the Ten Commandments states that no work must be performed on the Sabbath day without specifying what 'work' means. Haphazard instances appear here and there— the gathering of wood was prohibited; it was also forbidden to trade, to carry objects; to bring articles from outside into a house or to remove them from inside—but no full list of what was licit and illicit is available anywhere in Scripture. Yet it is obvious that in a matter of such private and public importance regulations must have been readily at hand. Indeed at a post-biblical stage these are extant and list no less than thirty-nine forbidden acts.

Perhaps the classic example of legal laconicism concerns another fundamentally important institution, divorce. The Bible does not treat it systematically (Deut. 24: 1–4); all we learn is that if a divorced woman who has remarried becomes free to enter matrimony for a third time, either because her second husband has died or because there has been a second divorce, in no circumstances may she renew her marital ties with her first husband. So divorce, even consecutive divorce, was an accepted social phenomenon, and it was procured, we discover accidentally, through the issue of a written document by the husband. But nowhere are we told on what *grounds* a marriage could be dissolved apart from the vague clause of impropriety. This term was understood to mean anything from causing the husband the smallest displeasure (such as spoiling his supper), to any form of sexual misbehaviour. A familiar illustration of this swing from the lax to the rigoristic is found in the Gospel of Matthew, chapter 19, where the Pharisees ask Jesus whether divorce is lawful *for any cause*, but are told that it is permitted in the case of unchastity alone (Vermes 1975*b*: 65–7). Here again, there must have been universally known rules relating to financial settlements, the form of the divorce bill, and so on (we now possess such deeds dating to the second century AD), but these essential details making good the omissions in Scripture were elaborated and transmitted for hundreds of years by the oral Torah only.

Gaps in a scriptural narrative can also be filled by means of *haggadic* exegesis. Genesis 12 recounts the migration of Abraham and Sarah to Egypt because of a severe famine in the land of Canaan. The patriarch, we are told, asked Sarah to conceal their true relationship, that they were a married couple, and say that she was his sister, explaining that if the Egyptians discovered the truth, they would certainly kill him. Their moral code apparently forbade the abduction of a man's wife, but considered a widow, irrespective of how she lost her husband, as available for remarriage. But the question arises: how did Abraham *know* that the beautiful Sarah would endanger his life? The Bible is silent on this point, but exegesis comes to the rescue, advancing all kinds of argument, rational and supernatural. The former, attested by the first-century AD Jewish historian Flavius Josephus (Jewish Antiquities i. 162), as well as by rabbinic interpreters (Midrash Rabbah: Exod. i. 22), implies that the Egyptians were well-known womanizers. Abraham, in consequence, required only a minimum of wordly wisdom to foresee what awaited him. A supernatural explanation is provided by one of the Dead Sea Scrolls: on the night of their arrival in Egypt, Abraham had a premonitory dream, which as a wise man he was able to interpret (Vermes 1975*a*: 217). By supplying either of these explanations, Bible exegesis not only renders the rough story smoother, but also resolves in advance any question which the readers or listeners are likely to ask.

In addition to its role as expounder of genuine—or imaginary— difficulties in the sacred books themselves, the oral Torah was also expected to deal with problems not envisaged in the Bible. Let us call this *applied* exegesis (Vermes 1975*b*: 62).

We have already seen, in connection with the canonization of Scripture, the change in the Pentateuch from legislation presupposing a multitude of temples to one that recognizes the Jerusalem Sanctuary alone. The destruction of this place of worship in 587 BC did not affect the legal and doctrinal position. The Jews who came back to Palestine from Babylonia obeyed the Deuteronomic statute and rebuilt the Second Temple on the ruins of the First. But what happened when, for theological or historical reasons, return to the status quo ante was no longer possible? To cite one case: following the unlawful deposition of the high priest Onias III by rival priests in the 170s BC (2 Macc. 4: 7–10), his son fled to Egypt and, Deuteronomy or no Deuteronomy, constructed there in the city of Leontopolis, in the district of Heliopolis, a new Jewish sanctuary (Josephus: Jewish Antiquities xiii. 62–8), justifying himself through scriptural exegesis, and a reinterpretation of Deuteronomy 12 in the light of Isaiah 19: 18–19, where the prophet proclaims:

'In that day there will be five cities in the land of Egypt which speak the language of Canaan and swear allegiance to the Lord of Hosts.
One of these will be called the City of the Sun (Heliopolis).
In that day there will be an alter to the Lord in the land of Egypt.'

Another Jewish group to imitate Onias in turning its back on the Jerusalem Sanctuary, though they refrained from erecting another temple, was the community of the Dead Sea Scrolls. Violently opposed to what they believed to be unlawful practices perpetrated by a wicked priesthood in Jerusalem, they found themselves on the horns of a dilemma. Scripture bade them to participate in Temple worship, but their consciences would not allow them to take part. They therefore *spiritualized* the Temple concept, deciding that during the age of perversion the 'offering of the lips', that is prayer, and a perfect life, would replace 'the flesh of the holocausts and the fat of sacrifice'. Their symbolical exegesis prepares that of St Paul for whom the Christian congregation is 'a holy Temple' (Eph. 2: 20–2) in which the faithful offer themselves as a 'living sacrifice' (Rom. 12: 1). Finally, when the Sanctuary was destroyed by the Romans in AD 70, the synagogue was assured of the divine presence, or any place where ten, or as few as two, men were gathered together to study Scripture (Mishnah: Aboth 3: 2, 6). Thus post-Destruction Judaism reactualized the law which originally sanctioned the plurality of temples (Exod. 20: 24):

'In every place where I cause my name to be remembered,
I will come to you and bless you.'

This practical type of exegesis plays a most useful part in the legal domain as well. For example, the Bible assumes that before marriage, girls are betrothed; but no rules relating to this important stage in the matrimonial process have been codified. The oral Torah deduces therefore, by means of an *a fortiori* reasoning, that since according to Exodus 21: 7 a father may sell his daughter into slavery, he may also 'sell' her into an arranged marriage. Or, as appears in a rabbinic saying (Lauterbach 1933–5: iii. 21):

If the father has the right to transfer his daughter from the state of potential betrothal to that of servitude, how much more so from potential to actual betrothal.

Among the many other roles of interpretative tradition, I must single out its use for foretelling the future; or more precisely, to demonstrate that events of the recent past, of the present time, and others expected to occur soon, correspond to the fulfilment of biblical prophecies. The scriptural precedent for this kind of exegesis appears in the second half of the Book of Daniel (ch. 9), where the author seeks to read the future destiny of his people by consulting Jeremiah's prediction concerning the seventy years of the Babylonian captivity. He is informed by the angel Gabriel that the prophet's words are cryptic, that the years are not to be taken literally, but should be understood as seventy weeks of years, (or 490 years) at the end of which redemption would come, shortly after the appointed end of the desolator. In less obscure terms, our pseudo-Daniel, living in the 160s BC, identifies the happenings of the reign of Antiochus Epiphanes with the events described by Jeremiah four centuries earlier, and tries vaguely to guess at their continuation, for his own days in this chronology represent the final phase of time.

Bible exegesis of this sort was common currency in inter-Testamental Judaism. It is enough to mention that in the Habakkuk Commentary among the Dead Sea Scrolls the entire historical context of the seventh-century BC prophecy announcing the invasion of Palestine by the Babylonians is moved forward almost six centuries by asserting that wherever Habakkuk speaks of the Chaldeans we must substitute Kittim, that is, Romans. There are numerous instances in rabbinic writings and in the New Testament. Various episodes of the life of Jesus, such as his having been conceived by a virgin (an interpretation recently the object of much-excoriated, though not unreasonable, episcopal doubt), his healing of the sick, his speaking in parables, his riding into Jerusalem on an ass, and so on, come about precisely in order to fulfil Scripture.

IV

My presentation of Scripture and tradition and their complex interconnections is drawing to a close. I have sketched the part played by both the spoken and written word in the making of the Bible and have examined the impact of canonization on its meaning and role in Judaism. I have analysed the structure, and investigated the function, purpose, and development of scriptural interpretation. In the little space that remains, I will endeavour to cast a retrospective glance at, and delineate, Scripture and the oral Torah in their fully evolved state. I should note here *en passant* that the explicit formulation of the rabbinic doctrine of two Torahs belongs probably to the turn of the eras. It is first attributed, rightly or wrongly, to Shammai, one of the great Pharisees of that epoch. Answering the question of a Gentile concerning the number of Torahs possessed by the Jews, he apparently replied: 'We have two: one oral, one written' (Babylonian Talmud: Shabbath 31*a*).

To turn first to the Bible, thought to have been originally composed by Moses, and according to a first-century AD view (4 Ezra 14), rewritten in its entirety by Ezra, for inter-Testamental and rabbinic Judaism it ceased in reality to be a product of space and time, and was transferred to the celestial sphere and to the age preceding the creation of the world. Not only were the Mosaic commandments acknowledged as copies of laws written on heavenly tablets and kept in a library on high until the predestined moment (if we are to believe the Book of the Jubilees, a mid-second-century BC composition), but according to one rabbinic tradition (Midrash Rabbah: Gen. i. 4) the Torah was created 2,000 years before even the universe came into being. Even more dramatically, Ecclesiasticus 24: 23, as well as rabbinic literature (Midrash Rabbah: Gen. i. 1), identifies 'the book of the Covenant of the Most High, the law which Moses commanded', with the eternal, creative wisdom of God itself.

Written in a holy tongue used since the beginning by God and his angels, the Bible is said to have been copied throughout the generations following immutable norms. Age-old spelling oddities survive even in modern computer-set editions of the Hebrew Scriptures.

They have been perpetuated because the rabbis were convinced that each peculiarity was endowed with significance. Take for instance the second account of the creation in Genesis 2:7, 'The Lord *formed* man.' The verb 'formed' (*wayyiṣer*) is not written with one *yod*, as is usually the case, but with two. This was done intentionally, we are told. The verb *wayyiṣer* ('he formed) being related to the noun *yeṣer* ('inclination'), the double *yod* is to show that man was formed with *two* inclinations, one towards good, the other towards evil (Targum Ps.-Jonathan to Gen. 2: 7).

A Bible scroll is held to be so numinous and holy that it is believed —no one knows why—to render the hands that touch it ritually unclean. Again, any book of Scripture is thought so sacred that it may be removed from a house on fire on the Sabbath (Mishnah: Shabbath 16: 1). But let me illustrate the Bible's standing with a directive given in the first post-biblical rabbinic code, the Mishnah (Megillah 3: 1): You may spend money obtained from the sale of a synagogue on buying an ark to house biblical scrolls. You may sell the ark to buy scroll wrappings. Their price may serve for the purchase of books containing the Prophets and the Writings. But if you sell these, the proceeds may only be employed for the acquisition of Torah scrolls. In brief, Scripture, especially the Law of Moses, is at the summit in the hierarchy of religious objects in Judaism.

As for the oral Torah, a phenomenon by nature evolutionary, it also tended by the end of the pre-Christian era to imitate written Scripture, to be backdated and conceived of as one half of the single complete revelation granted to Moses on the holy mountain. Many a precept, unwritten in the Pentateuch and patently the result of more recent legislation, has become known as a doctrine received by Moses from God. We are told that Moses was handed in advance everything from Scripture to the last exegetical minutiae of the rabbis (Babylonian Talmud: Berakhoth 5*a*):

What does Scripture teach, asks the Talmud, when it states, 'The Lord said to Moses . . . I will give you the tables of stone with the Torah and the commandment which I have written to instruct them' (Ex. 24: 12). The *tables of stone* are the Decalogue. The *Torah* is the Bible. The *commandment* is the Mishnah. *Which I have written* is the Prophets and the Writings. *To instruct them* is the Talmud.

Written Law and oral Torah both being Mosaic in this theological outlook, both are believed to be equally binding. The words of the scribes, advanced to clarify the import of Scripture, constituted for a time a distinct category of oral tradition. They were to be pressed with special emphasis according to the rabbis, even more strongly than a commandment directly demonstrable from the Bible. At the end, however, they, too, were traced back to Moses.

One of the characteristics of the oral Torah was its relative inaccessibility to the uninitiated. A published writing could easily fall into the wrong hands, whereas oral tradition could, theoretically at least, be controlled more comfortably. Hence new members of the Dead Sea community were required not merely to submit themselves to the Torah, but to do so 'in accordance with all that has been revealed of it to the sons of Zadok', the priestly guardians of Scripture. The latter, in their turn, were to observe the 'spirit of secrecy' towards outsiders, and conceal from them the true sense of the Law (Vermes 1975*a*: 79, 88). A rabbinic story has it that Moses was forbidden to record the oral Torah because God foresaw that the Gentiles would translate it and read it in Greek and declare, 'We are the children of the Lord.' The Jews would make the same claim and the scales would balance equally between the two. God would then tell the Gentiles that he recognized as his children only those who were acquainted with his secret doctrine, his *mysterion*. 'Your secret doctrine,' the Gentiles would ask. 'What is that?' The answer would be: 'It is the Mishnah' (Pesikta 5: 1).

But by the beginning of the third century AD, the Mishnah, the compilation and systematization of customary law by Rabbi Judah the Patriarch, succumbed to the common destiny of oral tradition and was redacted in writing. In fact, it was very soon chosen as one of the textbooks (the other being Scripture) taught and commented on in the rabbinic academies of Galilee and Babylonia, the Mishnah and its exegesis developing into the Talmud (which is short for Talmud Torah, the Teaching of the Torah). Ever since then Judaism has possessed its *written* oral law together with its Scripture. They are however not confused. To this very day, the traditional pious Jew worships God in the synagogue with a public recital of the Bible. (One of its Hebrew names is *Miqra*, which like the Arabic *Qur'ān*, means reading.) But if he wishes to discover how to behave in a given situation, he is unlikely to search the books of Moses and the Prophets, or even the Mishnah, but will consult the Talmud . . . and its commentaries.

To conclude: the overall function of the oral Torah has been to infuse with dynamism and vitality the religious message of the written Bible, the arrested spoken Word with a capital W. Its effect is to have enabled Scripture to maintain its impact until now on the mind and life of the believing Jew. And the same conclusion applies, *mutatis mutandis*, to the role of Scripture and Tradition among the scions of Judaism, Christianity, and Islam.

REFERENCES

Babylonian Talmud: *Der Babylonische Talmud*, ed. L. Goldschmidt, i–ix. Berlin: S. Calvary, 1897–1935.

——: *The Babylonian Talmud*, ed. I. Epstein, i–xxxv. London: Soncino, 1935–52.

Eusebius: *Praeparatio Evangelica*, book ix, ed. K. Mras. Berlin: Akademie-Verlag, 1954.

Ezra, 4: *The Apocrypha and Pseudepigrapha of the Old Testament*, ed. R. H. Charles, ii: 542–624. Oxford: Clarendon Press, 1913.

——: *The Old Testament Pseudepigrapha*, ed. J. H. Charlesworth, i: 517–59. London: Darton, Longman & Todd, 1983.

Josephus: *Jewish Antiquities*, iv–ix. The Loeb Classical Library. London: Heinemann, 1930–65.

Lauterbach, J. Z. (ed.) 1933–5; *Mekilta de-Rabbi Ishmael*, i–iii. Philadelphia: Jewish Publication Society.

Midrash Rabbah: *Midrash Rabbah*, ed. M. A. Mirkin, i–xi. Tel Aviv: Yavneh, 1956–67.

——: *Midrash Rabbah* (in English), ed. H. Freedman and M. Simon, i–xi. London: Soncino, 1951.

Mishnah: *Shishah Sidre Mishnah*, ed. H. Albeck and H. Yalon, i–vi. Jerusalem: Mosad Bialik; Tel Aviv: Devir, 1952–8.

——: *The Mishnah*, trans. H. Danby. London: Oxford University Press, 1933.

Moore, G. F. 1927–30: *Judaism in the First Centuries of the Christian Era*, i–iii. Cambridge, Mass.: Harvard University Press.

Palestinian Talmud: *Talmud Yerushalmi*, ed. Krotoschin, 1866.

——: *The Talmud of the Land of Israel*, trans. J. Neusner, in progress. Chicago: Chicago University Press, 1982– .

Pesikta: *Pesikta Rabbati*, ed. M. Friedmann. 1880.

——: *Pesikta Rabbati*, trans. W. G. Braude, i–ii. New Haven: Yale University Press, 1968.

Pritchard, J. B. (ed.) 1950: *Ancient Near Eastern Texts relating to the Old Testament*. Princeton, NJ: Princeton University Press.

Schürer, E. 1979: *The History of the Jewish People in the Age of Jesus Christ*, ii, ed. and rev. G. Vermes, F. Millar, and M. Black. Edinburgh: T. & T. Clark.

Targum Ps.-Jonathan: *Pseudo-Jonathan*, ed. M. Ginsburger. Berlin: S. Calvary, 1903.

——: *Targum Jonathan ben Uziel on the Pentateuch*, ed. D. Rieder. Jerusalem: privately published, 1974.

——: *The Targums of Onkelos and Jonathan ben Uzziel on the Pentateuch with the Fragments of the Jerusalem Targum from the Chaldee*, trans. J. W. Etheridge, i–ii. London: Longmans Green, 1862–5, repr. 1968.

——: *Targum du Pentateuque*, trans. R. Le Déaut and J. Robert, i–v. Paris: Le Cerf, 1978–81.

Vermes, G. 1973: *Scripture and Tradition in Judaism—Haggadic Studies.* 2nd edn. Leiden: Brill.

—— 1975a: *The Dead Sea Scrolls in English*, 2nd edn. Harmondsworth: Penguin.

—— 1975b: *Post-Biblical Jewish Studies.* Leiden: Brill.

THE MEANING OF LITERACY IN
EARLY MODERN ENGLAND

KEITH THOMAS

EVERYBODY today assumes that literacy is important. It is a stigma in the West for an adult to be unable to read or write and there are many agencies designed to prevent this from happening or to stamp it out when it does. In the Third World UNESCO and other bodies have large literacy programmes designed to raise the level of literacy in developing countries. Behind their activities lie the theories of linguists and anthropologists who maintain that the introduction of writing generates new mental processes. 'Writing restructures thought,' as Professor Ong puts it; and the transition from 'orality' to 'literacy' is represented as a crucial stage in human development, leading on to abstract thought, rationality, and 'modernity'. 'Literate and illiterate people', we are told, 'do think differently' (Barnes 1984: 159).

Some commentators, accordingly, seem to regard literacy as a tool, a piece of technology whose effects will always be the same. But our experience suggests that tools can have very different effects, depending on when they are used, for what purposes, and by whom. For this reason it is misleading to view 'literacy' as a single phenomenon and wrong to treat it as an autonomous mechanism of change, regardless of the particular circumstances. It may be better to regard it as something which takes different forms at different times and whose meaning, therefore, can only be studied in some specific context.

The particular context I have chosen is that of early modern England, by which I mean roughly England between 1500 and 1750. I want to try to assess what literacy meant at that time, why more people acquired it, and what were the social and mental effects of their doing so.

Of course it is not easy to do this. Early modern England was a rapidly changing society and it is not obvious how to distinguish the effect of growing literacy from that of other changes working in the same direction. The Russian psychologist A. R. Luria found this in the early 1930s. He made a fascinating exploration of the mental changes then being undergone by peasants in central Asia, but he never succeeded in separating the consequences of literacy from those of schooling, political change and collectivization (Luria 1976. Cf. Scribner and Cole 1981: 10–11, and Street 1984: 103).

The historian is in a much weaker position, for he cannot administer questionnaires or inkblot tests to the people of the past; many of their mental processes must forever remain hidden from him. What I have to say, therefore, is necessarily very tentative.

Moreover, by beginning in 1500 I am starting rather late. For by that time writing had long been established in England as a means of communication and record. The lawcourts had, three centuries earlier, made the crucial transition from oral memory to written record. Public and private administrators had long made extensive use of written documents for the conduct of business; and the preservation of records was so systematic that the volume of medieval documents housed in the Public Record Office today is greater than all the medievalists in the world have yet been able to peruse. Even peasants used written charters for the conveyance of land so regularly that, by the end of the thirteenth century, such documents had run into hundreds of thousands, perhaps millions (Clanchy 1979: 1, 34–5, and *passim*). In the Church, religion was founded upon scripture, written liturgies, and a huge mass of theological literature. At the universities texts and treatises nourished a complex intellectual life; while among the laity, reading for purposes of devotion, information, or amusement, was a steadily growing practice. Long before the end of the Middle Ages the ability to read and write had ceased to be the monopoly of a clerical élite (Aston 1984: 103, 106–8; Richardson and Sayles 1963: 269–83; Orme 1973: 11–56; Pantin 1976; Turner 1978; Kaeuper 1984; Moran 1985).

Early modern England, therefore, was not an oral society. But neither was it a fully literate one. Although many people could read and write, many others could not: and although documents and books played an increasing role in social life they by no means monopolized the means of communication and record. Indeed it is the interaction between contrasting forms of culture, literate and illiterate, oral and written, which gives this period its particular fascination.

During these two and a half centuries two obvious developments occurred. The first was the spread of the printed book, which had come to England in the later fifteenth century. Of books published in England before 1700, nearly 100,000 different titles or editions still survive and the total output, not to mention the import of books from abroad, was much greater. The second development was the more or less steady increase in the proportion of the population who were literate. This increase is less easy to quantify, partly because the evidence is incomplete, partly because so many different degrees of competence are involved. When we speak of 'literacy' today we mean the ability to read and write. But to read what and to write what? In early modern England there were so many kinds of written word, such a diversity of scripts, typefaces, and languages, that a simple contrast between 'literacy' and 'illiteracy' fails to register the complexity of the situation.

For example, when a child learned to read in Tudor England he started with the alphabet, usually pasted on a little board with a handle, like a ping-pong bat, and covered with a transparent piece of horn to protect it from grubby fingers: hence its name, a 'hornbook'. When he had learned the letters, usually in a sing-song, forwards and backwards, he went on to the Lord's Prayer, a Catechism, a Psalter, or a collection of prayers called a Primer (Tuer 1896; Baldwin 1943). What all these learning aids had in common was that they were usually printed in the Gothic type which we call 'black letter'—still used until recently for newspaper titles. For us, black letter is quite difficult to read by comparison with the 'roman' type which gradually superseded it. But for contemporaries it was the other way round: they found black letter easier. For that reason black letter was long retained for emphasis: it can be seen in James Harrington's political treatise, *Oceana* (1656), and it was long used for proclamations and Acts of Parliament. Black letter was the type for the common people; it survived into the eighteenth century in children's primers and in the ballads and romances published in chap-book form for consumption by the unsophisticated (Mish 1953). And it was a black-letter psalter which was usually proffered to convicted criminals to give them a chance to escape hanging by proving they could read and therefore claim benefit of clergy (Baker 1978: 329; Cockburn 1972: 300). Black-letter literacy, in short, was a more basic skill than roman-type literacy; and it did not follow that the reader fluent in one was equally at home in the other.

And even if he could manage both forms of type, it did not mean that he could decipher a written document. After all, everyone today can read a sixteenth-century book, but only a tiny minority can read an original sixteenth-century letter. Writing in the Tudor period, and indeed long after, was a different skill from reading. It was learned by older children and from a different teacher. It was a delicate task involving the making of quill-pens and the mixing of ink; and it required initiation into one of the many different scripts in vogue. The most common was the so-called Secretary hand, a Gothic cursive which, on first acquaintance, is impenetrable by the untrained modern reader. There were other stylized and even more difficult legal hands used for the records of the courts and for writing deeds and promissory notes. All these scripts had to be specially learned. The only Tudor hand which the modern reader can manage at sight is Italic, which was disseminated by Renaissance humanists and became common among the cultivated élite in the later sixteenth century (Hector 1966: 60–8).

The existence of all these different scripts meant that it was perfectly possible in the Tudor and early Stuart period for someone to be able to read print fluently, but to be quite incapable of deciphering a written document. For the only people who could easily read script were the privileged minority who had themselves learned to write it.

This inability of many contemporaries to read handwritten letters has misled many modern historians into thinking they could not read at all. For example, when we find two London bricklayers in 1599 picking up a 'writing' in the street and taking it to a scrivener to have it read (HMC Salisbury 1902: 260), we should not therefore assume that they were totally illiterate. When the Elizabethan Nonconformist John Penry wrote to his wife from gaol, he assumed that someone else would have to read his letter to her; but he also assumed that she could read the Bible and would teach their daughter to do so (Waddington 1854: 129–31, 141). It is likely, in short, that many individuals whom historians have assumed to have been absolutely unlettered were fluent readers of print, merely unable to decipher the sort of written document many of us would find impossible today.

The ability to read the printed word was thus the most basic form of literacy. Next came the ability to read and write written script. But beyond that there was a higher literacy, the knowledge of

Latin. 'The word illiterate in its common acceptation,' declared Lord Chesterfield in 1748, 'means a man who is ignorant of those two languages [Latin and Greek]'[1] (Strachey 1901: 230). Latin was the language of international scholarship: of nearly 6,000 books in the Bodleian Library in 1605, only 36 were in English (Shumaker 1972: xvi–xvii). Latin was also extensively used for legal and administrative documents and in medicine. In an area where grammar schools were plentiful, a smattering of Latin might be quite widely dispersed: an eighteenth-century inhabitant of the Lake District overheard one elderly labourer say to another, *'Frangam tibi caput'* (Watson 1817: 6). But such un-Wordsworthian vocabulary was rare on ordinary lips. Latin was essentially the prerogative of a social élite and a masculine one at that.

In the mid-seventeenth century many radical reformers urged that lawyers and doctors should give up using Latin. It was shameful, thought the regicide John Cook, 'that a subpoena should be served upon a countryman in Latin, when peradventure scarce anyone within five miles understands it' (Cooke 1646: 58). In the same spirit Henry Robinson urged the abolition of court hand, 'which to most people did nothing differ from exorcistical characters' (Robinson 1651: A2). For a short time in the 1650s all legal proceedings had to be in English: Latin, Law French, court hand, and other means of obfuscation were abolished (Latham 1959–60).[2] But they came back after the Restoration; and their continued use until 1733 meant that the legal world, like that of most professional and learned cultures, remained partly inaccessible to people who could read and write English but knew no Latin.

In the early modern period, therefore, there was an elaborate hierarchy of literacy skills; and this makes it hard to determine just what proportion of the population was 'literate'. Those historians who have produced estimates of the extent of illiteracy have relied exclusively upon one criterion: an individual's ability to sign his name, rather than making a mark, when affixing his signature to a formal document. On the basis of a large sample of signed documents, Dr David Cressy has calculated that, as late as the 1640s, 70 per cent of adult Englishmen and 90 per cent of English women were illiterate, that is unable to sign their names. He finds, however, great regional variations: in London only 22 per cent of men were illiterate; in Nottinghamshire over three-quarters were; and even within adjacent parishes the figures could vary enormously.

Over the whole period Dr Cressy estimates that male illiteracy declined, in fits and starts, from perhaps 90 per cent in 1500 to 55 per cent in 1714 and 40 per cent in the mid-eighteenth century. For women his estimates are much higher: 99 per cent illiterate in 1500; 75 per cent in 1714; 60 per cent in 1750. The gender difference was thus an enormous one; and so was the social difference. The greatest illiteracy was found at the bottom of the social scale, among the labourers and maidservants; the least was at the top, among the gentry and professional classes, who were wholly literate by 1600 (Cressy 1980: 176–7 and ch. 6).

But what do these totals of marks and signatures really tell us? In any individual case a mark does not necessarily mean that the person concerned could not write: he might have been ill at the time or he might have preferred to use the sanctifying symbol of the cross or to draw a shepherd's crook or pair of tailor's scissors or one of the myriad other devices with which even literate people customarily indicated their occupation and identity (Sisson 1928; King 1938: 379; Schoenbaum 1977: 37–8). Conversely someone who wrote his name could not necessarily write anything else (Collinson 1981: 31).[3]

The assumption made by most of those who believe in counting marks and signatures is that literacy figures based on signatures will overestimate the proportion of fluent writers, underestimate the proportion of not very good readers, but give a good indication of the proportion able to read fluently. They assume, in short, that a good reader was usually able to sign his or her name (Cressy 1980: 54; Schofield 1968: 323–4. Cf. Furet and Ozouf 1982: 16–17). This assumption is based on nineteenth-century evidence, but in my view (and that of others before me) (for instance Neuburg 1971: 96; Spufford 1979: 414) it is false for this period; and the calculations based on it greatly underrate the number of people who could read print with relative ease, but could not sign their names. For other evidence suggests that in this period the ability to read was much more widely diffused than the ability to write; and therefore even fluent readers and book-owners might sign their names with a mark. In Sweden, for example, the result of a campaign launched by the Lutheran Church in 1686 was that by 1740 over 90 per cent of the adult population in many rural parishes could pass a reading test. Moreover, this very high figure was achieved without a great expansion of formal schooling: children were taught to read, not in school, but by their parents and neighbours. But only a tiny percentage of the Swedes at this time could write: universal writing came only in the nineteenth century and it was learned at school (Graff 1981: ch. 8). To some extent the same was true of Britain. Professor T. C. Smout has discovered that, of a group of seventy-four Scottish women in the 1740s, only eight could write, but *all* of them could read the Bible fluently (Smout 1982). In early modern England even well-to-do women were notoriously bad at writing and their spelling was often dreadful. But they were not necessarily any worse at reading than the men. On the contrary many authors specifically addressed a female public (Salzman 1985: 111) and much of the teaching of children to read was in the hands of women.[4]

There is some reason, therefore, to think that Dr Cressy's figures for illiteracy in 1640—70 per cent men and 90 per cent women—are not just an underestimate of those who could read, but a spectacular underestimate; though we must always remember that, though many of these supposed illiterates could read books—'print hand', as they called it—they could not always read handwritten letters—'written hand' (Delamaine 1820: 601; Hey 1974: 190; Palliser 1982: 102; HMC Gawdy 1885: 23).

Early modern England, therefore, was a 'partially literate society' (Cressy 1980: 17) in which there coexisted people living at very different levels of intellectual sophistication. It was the age of Shakespeare, yet neither Shakespeare's father nor his daughter Judith could sign their names; and it was the age of Sir Isaac Newton, yet Newton's father could not sign his will, but drew a bird as his mark (Schoenbaum 1977: 37, 295; Foster 1928-9: 46). In the Tudor and early Stuart period it is easy to find examples of non-literate holders of important local offices: constables and church-wardens, mayors and town councillors, masters of City companies and governors of grammar schools;[5] even schoolteachers, like Elizabeth Snell of Watford, of whom it was reported in 1579 that 'she teacheth scholars to read and she herself cannot read' (Anglin 1980: 69). Inability to write did not necessarily exclude people from business success: witness Ambrose Crowley (d. 1720), who built up a great iron and steel business in Worcestershire and South Wales, yet always signed his name with a mark (Flinn 1962: 23). And total illiteracy was compatible with high technical skill: Joseph Browne, a Norwich coalheaver, could not read, but he was an excellent painter and, it was said in 1735, could copy old masters with great success (Denvir 1983: 134–5). John Boughton, a shepherd in Eynsham, was totally illiterate, but he played with such skill on the pipe and tabor that he used to be sent for to entertain the quality and was said in 1718 to have saved up an estate of £1,000 (Davis 1922: 141). The poet Crabbe later commented on the irony that men who could plough an immaculately straight furrow were capable of no more than a crooked scrawl when they came to sign the marriage register:

> Behold these marks uncouth! How strange that men,
> Who guide the plough, should fail to guide the pen:
> For half a mile, the furrows even lie;
> For half an inch the letters stand awry;
>   (Crabbe 1908: 65)

Literacy was in fact largely irrelevant to the pursuit of many occupations. Hangmen did not need to write (Young 1890: 421) and neither, thought the Jacobean writer Gervase Markham, did bailiffs or servants in husbandry (Markham 1635: 8–9). As Nicholas Breton put it: 'We can learn to plough and harrow, sow and reap, plant and prune, thresh and fan, winnow and grind, brew and bake, and all without book' (Breton 1966: 10). In the eighteenth century it was said that the Chiltern farmers 'entertain the worst opinion of books, as believing themselves above information in that way' (Ellis 1750: 79). Even today, business success need not involve literary skills: among Britain's gypsies it is the wealthiest families who are the least literate (Okely 1983: 64). In the early modern period there is no evidence to suggest that illiterates were less 'rational' than others in the conduct of their personal lives (Levine 1980–1).

What is perhaps more surprising in the early modern period is that illiteracy also proved compatible with political and religious activism and Nonconformity. It is often said that literacy is essential for political self-consciousness. Dr Peter Laslett writes that 'only the fully literate . . . were likely to be actively or potentially engaged in political activity . . . At least two-thirds of all mature males . . . were disabled [because of their illiteracy] from sharing to any great political upheavals of the seventeenth century' (Laslett also Oxenham 1980: 12). Yet all the evidence suggests from being disabled, such people were often in the forefront of religious and political upheaval. From the time of the Lollards onwards, many members of unorthodox Protestant sects had been unable to write, or sometimes even to read (Aston 1984: 199–202; Dickens 1964: 30). This was true of the early Elizabethan sectaries, like the group discovered at Wonersh, Surrey in 1561, many of whom could not read, or the congregation which petitioned the Queen in 1571, two-thirds of whom made marks (Hyland 1920: 103; Burrage 1912: 18; Weston 1955: 116–17, 124). As for the Brownists who went into exile in Amsterdam at the end of the century, their marriage register reveals that nearly a third of the men and over three-quarters of the women could not sign their names (Crippen 1905: 171). The preacher and expounder of scripture to an illicit conventicle at Dover in 1639 could not write, while in the 1640s the Baptist Andrew Debman, 'a cooper by trade, a sorry fellow that can neither write nor read', was nevertheless 'a great preacher among the sectaries' (Hamilton 1877: 81; Edwards 1646: 88). The Familists, the Fifth Monarchists, and the Quakers attracted illiterate supporters, as did the Muggletonians, some of whom were unable to decipher 'print hand' and had to have their leader's books read to them (Heal 1972: 218; Rogers 1653: 448; Vann 1969: 142; Delamaine 1820: 376, 601).

In the mid-seventeenth century, therefore, illiteracy was compatible with a high degree of religious heterodoxy. And it was certainly compatible with dramatic political action, whether by the 142 anti-enclosure rioters in Northamptonshire in 1607, all of whom made marks when they submitted afterwards to Sir Edward Montagu, or by the Diggers who set up communes in 1649 and issued remarkable manifestos, although in some cases unable to write (Wake 1935: xlviii; Thomas 1969: 61). Ann Carter, leader of the grain riots in Essex in 1629, had to have her letters written for her (Hunt 1983: 241). The Civil War armies, a contemporary tells us, contained 'many mechanics', of whom 'few were able to read and fewer to write their names' (Fuller 1660: 26).

It would be utterly wrong, therefore, to think that illiterates lived in some sort of mental darkness, debarred from effective participation in the great events of their time. From the Neolithic Revolution onwards, some of the most decisive developments in human history have been accomplished without the aid of writing. And even in the literate culture of early modern England inability to read and write did not necessarily mean intellectual simplicity:

'Many illiterate [are] of the exactest judgment,' wrote Richard Braithwaite in 1614 (Brathwayte 1614: 32).

How was it that people unable to read and write could function effectively in an increasingly literate world?

Part of the explanation is that they could draw on the services of others for access to the written word. Not being able to write then was rather like not being able to type or drive today: it could be a great inconvenience, but it was usually possible to get someone else to do it. In the early modern period much everyday writing was of a technical kind, involving legal documents, particularly relating to the borrowing of money and advancing of credit, in which everyone was deeply involved, so it was usually necessary to get a scrivener or legal expert to do it anyway. The well-to-do would dictate their letters to a secretary: many of the famous Lisle letters originated that way (Byrne 1981: 59). If a village constable could not write his presentments or passes for vagrants, he would get someone else to help him. A literate person in a country village could always supplement his income by writing accounts, letters, and bills for neighbours. The recently published diary of the Sussex shopkeeper Thomas Turner shows this practice at work in the mid-eighteenth century. Turner drafts bonds, writes wills, draws up inventories, charitable accounts, and tax returns, for all and sundry. Such semi-professional letter-writers were everywhere (Vaisey 1984: xxii. Cf. Sachse 1938: 4; Linnell 1950: x, 15, 43).

Reading could also be done by someone else. The Elizabethan government realized this when requiring its proclamations to be read aloud: 'considering the multitude of our good people are un-learned, and thereby not able by reading hereof to conceive our mind . . . we will that, beside the ordinary publication hereof . . . all curates in their parish churches shall . . . read this admonition to their parishioners' (Haynes 1740: 593). When notices and posters were displayed, a little group would gather and one would read the contents aloud to the others. A recipient of a legal document would look for a 'scholar' to read it to him (e.g. Roper 1907: 92). Clergymen recommended that those unable to read should keep a Bible in their houses nevertheless, so 'that when any come that can read, they may have it in readiness and not lose the opportunity that is offered' (Cressy 1980: 51). When Samuel Pepys went for a walk on Epsom Downs, he found a shepherd and his little boy reading the Bible to him, by themselves far away from houses and people (Pepys

1970–83, viii: 338). During the Civil War it was common for officers to read newsbooks and pamphlets aloud to their troops (Firth 1901: 229, 231); and in the eighteenth century newspapers were often read aloud.

Reading, after all, had begun as an oral activity. Most classical and medieval literature had been meant to be read aloud; and although silent reading had long been practised by the educated it had not yet become universal (Auerbach 1965: 243–7, 284; Crosby 1936; Saenger 1982). A proclamation of 1541 ordered that the English Bible placed in every parish church for general use should not be read 'with loud and high voices' during service times, but the implication was that it was aloud that it would be read (Hughes and Larkin 1964: 297).

So long as they had access to someone who would read, therefore, there was no reason why others needed to be cut off from the culture of the written word. The position of the illiterate was like that of the blind Sir Francis Englefield, who remarked in 1595 that for the past twenty-four years he had committed the reading and writing of all his letters and affairs to his secretary John Slade and felt no disadvantage, until Slade suddenly absconded (Loomie 1963: 48). Even Elizabethan rogues were able to provide themselves with false documents for protection, 'they having amongst them (of their own rank) that can write and read, who are their secretaries in this business' (Dekker n.d.: 95). As Dr Roger Schofield puts it, 'it only needs one or two members of normally illiterate groups who have acquired an ability to read, to read aloud to their friends and neighbours, for a bridge to be thrown across any supposed divide between exclusively literate and illiterate groups within society.' He concludes that in this period 'there was a large area in which there was effective participation in the literate culture by essentially illiterate people' (Schofield 1968: 312–13; also Thompson 1978: 155). So if writing structures thought in the way Professor Ong suggests, it will not be the thought only of the people who can write which will be affected. Literates and illiterates need not necessarily have different mental habits; and the illiterates of early modern England were in quite a different position from the non-literate inhabitants of purely oral societies. They lived in a world which was to a great extent governed by texts, even though they could not read them themselves.

Apart from using the services of others, those unable to write could also draw upon the various mnemonic devices which had been perfected during centuries of oral culture. The proverbs, rhymes, and formulaic expressions with which oral societies preserve their traditions did not disappear overnight with the coming of the printed book. The speeches of Elizabethan MPs were interlarded with proverbs, indeed sometimes consisted of nothing else.[6] It was only in the later seventeenth century that polite society discarded them. In the countryside agricultural lore was preserved in hundreds of proverbial maxims of the kind immortalized by Thomas Tusser (1984: 93):

> Sow barley in March, in April and May,
> The later in sand and the sooner in clay.

The Yorkshireman Henry Best records many husbandmen's sayings of this kind: 'A bad ewe may bring a bad lamb, yet she spoils but one; but an ill tup is likely to spoil many.' Stylized rhyming banter was a stock feature of rural conversation. Best heard a servant at a hiring fair, when asked what he could do, reply: 'I can sow, I can mow, and I can stack; and I can do my master too, when my master turns his back' (Woodward 1984: 6, 141. Cf. 153). Much practical wisdom was preserved in rhymes of this kind. The Tudor writer Fitzherbert even quotes seven lines of English hexameters to be recited each morning by a gentleman's servant when his master leaves the inn, in order to ensure that he has left none of his 'gear' behind (Fitzherbert 1882: 93).

Learning by rote was widely practised. It explains why an illiterate person really could teach a child to learn the ABC from a horn-book, rather like a weary optician today who has no need to look at his chart to know whether his patient is reading it correctly. Archbishop Ussher was taught to read by two aunts, both of whom had been blind from birth but knew large sections of scripture by heart (Parr 1686: 2). Memorization of the Bible had been common since the days of the Lollards (Aston 1984: 201). The Jacobean Puritan John Bruen had a servant who could not read or write, but who had memorized scripture and could identify the book and chapter from which any sentence came. He wore a leather girdle, long enough to go around him twice, and on it he tied knots. With its aid he could repeat a complete sermon when he got home (Hinde 1641: 56-8).

Such devices were common. Fitzherbert advised illiterate farmers to make marks on a stick to remind them of jobs which needed doing (Fitzherbert 1882: 92). Shepherds counted their sheep this way, notching symbols on a stick (Woodward 1984: 87). Tallies and notches were widely employed, whether by alehouse keepers reckoning the bill or by thieves counting the number of purses they had cut. A stick and a knife made pen and paper unnecessary (Nodal and Milner 1875: 8; Green 1856: 49; Thirsk 1967: 565; Ewbank 1963: 144). In nineteenth-century Whitby, milk-sellers used wooden tallies or 'nick-sticks' as they were called. A glossary explains that 'females in an interesting condition, when they have lost their reckoning, are said . . . to have lost their nick-stick' (Robinson 1875: 131–2).

It was possible indeed to be numerate but not literate. In 1725 Daniel Defoe told of a successful country shopkeeper who had his own accounting system:

He made notches upon sticks for all the middling sums, and with chalk for lesser things; he had drawers for every particular customer's name, which his memory supplied; for he knew every particular drawer, though he had a great many, as well as if their faces had been painted upon them; he had innumerable figures to signify what he would have written, if he could; and his shelves and boxes always put people in mind of the Egyptian hieroglyphics, and nobody understood anything of them but himself.

It was an odd thing to see him, when a country chap came up to settle accounts with him; he would go to a drawer directly, among such a number as was amazing; in that drawer was nothing but pieces of split sticks, like laths with chalk marks on them . . . every stick had notches on one side for single pounds, on the other side for tens of pounds, and so higher; and the length and breadth also had its signification, and the colour too; for they were painted in some places with one colour, and in some places with another; by which he knew what goods had been delivered for the money; and his way of casting up was very remarkable; for he knew nothing of figures, but he kept six spoons in a place on purpose, near his counter, which he took out when he had occasion to cast up any sum, and laying the spoons on a row before him, he counted them thus:

One, two, three, and another; one odd spoon, and t'other.
/   /   /   /   /   /

By this he told up to six; if he had any occasion to tell any further he began again . . . (Defoe 1841: 312–13).

We should, therefore, not underrate the calculating and mnemonic powers of the illiterate. As late as 1832 a clergyman in the Berkshire village of Buckland, giving some orders to the Oxford carrier, an elderly man, and seeing he took no notes, asked if he was sure he could remember them all, for the orders were complicated ones.

The carrier answered that he took no notes because he could not read or write, but that he carried his accounts in his head and that he had sixty-three different orders for his journey and often had more. 'The people at the parsonage told me that he never was known to make a mistake' (Mozley 1882: 289–90).

Nevertheless, illiteracy had its practical difficulties and the pressures to acquire some rudimentary literary skill were relentless. Anyone involved in business ran the risk of being cheated if he could not read a document or a set of accounts. Innumerable commercial disputes were provoked by the illiteracy of one or both parties, unaware of the obligations into which they had entered (Thirsk 1967: 566; Campbell 1960: 264–5; Palliser 1982: 102). Illiterate village officers could find it difficult to carry out their duties: a Wiltshire constable asked in 1616 to be released from his post, 'forasmuch as I am unlearned, and by reason thereof am constrained to go two miles from my house to have the help of a scrivener to read such warrants as are sent to me' (Cunnington 1932: 54). The churchwardens of Buttsbury, Essex, accused of allowing William Pinder to preach without first examining his licence, pleaded lamely that they had seen it, 'as they think, for . . . they saw a thing in writing with a red seal on it, which Pinder did tell them was a licence' (Slavin 1972: 189). One Worcestershire constable raised the hue and cry when handed a folded piece of paper by a servant girl, who had 'a purpose to be merry' (Brewer and Styles 1980: 27). Jacobean London was full of confidence tricksters who extracted money and goods by pretending to be sheriffs or constables and dangling some imposing piece of parchment before their illiterate victim, claiming it was a warrant (Middlesex Records 1928: 188). One English traveller, crossing the Alps and asked for his passport, produced by mistake a printed bill advertising some rope-dancers; the frontier guards let him through because they recognized the royal arms at the top of the paper (Veryard 1701: 102).[7]

It thus became increasingly common to require that holders of local offices should be literate and to discharge them if they were not. Since the fifteenth century, some City companies had required that their would-be apprentices should be able to read and write (Thrupp 1962: 158); and this condition became general. 'A youth brought up at school', wrote a contemporary, 'will be taken apprentice with less money than one illiterate' (Wase 1678: 33). It is not surprising, therefore, that it was in those trades most closely connected with the market economy that literacy was greatest (Cressy 1980: 131; Clark 1977: 188). To a large extent, the growth of literacy was determined by its practical utility. Shopkeepers, corndealers, colliery foremen, bailiffs, all found it easier to function if they could read and write. The expansion of trade created a new demand for commercial clerks; and that in turn led to the replacement of secretary hand by 'round' hand, because it could be written faster (Heal 1931: xxxiii). Economic reasons thus help to explain why literacy was greater in the towns than in the country, among traders than among labourers, and among men than among women. Though it was also a matter of unequal educational opportunity, for some form of schooling was virtually essential for learning to write; and that was available only to those whose parents who could afford to pay for it and to manage without their children's labour in the mean time. It is not surprising that the social distribution of writing skills closely reflected the hierarchy of wealth.

Practical utility apart, the other great source of pressure to acquire some literacy was religion. All the leaders of the post-Reformation Church maintained that the individual should be able to read the Bible in order to gain direct access to God's word. Even the exiled Jesuit leader Robert Persons wanted every village in England to have a schoolmaster 'to teach the children to write and read at the least, and to cast accounts, and to know the Christian doctrines' (Gee 1690: 260–1. Cf. Furet and Ozouf 1982: 60–1). It thus became a religious duty for parents to teach their children to read; and similar motives underlay most of the educational benefactions of the period. The activity of dedicated clergy sometimes explains the great variations between the degrees of literacy within adjacent parishes.

The essential feature of this religious pressure is that it related primarily to the ability to read, rather than to write (Furet and Ozouf 1982: 167–8). It is true that some of the godly thought it desirable to be able to take notes on the sermon, so as to discuss it afterwards;[8] they also urged the keeping of spiritual diaries and commonplace-books. But most religious injunctions to literacy relate to reading ability only; and this, I think, explains the apparent paradox presented by the existence of committed religious sectaries who were unable to sign their names. Historians nowadays play down the influence of religion upon the growth of literacy in England; they prefer to emphasize the practical value of literacy for economic life. But that is because by 'literacy' they mean writing ability. They have no figures for the numbers of those able to read; and for that the religious pressure was very strong.[9]

Early modern England thus abounds in evidence of increasing literacy and the spread of the printed word. Already in the fifteenth century the interiors of the churches had become lighter, so that the congregation could see to read; and after the Reformation the removal of stained glass was justified on similar grounds (Aston 1984: 123; Slack 1972: 295). On funeral monuments, the inscription became more important than the image of the deceased: it was by epitaphs, said a preacher, that 'the truest, and noblest and most inward parts of the dead are apt to be far more lively and properly set forth; the tools of carvers and pencils of painters being able to describe only their outsides' (Gurnay 1660: 52–3. Cf. Houlbrooke 1984: 205).

In daily life there was an ever-growing volume of written material, correspondence and records, diaries and accounts. Biblical texts were painted in the churches and printed ballads stuck on the walls of alehouses. Graffiti, scribbled in ink or chalk, or carved with a knife, were to be found on tables, desks, windows, walls, trees, and other customary places: 'All who come to [the] boghouse write,' as one author put it (Novak 1983: v. Cf. Anon 1788: 61). Both in the lawcourts and in intellectual life, the written document was given precedence over oral tradition. 'We are much more subject to mistake in speech [than in writing],' thought John Evelyn. 'Verbal reports we experimentably find so inconstant and apt to err . . . Nay, why (if this be otherwise) do men take such wondrous care about their deeds and legal evidences which concern their temporal estates . . . if writing be not more certain and less apt to err than words?' (Evelyn 1850: 425).

Printed books became ubiquitous. They were sold in the provinces as well as in London: in 1585 one Shrewsbury bookseller had a stock of 2,500 volumes (with 500 different titles) (Rodger 1958). Their growing presence can be observed in the domestic inventories of the middle classes (Clark 1976). Bibles and religious books were issued in vast numbers; and in the 1660s almanacs were selling over 400,000 per annum (Capp 1979: 44). Since the 1520s the written word had been extensively employed to influence public opinion; and every public controversy was accompanied by printed propaganda. In the later seventeenth century there was a deluge of cheap booklets, tales, jest-books, and ballads, hawked all over the country by peddlers and chapmen (Spufford 1981).

But what effect did all this have? How fundamentally did literacy and print transform English life?

It must be said at once that, for all their imperialistic potential, print and writing did not entirely displace the spoken word. Indeed I cannot imagine a society in which they ever could do so. In early modern England oral communication was still the chief means by which technical skills were transmitted, political information circulated, and personal relationships conducted. Of course, there were cookery books, medical books, and agricultural books, but recipes, medicines, and farming techniques were not normally learned that way. News still passed chiefly by word of mouth (Dodds 1971: 50; Levy 1982: 24). Newspapers appeared briefly during the 1640s and 1650s, but only in the eighteenth century did they become a regular feature of life. Meanwhile those who could read and write often used their skills in a strictly limited context, to read a letter or make out a bill. They did not necessarily become habitual book-readers. Practical literacy, in other words, did not imply cultural literacy. Moreover, only a tiny fraction of social knowledge was transmitted via the written word. To understand the weather or the crops or the daily meaning of human interaction it was necessary to learn to 'read' many other kinds of sign; and in such cases the illiterate was in no way at a disadvantage.[10]

Oral communication remained central, whether as speeches in Parliament, pleadings in the lawcourts, teaching in the schools, or preaching and catechizing in church. Despite their reliance on the Bible and the Prayer Book, the clergy still expected their flock to learn their articles of belief by heart and to listen to spoken sermons. And in the universities, despite much wishful thinking by professors (North 1890: 291; Elton, 1906: 182), the invention of the book conspicuously failed to abolish the academic lecture. Speech was long thought more direct and persuasive than print. When John King published his lectures on Jonah in 1597, he apologized for having 'changed my tongue into a pen, and whereas I spake before with the gesture and countenance of a living man, have now buried myself in a dead letter of less effectual persuasion' (Kinge 1597: *4). Meanwhile the high cost of books and the shortage of cheap paper meant that scholars did not always turn to books for ready reference but continued to rely heavily upon complicated mnemonic systems. Many thought it bad form for a preacher to write out his sermon: he was supposed to trust to his memory, not his notes.[11]

Sir Walter Pye, attorney in the Court of Wards, had plenty of records to hand, but he knew by heart the name of every English gentleman, his ancestors, pedigree, coat of arms, and chief mansion (Boyle 1744: 429). Thomas Fuller trained his memory so that he could repeat five hundred random words after hearing them only once; and in 1687 Sir William Petty claimed to have been almost as good at this trick, though it is revealing of changing attitudes that by then he thought such feats of memory 'of no use but to get the admiration of foolish people' (Pepys 1970–83, II: 23 n.; Lansdowne 1967: 284). Better means of information retrieval were coming in.

The spoken word was thus not easily ousted. Neither was the visual image. Protestantism was hostile to the visual representation of religious truths, whether by images or ritual. But, in society at large, public ceremony was still the chief means by which rank and hierarchy were demonstrated and social doctrines transmitted: whether in the ritual of Parliament and the lawcourts, or in the jockeying for precedence by aldermen's wives at a municipal feast, or by the annual perambulation in the villages, when the extent of the parish boundaries was impressed upon the younger members of the community. In the towns tradesmen identified their shops by hanging out signs: until the 1760s many London streets were obscured by a dense forest of painted boards, a form of popular heraldry of which only the signs outside public houses now remain (Heal 1947; Larwood and Hotten 1900: ch. 2). Merchants, farmers, and craftsmen had their own private marks, with which they inscribed the animals they owned, the merchandise they bought, and the buildings they erected. Even Protestant iconoclasts, hostile to religious images as such, liked to meditate on the meaning of allegorical pictures; the seventeenth century was the great age of the emblem book (Freeman 1948; Lewalski 1979: ch. 6).

Of course, literacy and print would ultimately diminish the importance of these visual symbols. Street signs gave way to numbers. The merchants' marks disappeared; and the emblem book was relegated to children's literature. Public ceremonial lost some of its importance. As Dr Johnson said, it was an age of ignorance which was an age of ceremony (Chapman 1930: 58). In the end literacy made it less necessary to 'act out' the social structure so frequently, just as it accustomed people to learn from written words without accompanying illustrations. An incidental effect of this would be to free pictorial art from the burden of informational content, thus making possible the idea of purely aesthetic expression. But all this was in the long run.

What about the short run? Did literacy develop abstract thinking, logical argument, a sense of power over language and all the other qualities claimed for it by Professor Ong, Professor Goody, and others (Goody 1977)? I have tried to show that illiterate people were neither foolish nor helpless. But it would be silly to imply that they were therefore capable of the scientific achievements of Gilbert, Harvey, or Newton. Writing, said Bacon, makes 'an exact man' (Bacon 1937: 205); and without writing there could have been no scientific revolution. Neither would there have been that extreme linguistic self-consciousness which characterizes the philosophy of Hobbes and Locke. This is not to deny that non-literate people had (and have) their own logic: it is merely to assert the obvious fact that theirs was not the logic which underlay European science, theology, and philosophy. As Locke himself remarked, 'We see men frequently dexterous and sharp enough in making a bargain, who, if you reason with them about matters of religion, appear perfectly stupid.' Abstract reasoning, he thought, was impossible for 'men of low and mean education, who have never elevated their thoughts above the spade and the plough, nor looked beyond the ordinary drudgery of a day-labourer. . . . Take . . . such an one . . . out of that narrow compass he has been, all his life, confined to, you will find him no more capable of reasoning than almost a perfect natural.' Locke himself certainly thought that his contemporaries lived at different cognitive levels (Locke 1824, ii: 333, 338; also i: 31–2; vi: 139, 157).

During these years the literate were developing a new attitude to the book. We see them learning to use it for quick reference, skimming rapidly in search of a passage, rather than plodding all the way through. Robert Beale tells us that he learned to absorb print 'by the swiftest glance of the eye, without the tediousness of pronouncing or articulating what I read'; and claims as a result to have saved much money by flicking through books in stationers' shops without actually buying them, the seventeenth-century equivalent of an afternoon in Blackwell's (Boyle 1744: 426). We also see the literate learning better techniques of indexing and a stricter sense of alphabetical order. In 1604 Robert Cawdrey had to inform readers of his *Table Alphabeticall . . . of . . . English Words* that, to use his dictionary, they would need to know by heart the order in which the letters of the alphabet came: 'as (b) near the beginning, (n) about the middest, and (t) towards the end. Now if the word which thou art desirous to find begin with (a) then look in the beginning of the Table, but if with (v) look towards the end . . .' (Cawdrey 1604: A4^v); and in 1624 the compiler of an index to the book of the merchants' gild of Carlisle had to begin his work by explaining the technique of foliation with 'a brief rule to find out every order contained in this book, that is to say the first leaf the figure 1, the second leaf the figure 2, and so constantly every leaf, the figure in order' (Ferguson and Nanson 1887: 93. Cf. Daly 1967; Willan 1962: xxiii).

We also see the emergence, or rather, the greater prevalence, of two distinct psychological types: the silent reader, 'lost in a book', antisocial and oblivious to his surroundings (Saenger 1982; Aston 1984: 133 n.; Vaisey 1984: 281–2); and the private diarist, entrusting his secret thoughts to papers which were intimately his: Sir Simonds D'Ewes, himself a great diarist, could declare in Parliament in 1641 that the unauthorized search of a man's papers was 'a greater injury than the imprisonment of the body' (Notestein 1923: 168).[12]

Such an introspective relationship with the written word was increasingly common in the early modern period and so, we may guess, were the losses which literacy brought in its train: a memory ruined by speed-reading, an inability to retain long verbal instructions or to sit still through a lecture, perhaps even emotional deprivation stemming from a retreat from other forms of verbal and physical expression, reflected in a buttoned-up, more inhibited personality and a preference for communication by paper rather than face to face (Bantock 1966; Oxenham 1980: 124).

These are speculations. What is certain is that the uneven social distribution of literacy skills greatly widened the gulf between the classes. Bishop Butler described the result in a sermon in 1745. Until a few centuries ago, he said, 'all ranks were nearly upon a level', so far as reading and writing were concerned. But now the poor were 'more inferior . . . than they were in times past'. If they remained illiterate, they would be 'upon a greater disadvantage, on many accounts, especially in populous places, than they were in the dark ages: for they will be more ignorant comparatively with the people about them than they were then; and the ordinary affairs of the world are now put in a way which requires that they should have some knowledge of letters, which was not the case then' (Butler 1897: 294–5).

The same was true of women. They too were at a new disadvantage, so long as there prevailed what Martin Billingsley called 'that ungrounded opinion of many, who affirm writing to be altogether unnecessary for women' (Billingsley 1618: C 1^v). In the eighteenth century the decline of Latin would emancipate the female reader. But in the seventeenth century women were normally shut out from high culture. We can only speculate about the relationships between highly literate husbands and their semi-literate wives. John Winthrop, future governor of Massachusetts Bay, tells us how, perusing the letters of his first wife, he 'observed the scribbling hand, the mean congruity, the false orthography and broken sentences, etc; and yet found my heart not only accepting of them, but delighting in them, and esteeming them far above more curious workmanship in another; and all from hence . . . I loved her' (Winthrop Papers, 1929: 203). But Winthrop was not worried by his wife's semi-literacy because, as his words reveal, he still thought of writing as mere 'workmanship', a technical skill; whereas many of his contemporaries were coming to regard it as an integral part of human identity; for them illiteracy was a shame and a stigma. By 1684 Richard Steele could declare that someone unable to read or write, or 'to convey his mind with any certainty to his distant friends . . . but by assistance from others' was 'scarce to be reckoned among rational creatures' (Steele 1684: 40–1).[13] It is not difficult to guess what effect this assumption had upon attitudes to women and the poor.

The unequal spread of literacy thus gave a new cultural dimension to social differences previously founded on wealth and power. It reinforced the existing social hierarchy by enabling the upper classes to despise their inferiors as 'illiterate clowns', unentitled to any share in government: in due course Jeremy Bentham would propose that non-readers should not be allowed to vote (Bentham 1983: 29). In the seventeenth century there were some who did not want the poor taught to read and write, lest they should gain ideas above their station. 'When most was unlettered, it was so much a better world,' the Duke of Newcastle told Charles II; and in Virginia in 1671 Sir William Berkeley rejoiced that there were no free schools or printers there, 'for learning has brought disobedience, and heresy, and sects into the world, and printing has divulged them,

and libels against the best government. God keep us from both!'
(Strong 1903: 189; Bremner 1970: 90.) It is easy to see why the
Levellers and other seventeenth-century radicals set so much store
by universal literacy as a means to popular emancipation. They
welcomed the printing press because it democratized information
by making it widely available and giving new opportunities for self-
education and independent thought (Brailsford 1961: 534; Haller
and Davies 1964: 384; Hill 1974: 68). Conversely, many eighteenth-
century conservatives were afraid that if the poor learned to read
and write they would become seditious, atheistical, and discontented with their humble position. They therefore concluded, as
one of them put it, that 'The art of writing is not necessary to a
performance of the duties of the poor'; or, as another said, 'Some
degree of ignorance is necessary to keep them subordinate' (Ruggles
1793: Anon 1788: 58).

But literacy is not necessarily subversive of existing social forms
and in early modern England it is very doubtful whether it did much
at first to undermine the prevailing social order. Certainly the
clergy did not think so; for most of them saw literacy as a means of
reinforcing the status quo, by instilling godliness, civility, and law-
abiding behaviour. Reading, it was said, would 'prevent much of
that ignorance and wickedness that is found amongst our poor
people, and bring them to sobriety and virtue' (Firmin 1681: 8).
When Henry VIII placed an English Bible in every parish church he
did so, not only so that his subjects might read of God's goodness,
but also so that they should 'learn thereby to observe God's commandments, and to obey their sovereign lord and high powers, and
. . . to use themselves according to their vocations . . . without
murmur or grudgings' (Hughes and Larkin 1964: 297). And when
benefactors founded reading schools, they did so in order that
children might 'be better able to read the Holy Scriptures, and
therein to learn their duty' (Beazley 1908: 31).

Literacy thus appeared to the authorities as a route to obedience
and docility. It enabled the government to penetrate more deeply,
saturating the country with proclamations, injunctions, homilies,
and visitation articles; and it helped the clergy to bring the population to a new type of religion based on the book. It was from the
illiterate that the real threat came: what Richard Baxter called 'the
tinkers and sow-gelders and crate-carriers and beggars and barge-
men, and all the rabble that cannot read' (Powicke 1926: 182). Such
people were perceived as vulnerable to sectarianism, radicalism,

and atheism. For experience showed that even the most powerful ministry could make no impact upon 'an ignorant and unlearned congregation' (Annesley 1677: 214. Cf. Schlatter 1940: 35-7). For those who wished to preserve the social order there was thus a dilemma: either one allowed the poor to read and took the risk that they might read unsuitable matter and become discontented and seditious. Or one left them illiterate and faced the certainty that orthodox religion and morality would pass them by. On the whole, the consensus in this period was that literacy should be encouraged because it did more to support the social order than to subvert it.

But if literacy was potentially a conservative force, what about the printed word? Did it not subvert orthodoxy by making information more widely available and enabling the individual to reach his own independent conclusions? Of course, to some extent it did. At the very least, the vast expansion of print gave the ordinary reader new models to imitate, a greater awareness of the past and of other societies, a wider sense of the possible, and a general consciousness that things might be other than they were. There is indeed some evidence to suggest that literate people were more restless, less satisfied with their place in society, readier to move elsewhere, or even to emigrate overseas in search of new opportunities (Marshall 1969:. 304; Graff 1981: 189-90; Wrightson 1982: 196-7).

But there are two reasons why we should not exaggerate the impact of print.

The first is that printing did not involve a total break with the past. There was a large reading public in the later Middle Ages; and its relationship to the written word was not very different from what it became in the age of print (Saenger 1982). There was much continuity between the content of medieval manuscripts and of printed books. Until 1640 religious works still accounted for nearly half the press's output and new literary genres were slow to evolve (Klotz 1937-8). The most important ones, the newspaper, the magazine, and the novel, were not really launched until after 1700. Meanwhile a great deal of medieval literature continued to circulate. Of course, printing made books cheaper and more easily available, but the difference in scale of output, though considerable, should not be exaggerated, for some medieval texts had circulated in hundreds of copies (Febvre and Martin 1976: 28; Grafton 1980: 273-4, 280). It is easy to see, therefore, why, half-way through the seventeenth century, Thomas Hobbes could confidently conclude that 'the invention of printing, though ingenious, compared with the invention of letters, is no great matter' (Hobbes 1651: ch. 4).

The second reason why printing did not instantly undermine existing authority is that, for the first two centuries of its existence, it was very strictly controlled by the government and the Church (Loades 1974; Hill 1985; ch. 2). Of course, there were moments when the censorship broke down, resulting in the illicit distribution of Lutheran books under Henry VIII, Protestant ones under Mary, and Catholic ones under Elizabeth; and there were illegal presses, like that which put out the scurrilous Marprelate tracts attacking the Elizabethan bishops (Rostenberg 1971). In the 1640s, with the Civil War, all controls seemed to have lapsed altogether and the result was an extraordinary output of heterodox ideas of a kind which would not have been allowed before or afterwards. But normally the system of state licensing, which lasted until the end of the seventeenth century, had a deeply inhibiting effect upon printed publication,[14] and the press was a powerful influence in the hands of those who already wielded political power. The almanacs helped to keep alive an awareness of political and religious diversity (Capp 1979: 286–7), but most of the literature aimed directly at the lower classes was politically anodyne: most typically, it comprised either religious tracts or chap-books, ballads and romances of a trivializing, escapist, and often highly traditional kind. Some of it, notably the joke-books, had subversive implications,[15] and, of course, anything could be read in a radical way, even the Bible (perhaps especially the Bible). One observer thought that even the chap-book romances would give the poor ideas above their station: 'What ploughman who could read the renowned history of Jack Hickerthrift, or the story of the Seven Wise Men of Greece, would be content to whistle up one furrow, and down another, from the morning dawn to the setting of the sun?' (Anon 1788: 58.) But although it is possible that any fiction could be unsettling, it is clear that, for the most part, unorthodox ideas were much more likely to circulate orally or in manuscript than in print.

Meanwhile the effect of printing was to undermine the independence of popular oral tradition. As we have seen, people did not need to be able to read to be affected by literature culture; as a result, oral and literary forms rapidly intermingled. In modern times, students of folk-song and popular traditions have found, time and again, that their material has been, as it were, 'contaminated' by literary influences. At least 80 per cent of the folk-songs collected in the early twentieth century, for example, turn out to have been derived from earlier printed broadsides. It has been suggested that it was in the early modern period that the change occurred from inventing popular songs to memorizing them from a printed text. But all the evidence indicates that this intertwining of oral and literary tradition goes further back into the Middle Ages. Authentic oral tradition, unaffected by any written text, is never easy to find (Schmidt 1978; Spufford 1981: 9, 11–12, 229–31; Wrightson 1982: 195–6; Thomas 1984: 7–8).

The printed word thus helped to diminish the possibility of a genuinely independent 'folk' tradition. It also disparaged vernacular forms of verbal expression as inferior and incorrect. Printing standardized spelling and outlawed regional dialect and vulgar idioms. The language it used was that of London and the universities, not that of lower-class speech. Written literacy was the literacy of the educated classes; it was almost impossible to acquire it without also absorbing the values and social attitudes of polite metropolitan culture. The result was that in the eighteenth century the reading habits and literary tastes of a self-educated provincial tradesman did not differ very much from those of the social élite in the metropolis (Barrell 1985: 138). Those who did not aspire to imitate their betters had to be content with an inferior brand of literature designed by commercial publishers for a popular market (cf. Porter 1984: 248–9). The printed word thus either educated an imitative audience in accepted views or confirmed a passive one in a position of cultural inferiority. That is why some critics regard literacy as a means not of popular emancipation, but of upper-class hegemony and oppression. Put that way, it sounds too much like a conspiracy. In fact, the continuing tendency of print to reinforce already established values was not the result of a plot on anyone's part, but the almost inevitable consequence of an imitative social structure and a free market in printed literature.

The spread of literacy in early modern England, therefore, did not noticeably alter the direction in which society was moving anyway. Neither did it have more than a gradual effect upon people's mental habits. What it did do was to consolidate the authority of the educated classes over their inferiors and to impoverish and disparage other forms of expression. Of course, literacy and the printed word also widened people's horizons and opened up new possibilities. But, as with so many other social changes something had been lost as well as gained.

NOTES

In all quotations from contemporary sources, the spelling and punctuation have been modernized.

1. According to the *Oxford English Dictionary*, the first British (as opposed to American) use of the term 'literacy' to mean the ability to read and write was not until 1895.

2. Though one contemporary asked: 'What are we the better for the Englishing the law? Are not the lawyers as complete knaves in plain English as they are in their other language?' (Rogers 1653: 222).

3. For an attempt to discriminate between signatures of varying fluency see Longuet (1978).

4. This is an impression based on a wide range of scattered evidence. For some suggestive corroboration see Peyton (1928: 293); Wilkinson (1928: 119); Spufford (1979: 434–5); Anglin (1980: 69).

5. For some, not unrepresentative, examples see Brewer and Styles (1980: 27–8); Hyland (1920: 309–10); Atkinson (1963: 72); Underdown (1971: 319); Hammer (1978: 18); Howell (1967: 14); Lilly (1822: 26); Page (1905: 391).

6. In 1601 the contribution made by Thomas Jones, MP for Hereford, to the debate on a bill to avoid double debts ran as follows: 'It is now my chance to speak something, and that without humming or hawing. I think this law is a good law; even reckoning makes long friends; as far goes the penny as the penny's master. *Vigilantibus non dormientibus jura subveniunt.* Pay the reckoning over night, and you shall not be troubled in the morning. If ready money be *mensura publica*, let every man cut his coat according to his cloth. When his old suit is in the wain, let him stay till that his money bring a new suit in the increase. Therefore I think the law to be good, and I wish it a good passage.' (Townshend 1680: 283, cited by Wilson 1941: 182–3.)

7. I cannot be the only person to have gained admission to the Bodleian Library by inadvertently showing my Barclaycard.

8. The godly John Bruen left to his heirs the results of over thirty-five years of note-taking on sermons, lectures, and exercises in 'so many volumes of manuscripts, under his own hand, set up in a comely order in his own study as is scarce credible to report' (Hinde 1641: 102).

9. It has been argued that in France a distinction should be drawn between the spread of reading ability, for which religious influences were crucial, and the rise of full literacy, which depended on the spread of the market economy (Furet and Ozouf 1982: 304).

10. I owe this point to discussion with Dr Stuart Clark.
11. For conflicting evidence on this complicated subject, see Anon (1851: 106) and Mitchell (1932: 16–26).
12. His point, however, was that such a search would implicate the suspect's correspondents as well.
13. It was asserted a little later that, in country villages, the inability to read or write was a defect 'accounted so scandalous that it is an encouragement and spur to others to avoid the same common disparagement' (B.,F. 1701: 44).
14. In 1636 John Vicars was of the opinion that 'MS are now the best help God's people have to vindicate the Truth, printing being nowadays prohibited to them, especially if their writings have any the least tang or tincture of opposition to Arminianism, yea or even to Popery itself' (Boas, 1935: 89).
15. A popular Elizabethan writing-book invited its readers to transcribe the following sentiment (attributed to Plato): 'All men are by nature equal, made all by workman of like mire, and, howsoever we deceive ourselves, as dear unto God is the poorest beggar, as the most pompous prince living the world' (Beau Chesne and Baildon 1602: B1). Some important (and still unanswered) questions about the effects of popular literature in this period are raised by Reay (1983: 245–7).

REFERENCES

Andrews, C. Bruyn (ed.) 1970: *The Torrington Diaries*. New York and London.

Anglin, J. P. 1980: 'The Expansion of Literacy: Opportunities for the Study of the Three Rs in the London Diocese of Elizabeth I', in *Guildhall Studies in London History*, 4.

Annesley, Samuel (ed.) 1677: *The Morning-Exercise at Cripplegate: or Several Cases of Conscience Practically Resolved*, 4th edn. London.

Anon 1788: *Variety: a Collection of Essays*. London.

Anon 1851: *College Life in the Time of James the First, as illustrated by an Unpublished Diary of Sir Symonds D'Ewes*. London.

Aston, Margaret 1984: *Lollards and Reformers. Images and Literacy in Late Medieval Religion*. London.

Atkinson, Tom 1963: *Elizabethan Winchester*. London.

Auerbach, Erich 1965: *Literary Language and its Public in Late Latin Antiquity and in the Middle Ages*, trans. R. Manheim. London.

B., F. 1701: *Of Education with Respect to Grammar Schools*. London.

Bacon, Francis 1937: *Essays* (World's Classics). London.

Baker, J. H. (ed.) 1978: *The Reports of Sir John Spelman*, ii (Selden Society). London.

Baldwin, T. W. 1943: *William Shakespeare's Petty School*. Urbana, Ill.

Bantock, G. H. 1966: *The Implications of Literacy*. Leicester.

Barnes, A. E. 1984: Review of D. Weinstein and R. Bell, *Saints and Society* (Chicago 1982) and P. Brown, *The Cult of the Saints* (Chicago 1981) in *Journal of Social History*, 18: 157–61.

Barrell, John 1985: Review of *The Diary of Thomas Turner*, *TLS*, 8 Feb., p. 138.

Beau Chesne, John de, and John Baildon 1602: *A Booke Containing Divers Sortes of Hands*, rev. edn. London.

Beazley, F. C. 1908: 'Notes on the Parish of Burton in Wirral', *Transactions of the Historic Society of Lancashire and Cheshire*, lix.

Bentham, Jeremy 1983: *Constitutional Code*, i, eds. F. Rosen and J. H. Burns. Oxford.

Billingsley, Martin 1618: *The Pen's Excellencie*. London.

Boas, Frederick S. (ed.) 1935: *The Diary of Thomas Crosfield*, London.

Boyle, Robert 1744: *The Works of the Honourable Robert Boyle*, v. London.

Brailsford, H. N. 1961: *The Levellers and the English Revolution*, ed. Christopher Hill. London.

Brathwayte, Richard 1614: *The Schollers Medley*. London.

Bremner, Robert H. (ed.) 1970: *Children and Youth in America. A Documentary History*, i. Cambridge, Mass.

Breton, Nicholas 1966: *The Court and the Country* (1618), in *The Works in Verse and Prose of Nicholas Breton*, ii, ed. A. B. Grosart. New York.

Brewer, John, and John Styles (eds.) 1980: *An Ungovernable People. The English and their Law in the Seventeenth and Eighteenth Centuries*. London.

Burrage, Champlin 1912: *The Early English Dissenters*, ii. Cambridge.

Butler, Joseph 1897: *Sermons*, ed. W. E. Gladstone. Oxford.

Byrne, Muriel St Clare (ed.) 1981: *The Lisle Letters*, i. Chicago and London.

Campbell, Mildred 1960: *The English Yeoman under Elizabeth and the Early Stuarts*. London.

Capp, Bernard 1979: *Astrology and the Popular Press. English Almanacs 1500–1800*. London.

Cawdrey, Robert 1604: *A Table Alphabeticall, conteyning and teaching the True Writing, and Understanding of Hard Usuall English Wordes*. London.

Chapman, R. W. (ed.) 1930: *Johnson's Journey to the Western Islands of Scotland*. London.

Clanchy, M. T. 1979: *From Memory to Written Record, England 1066–1307*. London.

Clark, Peter 1976: 'The Ownership of Books in England, 1560–1640: the

Example of Some Kentish Townsfolk', in L. Stone (ed.): *Schooling and Society*. Baltimore.

—— 1977: *English Provincial Society from the Reformation to the Revolution*. Hassocks, Sussex.

Cockburn, J. S. 1972: *A History of English Assizes 1558–1714*. Cambridge.

—— (ed.) 1977: *Crime in England 1550–1800*. London.

Collinson, Patrick 1981: 'The Significance of Signatures', *TLS*, 9 Jan.

Cooke, John 1646: *The Vindication of the Professors and Profession of the Law*. London.

Crabbe, George 1908: *The Poetical Works*, ed. A. J. Carlyle and R. W. Carlyle. London.

Cressy, David 1980: *Literacy and the Social Order, Reading and Writing in Tudor and Stuart England*. Cambridge.

Crippen, T. G. 1905: 'The Brownists in Amsterdam', in *Transactions of the Congregational History Society*, ii (3).

Crosby, Ruth 1936: 'Oral Delivery in the Middle Ages', *Speculum*, xi.

Cunnington, B. Howard (ed.) 1932: *Records of the County of Wilts*. Devizes.

Daly, Lloyd W. 1967: *Contributions to a History of Alphabetization in Antiquity and the Middle Ages* (Collection Latomus, xc). Brussels.

Davis, F. N. (ed.) 1922: *Parochial Collections (Second Part) made by Anthony à Wood, M.A., and Richard Rawlinson, D.C.L., F.R.S.* Oxfordshire Record Society, Oxford.

Defoe, Daniel 1841: *The Complete English Tradesman*, i. Oxford.

Dekker, Thomas (n.d.): *The Guls Hornbook and the Belman of London*. Temple Classics. London.

Delamaine, Alexander 1820: *A Volume of Spiritual Epistles . . . by . . . John Reeve and Lodowick Muggleton*. London.

Denvir, Bernard 1983: *The Eighteenth Century. Art, Design and Society 1689–1789*. London.

Dickens, A. G. 1959: *Lollards and Protestants in the Diocese of York 1509–1558*. London.

—— 1964: *The English Reformation*. London.

Dodds, Madeline Hope, and Ruth 1971: *The Pilgrimage of Grace 1536–1537 and the Exeter Conspiracy 1538*, i. London.

Edwards, Thomas 1646: *Gangraena*, iii. London.

Ellis, William 1750: *The Modern Husbandman*, i. (3). London.

Elton, Oliver 1906: *Frederick York Powell*, i. Oxford.

Evelyn, John 1850: *The History of Religion*, i. ed. R. M. Evanson. London.

Ewbank, Jane M. 1963: *Antiquary on Horseback* (Cumberland and Westmorland Archaeological and Antiquarian Society, extra series, xix).

Febvre, Lucien, and Henri-Jean Martin 1976: *The Coming of the Book. The Impact of Printing 1450–1800*, (trans. D. Gerard; ed. G. Nowell-Smith and D. Wootton. London.

Ferguson, R. S., and W. Nanson 1887: *Some Municipal Records of the City of Carlisle* (Cumberland and Westmorland Antiquarian and Archaeological Society).

Firmin, Thomas 1681: *Some Proposals for the Imployment of the Poor*. London.

Firth, C. H. (ed.) 1901: *The Clarke Papers*, iv. Camden Society.

Fitzherbert, Master 1882: *The Book of Husbandry* (1534), ed. W. W. Skeat. English Dialect Society.

Flinn, M. W. 1962: *Men of Iron. The Crowleys in the Early Iron Industry*. Edinburgh.

Foster, C. W. 1928–9: 'Sir Isaac Newton's Family', *Reports and Papers of the Architectural Societies of . . . Lincoln . . . York . . . Leicester*, xxxix.

Freeman, Rosemary 1948: *English Emblem Books*. London.

Fuller, Thomas 1660: *Mixt Contemplations in Better Times*, ii, London.

Furet, Francois, and Jacques Ozouf 1982: *Reading and Writing. Literacy in France from Calvin to Jules Ferry*. Cambridge.

Gee, Edward 1690: *The Jesuit's Memorial for the Intended Reformation of England*. London.

Goody, Jack 1977: *The Domestication of the Savage Mind*. Cambridge.

Graff, Harvey J. (ed.) 1981: *Literacy and Social Development in the West: a Reader*. Cambridge.

Grafton, Anthony 1980: 'The Importance of being Printed', in *Journal of Interdisciplinary History*, xi.

Green, Mary Anne Everett (ed.) 1856: *Diary of John Rous* (Camden Society).

Gurnay Edmund 1660: *Gurnay Redivivus, or an Appendix unto the Homily against Images in Churches*. London.

Haller, William, and Godfrey Davies 1964: *The Leveller Tracts 1647–1653*, repr. Gloucester, Mass.

Hamilton, William Douglas (ed.) 1877: *Calendar of State Papers, Domestic Series, of the Reign of Charles I, 1639–40*. London.

Hammer, Carl I., Jr., 1978: 'Anatomy of an Oligarchy: the Oxford Town Council in the Fifteenth and Sixteenth Centuries', in *Journal of British Studies*, 18.

Haynes, Samuel 1740: *A Collection of State Papers*. London.

Heal, Ambrose 1931: *The English Writing-Masters and their Copy-Books 1570–1800*. Cambridge.

—— 1947: *The Signboards of Old London Shops*. London.

Heal, Felicity 1972: 'The Family of Love and the Diocese of Ely', in

D. Baker (ed.), *Schism, Heresy and Religious Protest*. Studies in Church History, ix. Cambridge.

Hector, L. C. 1966: *The Handwriting of English Documents*, 2nd edn. London.

Hey, David 1974: *An English Rural Community. Myddle under the Tudors and Stuarts*. Leicester.

Hill, Christopher 1974: *Change and Continuity in Seventeenth-Century England*. London.

—— 1985: *The Collected Essays of Christopher Hill*, i. Brighton.

Hinde, William 1641: *A Faithfull Remonstrance of the Holy Life and Happy Death of Iohn Bruen*. London.

HMC Gawdy 1885: *Historical Manuscripts Commission. Report on the Manuscripts of the Family of Gawdy*. London.

HMC Salisbury 1902: *Historical Manuscripts Commission. Calendar of Manuscripts of the Most Honourable the Marquis of Salisbury*, ix. London.

Hobbes, Thomas 1651: *Leviathan*. London.

Houlbrooke, Ralph A. 1984: *The English Family 1450–1700*. London.

Howell, Roger 1967: *Newcastle upon Tyne and the Puritan Revolution*. Oxford.

Hughes, Paul L., and James F. Larkin (eds.) 1964: *Tudor Royal Proclamations*, i. New Haven and London.

Hunt, William 1983: *The Puritan Moment. The Coming of Revolution in an English County*. Cambridge, Mass.

Hyland, St George Kieran 1920: *A Century of Persecution under Tudor and Stuart Sovereigns from Contemporary Records*. London.

Kaeuper, Richard W. 1984: 'Two Early Lists of Literates in England, 1334, 1373', in *English Historical Review*, xcix.

King, J. E. (ed.) 1938: *Inventory of Parochial Documents in the Diocese of Bath and Wells and the County of Somerset*. Taunton.

Kinge, John 1597: *Lectures upon Jonas delivered at Yorke*. Oxford.

Klotz, Edith L. 1937–8: 'A Subject Analysis of English Imprints for every Tenth Year from 1480 to 1640', in *Huntington Library Quarterly*, i.

Lansdowne, Marquis of (ed.) 1967: *The Petty-Southwell Correspondence 1676–1687*, repr. New York.

Larwood, Jacob, and John Camden Hotten 1900: *The History of Signboards*, 11th edn. London.

Laslett, Peter 1983: *The World We Have Lost*, 3rd edn. London.

Latham, R. E. 1959–60: 'The Banishment of Latin from the Public Records', in *Archives*, 4.

Levine, David 1980–1: 'Illiteracy and Family Life during the First Industrial Revolution', in *Journal of Social History*, 12.

Levy, F. J. 1982: 'How Information spread among the Gentry, 1550–1640', in *Journal of British Studies*, xxi.

Lewalski, Barbara Kiefer 1979: *Protestant Poetics and the Seventeenth-Century Religious Lyric.* Princeton, NJ.

Lilly, William 1822: *William Lilly's History of His Life and Times . . . by himself.* London.

Linnell, C. D. (ed.) 1950: *The Diary of Benjamin Rogers, Rector of Carlton 1720–71.* Publications of the Bedfordshire Record Society, xxx.

Loades, D. M. 1974: 'The Theory and Practice of Censorship in Sixteenth-Century England', in *Transactions of the Royal Historical Society*, 5th series, 24.

Locke, John 1824: *The Works of John Locke*, 12th edn., nine vols. London.

Longuet, Yves 1978: 'L'Alphabétisation à Falaise de 1670 à 1789', in *Annales de Normandie*, 28.

Loomie, Albert J. 1963: *The Spanish Elizabethans.* New York.

Luria, A. R. 1976: *Cognitive Development. Its Cultural and Social Foundations*, trans. M. Lopez-Morillas and L. Solataroff; ed. M. Cole. Cambridge, Mass.

Markham, Gervase 1635: *The English Husbandman*, i. London.

Marshall, J. D. 1969: 'Some Aspects of the Social History of 19th-Century Cumbria: (i) Migration and Literacy', in *Transactions of the Cumberland and Westmorland Antiquarian and Archaeological Society*, lxix.

Middlesex Records, 1928: *Middlesex County Records. Reports by the Late W. J. Hardy and W. Le Hardy.* Fakenham and London.

Mish, Charles C. 1953: 'Black Letter as a Social Determinant in the Seventeenth Century', in *Publications of the Modern Language Association*, lxviii.

Mitchell, W. F. 1932: *English Pulpit Oratory from Andrewes to Tillotson.* Cambridge.

Moran, Jo Ann Hoeppner 1985: *The Growth of English Schooling, 1340–1548. Learning, Literacy and Laicization in Pre-Reformation York Diocese.* Princeton, NJ.

Mozley, T. 1882: *Reminiscences chiefly of Oriel College and the Oxford Movement*, i.

Neuburg, Victor E. 1971: *Popular Education in Eighteenth Century England.* London.

Nodal, John H., and George Milner 1875: *A Glossary of the Lancashire Dialect*, i. English Dialect Society. London.

North, Roger 1890: *The Lives of . . . Francis North . . . Sir Dudley North: and . . . Dr. John North*, ii, ed. Augustus Jessopp. London.

Notestein, Wallace (ed.) 1923: *The Journal of Sir Simonds D'Ewes from the Beginning of the Long Parliament to the Opening of the Trial of the Earl of Strafford.* New Haven.

Novak, Maximillian E. 1983: (introduction to) *The Merry-Thought: or, The Glass-Window and Bog-House Miscellany*, parts 2–4 (1731–?). Augustan Reprint Society. Los Angeles.

Okely Judith 1983: *Changing Cultures. The Traveller-Gypsies.* Cambridge.

Orme, Nicholas 1973: *English Schools in the Middle Ages.* London.

Oxenham, John 1980: *Literacy. Writing, Reading and Social Organisation.* London.

Page, William (ed.) 1905: *The Victoria County History of the County of Durham*, i. London.

Palliser, D. M. 1982: 'Civic Mentality and the Environment in Tudor York', in *Northern History*, xviii.

Pantin, W. A. 1976: 'Instructions for a Devout and Literate Layman', in J. J. G. Alexander and M. T. Gibson (eds.), *Medieval Learning and Literature.* Oxford.

Parr, Richard 1686: *The Life of . . . James Usher, Late Arch-Bishop of Armagh.* London.

Pepys, Samuel 1970–83: *The Diary of Samuel Pepys*, i–xi, eds. Robert Latham and William Matthews. London.

Peyton, Sidney A. (ed.) 1928: *The Churchwarden's Presentments in the Oxfordshire Peculiars of Dorchester, Thame and Banbury.* Oxfordshire Record Society.

Pollexfen, Henry 1697: *A Discourse of Trade and Coyn.* London.

Porter, Roy 1984: 'Spreading Carnal Knowledge or Selling Dirt Cheap . . .', in *Journal of European Studies*, 14.

Powicke, Frederick J. (ed.) 1926: 'The Reverend Richard Baxter's Last Treatise', in *Bulletin of the John Rylands Library*, 10.

Reay, Barry 1983: 'Popular Literature in Seventeenth-Century England', in *Journal of Peasant Studies*, 10.

Richardson, H. G., and G. O. Sayles 1963: *The Governance of Mediaeval England from the Conquest to Magna Carta.* Edinburgh.

Robinson, Henry 1651: *Certain Considerations in order to a more speedy, cheap and equal distribution of Justice throughout the Nation.* London.

Robinson, F. K. 1875: *A Glossary of Words used in the Neighbourhood of Whitby.* English Dialect Society. London.

Rogers, John 1653: *Ohel or Beth-Shemesh. A Tabernacle for the Sun.* London.

Rodger, A. 1958: 'Roger Ward's Shrewsbury Stock: an Inventory of 1585', in *The Library*, 5th series, xiii.

Roper, William Oliver 1907: *Materials for the History of Lancaster*, i. Chetham Society.

Rostenberg, Leona 1971: *The Minority Press and the English Crown.* Nieuwkoop.

Ruggles, Thomas 1793: *The History of the Poor*, ii. London.

Sachse, William L. (ed.) 1938: *The Diary of Roger Lowe of Ashton-in-Makerfield, Lancashire, 1663–74.* London.

Saenger, Paul 1982: 'Silent Reading: Its Impact on Late Medieval Script and Society', in *Viator*, 13.

Salzman, Paul 1985: *English Prose Fiction 1558–1700*. Oxford.

Schlatter, Richard B. 1940: *The Social Ideas of Religious Leaders 1660–1668*. London.

Schmidt, Paul Gerhardt 1978: 'The Vision of Thurkill', in *Journal of the Warburg and Courtauld Institutes*, 41.

Schoenbaum, S. 1977: *William Shakespeare. A Compact Documentary Life*. Oxford.

Schofield, R. S. 1968: 'The Measurement of Literacy in Pre-Industrial England', in J. Goody (ed.), *Literacy in Traditional Societies*. Cambridge.

Scribner, Sylvia, and Michael Cole 1981: *The Psychology of Literacy*. Cambridge, Mass.

Shumaker, Wayne 1972: *The Occult Sciences in the Renaissance*. Berkeley, Los Angeles and London.

Sisson, Charles 1928: 'Marks as Signatures', in *The Library*, 4th series, 9.

Slack, Paul 1972: 'Religious Protest and Urban Authority: The Case of Henry Sherfield, Iconoclast, 1633', in D. Baker (ed.), *Schism, Heresy and Religious Protest*. Studies in Church History, 9. Cambridge.

Slavin, Arthur J. (ed.) 1972: *Tudor Men and Institutions*. Baton Rouge, La.

Smout, T. C. 1982: 'New Evidence on Popular Religion and Literacy in Eighteenth-Century Scotland', in *Past and Present*, 97.

Spufford, Margaret 1979: 'First Steps in Literacy: the Reading and Writing Experiences of the Humblest Seventeenth-Century Spiritual Autobiographers', in *Social History*, 4.

—— 1981: *Small Books and Pleasant Histories. Popular Fiction and Its Readership in Seventeenth-Century England*. London.

Steele, Richard 1684: *The Trades-Man's Calling*. London.

Strachey, Charles (ed.) 1901: *The Letters of the Earl of Chesterfield to His Son*, i. London.

Street, Brian V. 1984: *Literacy in Theory and Practice*. Cambridge.

Strong, S. Arthur 1903: (comp.): *A Catalogue of Letters and Other Historical Documents exhibited in the Library at Welbeck*. London.

Thirsk, Joan (ed.) 1967: *The Agrarian History of England and Wales*, iv. Cambridge.

Thomas, Keith 1969: 'Another Digger Broadside', in *Past and Present*, 42.

—— 1984: *The Perception of the Past in Early Modern England*. Creighton Trust Lecture. London.

Thompson, E. P. 1978: 'Eighteenth-Century English Society: Class Struggle without Class?', in *Social History*, 3.

Thrupp, Sylvia L. 1962: *The Merchant Class of Medieval London (1300–1500)*. Ann Arbor.

Townshend, Heywood 1680: *Historical Collections: or An Exact Account of the Four Last Parliaments of Queen Elizabeth*. London.

Tuer, Andrew W. 1896: *History of the Horn-Book*, 2 vols. London.

Turner, Ralph V. 1978: 'The Miles Literatus in Twelfth- and Thirteenth-Century England: How Rare a Phenomenon?', in *American Historical Review*, 83.

Tusser, Thomas 1984: *Five Hundred Points of Good Husbandry*. Oxford.

Underdown, David 1971: *Pride's Purge*. Oxford.

Vaisey, David (ed.) 1984: *The Diary of Thomas Turner 1754-1765*. Oxford.

Vann, Richard T. 1969: *The Social Development of English Quakerism 1655-1765*. Cambridge, Mass.

Veryard, E. 1701: *An Account of Divers Choice Remarks . . . taken in a Journey through the Low-Countries, France, Italy, and Part of Spain*. London.

Waddington, John 1854: *John Penry the Pilgrim Martyr, 1559-1593*. London.

Wake, Joan (ed.) 1935: *The Montagu Musters Book, A.D. 1602-1623*. Northamptonshire Record Society.

Wase, Christopher 1678: *Considerations concerning Free-Schools, as Settled in England*. Oxford.

Watson, Richard 1817: *Anecdotes of the Life of Richard Watson, Bishop of Landaff: written by himself*. London.

Weston, William 1955: *The Autobiography of an Elizabethan*. London.

Wilkinson, John T. 1928: *Richard Baxter and Margaret Charlton*. London.

Willan, T. S. (ed.) 1962: *A Tudor Book of Rates*. Manchester.

Wilson, F. P. 1941: 'Shakespeare and the Diction of Common Life', in *Proceedings of the British Academy*, xxvii.

Winthrop Papers 1929: *Winthrop Papers*, i. Massachusetts Historical Society.

Woodward, Donald (ed.) 1984: *The Farming and Memorandum Books of Henry Best of Elmswell, 1642*. British Academy.

Wrightson, Keith 1982: *English Society 1580-1680*. London.

Young, Sidney 1890: *The Annals of the Barber-Surgeons of London*. London.

LITERACY AND CULTURAL IDENTITY
IN THE HORN OF AFRICA:
THE SOMALI CASE

IOAN LEWIS

I

LANGUAGES, Samuel Johnson remarked, are the 'pedigrees of nations'. This view of the political significance of language is endorsed by those modern political scientists who define a nation as those people 'who speak the same language' (Minogue 1967: 154). Other students of nationalism go further and add literacy as an indispensable qualification for the development of effective national identity (Gellner 1983). This, of course, is in line with Professor Ong's assertion, in the opening chapter of this book, that writing 'heightens consciousness'.

In the Horn of Africa, three of the world's great literate traditions have contended and interpenetrated for over a thousand years, producing extreme nationalist conflict, which would seem at first sight to demonstrate all too graphically the validity of this thesis. However, as I would like to suggest, by considering the very recent introduction of widespread mother-tongue literacy among the previously oral Somali, the relationship between nationalism and literacy seems rather more equivocal. In Ethiopia, where again widespread literacy is a modern phenomenon, there is a more complex relationship between nationalism and writing. This arises from the fact that the politically dominant peoples who, following their rulers' conversion in the fourth century, have appropriated Christianity, possess their own indigenous literate tradition which has become the medium for Christian worship and teaching. Here one might perhaps say that it is Christianity rather than literacy that has heightened (ethnic) consciousness. Later, as we shall see, modern mass literacy campaigns waged in the name of 'nation-building' have, paradoxically, stimulated reactive counter-nationalistic sentiments and aspirations.

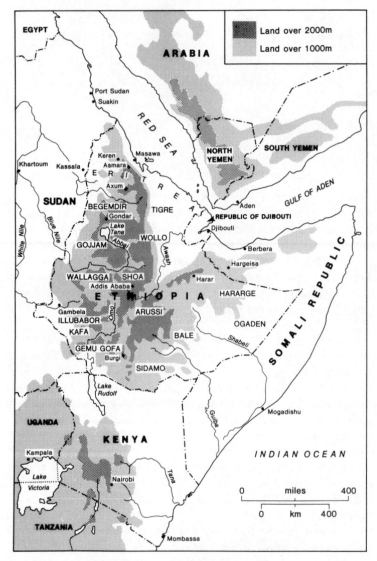

The Eastern Horn of Africa

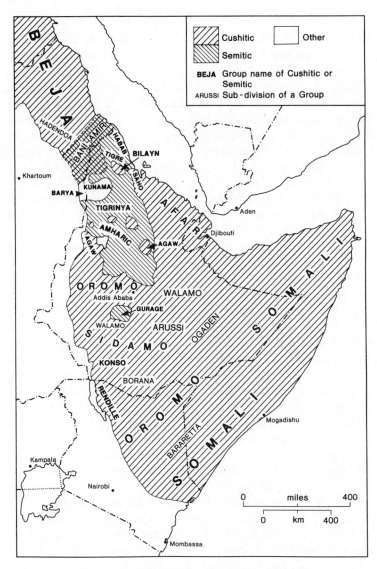

Languages and Peoples of the Horn of Africa

II

The three great (literate) traditions represented in the Horn of Africa are of course Judaism, Christianity, and Islam. Although the first is most directly associated with the so-called 'Black Jews'— the indigenous Falashas, the Judaic tradition also strongly colours the politically dominant Christian tradition of the Semitic-speaking Tigreans and Amharas who have controlled Ethiopia since its foundation at Axum (see Ullendorff 1968; Jones and Monroe 1935). Commanding the Ethiopian highlands where they live as settled farmers, these two ethnic groups are hierarchically organized into a ruling military stratum, clergy, and lay peasantry. Christianity has been firmly indigenized in this dominant local *literate* tradition, first in the liturgical language, Ge'ez, and later in the related Tigrinya and Amharic. These three Semitic languages are similar in relationship to the Romance languages, with Ge'ez equivalent to Latin, Tigrinya to Italian, and Amharic to French. Since the Amharic-speaking Amharas succeeded in installing themselves as the ruling ethnic group in this expanding Christian conquest state some 700 years ago, their language has been known officially as 'the language of the King', with Amharicized Ge'ez providing the medium in which the official court scribe, or 'writer of orders' and 'keeper of the seal', later styled 'Minister of the Pen', recorded royal decisions. While mainly oral Amharic was thus the language of government, Ge'ez remained, like Latin, the ecclesiastical and literary language.

The historic mandate of the Amhara ethnic élite to conquer and convert neighbouring peoples in the name of the Lion of Juda was conveyed and enshrined in the famous national epic in Ge'ez, *The Glory (or Pride) of Kings (Kebra Nagast)*, written, if not composed, in the fourteenth century. This unique royal charter which traces the origins of Ethiopian kingship to the legendary Menelik I, issue of Solomon and the Queen of Sheba, is like the Old Testament for the Hebrews, or the Koran for the Arabs, the repository of profound national and religious feelings (Ullendorff 1960: 144). It constitutes, as Donald Levine (1974: 92) aptly puts it, 'a national script' for the Christian Ethiopian state which, by this time (the fourteenth century), led by the bellicose King 'Amda Zion ('Pillar of Zion': 1314–44), was already locked in protracted religious wars with the surrounding Muslim principalities and peoples, including illiterate Cushitic-speaking lowland pastoralists such as the Somali.

Although the Somali *oral* tradition lays claim to the sixteenth-century Muslim conqueror, Ahmed Gran (1506–43), under whose fierce attacks the Amhara kingdom almost collapsed, there was little direct contact between the two ethnic groups until the closing decades of the nineteenth century and the colonial partition of the Somali nation in which, with its new European guns and rifles, Ethiopia participated under Menelik II, the founder of the modern empire state. In this scramble for new possessions, Menelik was as emphatic as his European competitors (the French, British, and Italians) in stressing his god-given civilizing mission to share the benefits of Christianity with new, 'heathen' subjects. This long history of isolation (familiar from Gibbon's famous rotund reference[1]), religious animosity and sometimes accommodation with Islam and, in the modern era, military conflict with European powers has, naturally, sharpened Ethiopian nationalism.

Just as it had appropriated and indigenized Christianity, the Amhara core national culture of this expanding African Habsburg empire absorbed new subject groups, offering the possibility of assimilation and upward mobility with conversion and Amharicization—for both Menelik and Haile Selassie the key to integrating Ethiopia's ethnic mosaic. Ethiopia thus pioneered the 'nation-building' process characteristic of most post-colonial African states, with literacy in the mother tongue of the Amhara élite the final signature of full citizenship. The surge of ethnic consciousness aroused by modernization under Haile Selassie led after the 1974 Revolution, to which it had contributed, to literacy campaigns utilizing the Amharic script to write several of the other languages of the eighty-five officially recognized 'nationalities'. Before the Revolution only Amharic (and Ge'ez) could be written;[2] after the Revolution only Amharic could be written. Ethiopia had now, literally, a national (or nationalizing) script.

III

Despite their early conversion to Islam, reflecting their proximity to Arabia, and peripheral involvement in the ephemeral Islamic states which encircled Ethiopia in the Middle Ages, the Somalis, so far as we know, had not previously translated their strong sense of *cultural* nationalism into political terms. They had never constituted a state. It was characteristic also of their mixed Islamic literary and Somali oral heritage that although this first manifestation of nationalism, coinciding with Ethiopian, British, and Italian colonial penetration, was couched in the classic Muslim form of a jihad, led by a sophisticated Somali sheikh well versed in Arabic literacy, its success depended crucially on this man's power of oratory and his genius—still widely recognized—as a major *oral* poet. I refer, of course, to the fiery Somali crusader, Sayyid Muhammad Abdille Hassan, whose guerrilla forces defied the Christian colonizers of his people from 1900–20. His banner was the banner of Islam, his book the Holy Koran, but his battle cry was delivered in oral Somali—not written Arabic. (His oral legacy has provided, retrospectively, an oral charter for modern Somali nationalism including literacy in the mother tongue.)

Arabic is the language of the Koran, which, ideally, should be transmitted in Arabic. From the time of their adoption of the faith centuries ago, the Somalis have had access to Arabic, the language of Islam. But despite a vernacular tradition of Arabic instruction going back to the twelfth century (see Lewis 1969: 75–82) Arabic has remained the prisoner of its exalted status as the word of God, the magical language of religion, known orally and to some extent written only by religious specialists and a few merchants and sailors. Indeed the distinction between these religious specialists (*Wadaaddo*) and the warrior (*Waranleh*) laiety (who form the majority) constitutes the most pervasive division (after that of gender) in the strongly egalitarian social system of the Somalis. The two roles are complementary since the warriors need holy mediators to regulate their internal problems and to negotiate on their behalf with God. Thus, traditionally, these exponents of Islam, with limited literacy in Arabic, teach the Koran in itinerant religious schools, solemnize marriage, divorce, and death, assess damages in disputes, mediate and dispense blessings and therapeutic potions. The subordination of their restricted literacy tradition to the priorities of this primary oral culture is epitomized in the regular oral treatment which these religious specialists provide for illness. This remedy (not, of course, unique to Somalia) involves the literal imbibing of holy writ, by drinking a decoction, made by washing into a cup powerful passages from the Koran transcribed on a piece of paper.

Despite (and because of) its unique religious significance, Arabic remained marginal, restricted to ritual contexts, and to external trade. It was not indigenized, and the Arabic script was similarly little used to transcribe the vigorous, dominant medium-oral Somali (for which it is not, in any case, linguistically an altogether perfect vehicle). The men of God who controlled this prestigious, if minority, literate tradition clearly had vested interests in maintaining its exclusiveness and they were also not necessarily anxious to extend its use to promote written Somali. Equally, some Somalis suggest that, as a people proudly tracing their origins (through painstakingly constructed *written* genealogies) to the family of the Prophet Muhammad, they were reluctant to advertise to the literate Arab world that Arabic was not actually their mother tongue.

Undersigned or underwritten, in this fashion, by the language of the faith, oral Somali well served the needs of a highly articulate and linguistically self-conscious people. Language was primarily for communication, and complicated messages were regularly encoded in poetic form for accurately memorized, rapid word-of-mouth transmission among mobile nomads—a mode of communication which B. W. Andrzejewski (1982: 75) calls the 'oral postal service'. In this populist oral culture, poetry in many different genres, and oratory, occupied the centre of the stage. Opinion within one's own clan and outside it was influenced and formed by poems and oratory which captured the imagination of the listener. Reputations depended crucially on skill in these arts which also entailed possessing a good command of the seemingly endless store of Somali proverbs. As the Somali historian Said Samatar (1982: 75) points out, the Somali term for orator (*'Odkar*), means literally 'capable of speech', implying that those who lack oratorial skill are, virtually, incapable of speech, literally dumb. Without going into details, let me simply say here that poems (frequently containing archaic expressions), seldom exceeding a hundred lines, were composed and recited verbatim (usually in the form of a chant), either by their authors or by reciters aided by the alliteration and scansion principles of the different genres. Thousands of poems going back well over a hundred years survive into the present, remembered for their artistic perfection and eloquence, a heritage endlessly replenished by new compositions (Andrzejewski and Lewis 1964: 130). Poets and poetry reciters regularly possess a memorized repertoire extending up to fifteen hours of 'playback' time.

In this highly articulate oral culture, words are viewed as things
—not in the magical vein at times associated with orality—but
rather as instruments, capable of inflicting deadly wounds which
entail claims for compensation for defamation (*haal*), paralleling
those applicable to physical assault (*haq*). As a line from a famous
poem on ingratitude by Salaan 'Arrabey (d. 1940) puts it: 'The
tongue is like a sword cutting off life.' These two systems of aggres-
sion, 'speech feud' and 'blood-feud', are apt to intersect and
reinforce each other. As a traditional Somali elder puts it reflec-
tively: 'Camels are looted and men killed because of poetry. The
more camels a clan owns, the greater their resources. Camels bring
men together. If a clan loots camels and kills men from another
clan, the injured clan may bide their time and not rise in immediate
revenge. But if the victorious clan attempt, as they often do, to im-
mortalize their victory in verse, then the looted clan feels humiliated
and immediately seeks to remedy their honour and avenge their
wrongs. Thus revenge follows revenge and feud, feud' (Samatar
1982: 27).

If words can so directly harm, they can also heal. Famous pacifi-
catory poems thus find their place in the Somali oral heritage as,
for example, the famous appeal addressed successfully by Salaan
'Arrabey to rival clan segments to draw back from battle (Andrzejewski and Lewis 1964: 130):

> The day the 'Umar Daahir
> Cut themselves to pieces in the battle
> Of 'Alool'ad, he who was present then
> And who also knows what happened at the battle
>   of Meygaag 'Iidan,
> Knows to the full
> The horror and the turmoil of war
> And understands its real nature;
> Oh clansmen, stop the war!

IV

The first significant initiative towards literacy arose out of this oral
culture itself when, in the wake of the expansion of colonial rule
following Sayyid Muhammad's defeat in 1920, a prominent elder
of one of the major north-eastern clans (then under Italian juris-
diction) invented the first, phonetically perfect script for Somali.

b t ǧ ḥ ḫ

d z s ǰ g

ḍ c f q k

l m n h

i u o a e

y, ī w, ū ō ā ē

1 2 3 4 5

6 7 8 9. 0

This Osmaniya script, as it became known after its inventor's name, is written from left to right, unlike Arabic, and some of its characters are reminiscent of Amharic letters.

When twenty years later the first modern Somali Nationalist Organization was launched in what was then British occupied (Italian) Somalia, this 'Somali writing', as it became known, acquired a new and wider impetus as a vehicle for nationalism. This was in line with the motives which had inspired the inventor who felt that national pride required his mother tongue now to be a written language. This would also facilitate communication between widely separated cells of the new nationalist organization in a script which would be indecipherable to the European and Ethiopian adminstrative authorities.

By 1947, when the Somali Youth League had become firmly established as the main nationalist party, the promotion of this script was one of its four major policy aims. However, changes in the leadership of the League soon led to a fierce debate between Osmaniya supporters and advocates of Arabic viewed as the natural medium for a Muslim nation. The possibility of using Latin characters to write Somali also began to be examined by some nationalists. In 1957, three years before Somalia attained full independence, the Somali Youth League government printed a page of the official newspaper in Somali, transcribed in Roman characters. This bold experiment produced such a violent reaction, particularly on the part of traditional religious leaders, that it was not repeated. The pro-Arabic lobby denounced the use of the Latin script with the derogatory, punning slogan: *Laatiin waa laa diin* (Latin is irreligion).

At independence in 1960, the Somali Republic (comprising the former British and Italian Somalilands) thus found itself with three *written* languages: Arabic, English, and Italian. This confusing situation made it all the more urgent to solve the problem of finding an acceptable script for Somali. In 1966 a distinguished UNESCO Commission of linguists led by B. W. Andrzejewski added its weight to the choice of Latin. But public opinion remained divided and volatile and the Somali government hesitated.

It was left to the military who seized power in 1969 to resolve the issue. Following what for some years had been the informal practice in the police and army, in 1972 General Siyad's regime adopted a very practical Roman script for the national language.[3] What has

been hailed as the 'Somali miracle of instant literacy' was achieved
with the launching in 1973 of a concerted urban literacy campaign.
Government officials were enlisted in 'crash courses' in the new
script, with the prospect of losing their positions if they failed.
Adult literacy classes drew large and enthusiastic attendances from
the most educationally deprived sectors of the urban population,
including women. In this 'Cultural Revolution', as it was pro-
claimed by the Minister of Information and National Guidance, the
next step was to extend literacy to the neglected nomads who form
the majority of the population. Accordingly, in the late summer of
1974, a task force of 30,000 secondary-school students and teachers
was dispatched in truckloads to the interior, to teach the nomads to
read and write and to impart the basic principles of scientific
socialism, now the official policy of the state. These privileged
urban students were thus to share the fruits of the 'Glorious Revolution' (as the coup was retrospectively named) with their nomadic
comrades. The guiding slogan, provided by the Head of State
himself was: 'If you know teach; if you don't learn.' As the
General explained in a major public speech on 8 March 1974,
marking Women's International Day: 'The key . . . is to give
everybody the opportunity to learn reading and writing. . . .
It is imperative that we give our poeple modern revolutionary
education . . . to restructure their social existence . . . It
will be the weapon to eradicate social balkanization and fragmentation into tribes and sects. It will bring about an absolute
unity and there will be no room for any negative foreign cultural influences.'

The goals of modernization, nationalism, and independence are
all fused here: a modern, integrated nation consists of those who
not only 'speak the same language' but also read and write it. (All
this, of course, is very much in the spirit of Professor Ernest
Gellner's theories of nationalism, although I have no reason to
think that General Siyad's ideas come from this source.)

As it happened, I was in Somalia in the summer of 1974 and saw
the beginnings of the acute drought which was to turn this 'Rural
Prosperity Campaign', as it was originally called, into a humane
and well-organized famine relief operation. The emphasis quickly
shifted to endeavouring to meet the survival needs of the drought-
stricken nomads, who, once they had been grouped in relief camps,
were readily induced to join literacy classes.

With a substantial drift back to the nomadic economy, after several years of good rains, it has obviously been difficult, despite considerable effort, to sustain high levels of rural literacy. It is officially claimed that over 1.5 million people participated in these two literacy campaigns and that by 1982 400,000 of the urban population were literate, in addition to the half million children enrolled in school where written Somali had also been established. These generous figures may also include some of the refugees who poured into Somalia after the Somali–Ethiopian conflict of 1977/8. More accessible statistics of Somali literacy can be gleaned from the records kept at the BBC Somali programme of listeners' letters received from the Horn of Africa. These increased from a figure of 2,500 in 1973 to over 6,500 in 1983 when the proportion written in Somali had risen in the same period from 12 per cent to 90 per cent.[4]

However difficult it may be to gauge the numerical strength of the new literacy, there is no gainsaying its popularity or its genuinely populist character. In contrast to literacy in foreign languages such as Arabic, Italian, and English which previously favoured the educated élite, in their own mother tongue many people who have had no experience of 'modern education' have greater mastery of the Somali vernacular than those brought up in towns and trained mainly in these foreign traditions. This new mother-tongue literacy also corrects the sex bias of previous forms of formal education, including Arabic, which gave men a great advantage over women. It is not surprising that this populist measure should perhaps be the most popular of all those introduced by the present Somali government.

This revolution in Somali literacy has naturally created a corresponding demand for reading material as well as stimulating new forms of literary production. In addition to the official news, stories, and other material published in the daily *October Star*, the ideological bureau of the Somali Revolutionary Socialist Party has produced a flood of propagandist pamphlets and manuals in addition to its monthly organ, 'Struggle' (*Halgan*). Hundreds of school textbooks as well as primers for adult literacy have been prepared by the curriculum department of the Ministry of Education.

These all stress Somali language and literature, and make extensive use of 'traditional' poetry, presented in verbatim form. Here, as elsewhere, where new work is produced, the scansion patterns and alliteration of oral poetry have been carried over intact into written poetry, even when the theme is current politics.

Having mastered the new script, poets now readily compose directly at the typewriter, sometimes, it has to be admitted, within office hours. I remember in this connection an early visit I made—with some trepidation—to the Censorship Office to seek a permit to take photographs. Entering what seemed to me a rather sinister office, I found myself confronting a young military officer who knew me—although I did not immediately recognize him. After he had introduced himself and before I could explain the purpose of my visit, he invited me to read the document he was assiduously typing and which I assumed might contain classified information (possibly relating to myself). To my surprise, the Censorship Officer was actually engaged in composing rather explicit love poems which he was anxious to publish.

Over six million copies of books had been printed on the national press by the late 1970s. These included the first Somali novels, and written plays, as well as scholarly dictionaries, collections of poetry and traditional folklore, and history books edited by the Somali Academy of Science and Culture whose first President (Shireh Jama Ahmad) had devised the Latin Somali script. There were also translations from works by foreign authors as diverse as Brecht and G. A. Henty, as well as less celebrated writers—as I discovered when, purely by chance, I stumbled upon a group of keen translators, busily rendering some of my own accounts of Somali history into Somali.

More novel in a culture which, unlike Christian Ethiopia, has no tradition of visual art, are the propagandist posters and office and shop signs which literacy has encouraged. During the era of Scientific Socialism, these included posters at Orientation Centres displaying the revolutionary trinity: *Jaalle* Markis (as the Somalis call him), *Jaalle* Lenin, and *Jaalle* Siyad. At a less elevated level one could notice various new names for restaurants and stores, including after the introduction of television in the capital Mogadishu, a shop (*daas*) called *'Daaski Dallas'*!

This remarkable development in mother-tongue literacy producing what has been called a unique 'orally written literature' (Andrzejewski 1984: 227–9) was with little doubt the most popular and effective of a package of modernizing measures. These included the official abolition of the clan loyalties that traditionally divided the nation, and, indeed, the complete replacement of kinship, by comradeship in the lofty name of Scientific Socialism (see Lewis 1980: 209–25). These secular innovations once again brought to the fore the complex issue of Somali Islamic identity. To reassure the local guardians of the faith, and for other strategic reasons, Somalia prudently joined the Arab League in 1974, thus respecting the ancient twin pillars of Somali society: the lay and the religious.

V

In the historical context we have briefly sketched, it is clear, I think, that having experienced for centuries the rivalry between the Amharic Christian and Arabic Muslim literate traditions, swelling sentiments of national pride fired the Somali quest for a national script. As Ong and other students of literacy argue, has literacy then actually increased national consciousness? This, as we have seen, was according to President Siyad one of the major objectives in introducing Somali writing. This is also the conclusion of the Somali political scientist who has made the closest study of the problems of writing his native tongue. 'The writing . . . of the language has', he says, 'facilitated national integration, and . . . strengthened Somali identity . . .' (Adam 1983: 41). Although I cannot cite other than random personal impressions, in the wake of the national literacy campaigns, at least in urban centres in Somalia, there did seem to me to be a discernible increase in Somali linguistic self-consciousness and national pride. Certainly such nationalist sentiment found enthusiastic expression in 1977 in the initially intoxicatingly successful, but ultimately disastrous campaign to liberate the Ogaden region of eastern Ethiopia (ethnically Western Somalia). By this time, following the Ethiopian Revolution of September 1974, and the ensuing power struggle in Addis Ababa, Ethiopia had become extremely vulnerable, and the Western Somali Liberation Front guerrilla forces were able to drive out the Ethiopian garrisons, encountering less resistance than had been anticipated. As they liberated each settlement, the WSLF proudly replaced all the Amharic signs and notices with announcements in the new Somali script and opened schools to teach Somali writing. To the bitter dismay of Somali ambitions, all this was quickly swept away when, a few months later after the superpower summersault which brought the Soviet Union to Ethiopia's side, Russian- and

Cuban-supported Ethiopian forces reconquered the Ogaden. Those Somalis who remained in the region, rather than flooding into Somalia as refugees, if they wished to write their language had now to do so in Amharic characters. This restoration of linguistic hegemony has encouraged other ethnic nationalist movements in Ethiopia, such as that of the vast Oromo nation (the largest ethnic group in the Horn of Africa), to follow the Somali initiative in using Latin characters to write their national language which belongs to the same Cushitic family.

Events in the bitter years since the Ogaden débâcle indicate that while the 'instant literacy' we have examined may have fuelled nationalist feeling inside the Somali Republic and in the adjacent Ogaden prior to the 1977/8 Somalia–Ethiopia conflict, it did not produce a radical and sustained transformation of nationalism into a modernist mode of the type associated with literacy by Gellner and others. In defeat, patriotism has been replaced by rancorous clan strife which, far from being eradicated by the regime of Scientific Socialism, has in fact become the primary recipe for survival.

The resurgence of this powerful oral political tradition at the disposition of those who control state literacy may seem a little paradoxical. But written or unwritten, language is after all a means of expression, not an end in itself. And it is not only written Somali that is involved here. We have, in fact, so far quite ignored, and now touch on in conclusion, what, in the short term at least, seems much more significant in its general social and political implications than Somali writing, impressive though that is. I refer, of course, to what Ong calls 'secondary orality'. By the time literacy had made its dramatic entry on the Somali stage, the transistor revolution was already firmly entrenched, reinforcing and infinitely extending and amplifying Somali oral culture. The highly articulate Somalis, as might be anticipated, took to radio, telephone, loudspeaker and tape recorder with marked enthusiasm. Once cheap transistor radios and casette recorders became readily available in the late 1960s and early 1970s, they became immediately extremely popular, sweeping Somali culture into the exciting world of secondary orality. Today, it would scarcely be an exaggeration to say that almost every nomadic family has a radio and, from being a nation of bards, the Somalis have rapidly also become a nation of radio buffs, listening avidly to Somali broadcasts from local stations and from places as distant as Cairo, London, and Moscow. In this context, as they produce new works, poets now frequently use tape recordings to supplement their memories.

New pop radio songs (*Heello*), with musical accompaniments (Johnson 1974) beat out the party line. Opponents of the regime, inside and outside the country, compose stinging attacks on its leaders, sometimes in the form of opaque love songs. As in traditional Somali politics, the President's poets exchange vitriolic verse with his opponents outside Somalia. These vigorous poetical polemics constitute oral chain letters, stored in cassettes which circulate round the Somali communities scattered all over the world. There are whole cycles of such poetic exchanges, composed to alliterate in a particular letter—such as 'Siinleh'—the 'S'-chains, and 'Dalleh' —the 'D'-chains for example. In this surge of electronic rhetoric Somali politics retains its overwhelmingly oral character, bypassing the written word which, if indispensable in certain contexts, falls into second place as an ancillary medium for communication—an extension in writing of oral culture in which there was already a tendency towards fixed forms. In this vein also, in the Somali interior today, those with some knowledge of the new script are assuming the subsidiary clerical (letter-writing) functions of the traditional religious specialists whose medium was Arabic. Here lay literacy directly confronts the religious literacy in Arabic which is the only 'traditional' form of literacy known to the Somali.

Thus, literacy which, symbolically as much as literally, is such a central element in the Ethiopian (Amhara) national consciousness, remains, I believe, peripheral to Somali identity, where the stress is primarily on orality. Across the border, within the Ethiopian pluralist mosaic, the extension of literacy in Amharic characters, inflames reactive sentiments of ethnic nationalism amongst those non-Amhara peoples who, like the Somali, would write their own language in their own way. In this case, the rejection of unacceptable literacy heightens national consciousness.

NOTES

1. 'Encompassed on all sides by the enemies of their religion, the Aethiopians slept near a thousand years, forgetful of this world, by whom they were forgotten' (Gibbon 1957, v: 69).

2. In Eritrea, more currency was allowed to Tigrinya and, of course, Ge'ez remained as a specialized archaic religious medium. Arabic was also used as a written medium by literate Muslims.
3. This had been developed by one of the first President of the Somali National Academy of Culture, Shirre Jama Ahmad, founder of the first Somali literary magazine (*The Light of Knowledge and Education*).
4. Figures kindly supplied by the BBC Somali Programme, London.

REFERENCES

Adam, H. M. 1983: 'Language, national self-consciousness and identity—the Somali experience', in I. M. Lewis (ed.), *Nationalism and Self-Determination in the Horn of Africa*, 31–42. London: Ithaca Press.

Andrzejewski, B. W. 1982: 'Alliteration and Scansion in Somali Oral Poetry and their Cultural Correlates', in V. Görög-Karady (ed.), *Genres, Forms, Meanings: Essays in African Oral Literature*, 68–83. Oxford: Journal of the Anthropological Society of Oxford.

—— 1984: 'Somali Literature', in L. S. Klein (ed.), *Encyclopedia of World Literature in the Twentieth Century*, iv: 277–9. New York: Frederick Ungar.

—— and I. M. Lewis 1964: *Somali Poetry*. Oxford: Clarendon Press.

Gellner, E. 1983: *Nations and Nationalism*. Oxford: Basil Blackwell.

Gibbon, E. 1957: *The Decline and Fall of the Roman Empire*, Everyman edn. London.

Johnson, J. W. 1974: *Heellooy, Heelleellooy: the development of the genre Heello in modern Somali poetry*. Bloomington: Indiana University Press.

Jones, A. H. M. and E. Monroe 1935: *A History of Ethiopia*. Oxford: Clarendon Press.

Laitin, D. 1977: *Politics, Language and Thought: the Somali Experience*. Chicago: Chicago University Press.

Levine, D. 1974: *Greater Ethiopia*. Chicago: Chicago University Press.

Lewis, I. M. 1969. 'Sharif Yusuf Barkhadle: the blessed saint of Somaliland', in *Proceedings Third International Congress of Ethiopian Studies*, 75–82. Addis Ababa.

—— 1980: *A Modern History of Somalia*. London: Longman.

Minogue, K. 1967: *Nationalism*. London: Batsford.

Samatar, S. S. 1982: *Oral Poetry and Somali Nationalism*. Cambridge: Cambridge University Press.

Ullendorff, E. 1960: *The Ethiopians*. London: Oxford University Press.

—— 1968: *Ethiopia and the Bible*. London: Oxford University Press.

NEW TECHNOLOGIES IN PRINTING
AND PUBLISHING: THE PRESENT
OF THE WRITTEN WORD

ADAM HODGKIN

AUTHORS, publishers, printers, and readers tend to think of the new information technologies as ways of helping them to do what they already do, only more efficiently, more cheaply, or more quickly. The new technologies can help us in these ways, but they also change the nature of what we are trying to do. It is not simply a matter of producing new books by a new method or of reading the classic texts through a computer screen; if we want to gain the benefits of this new technology we have to understand the ways in which it will allow writers to write different kinds of books and also permit readers to construe texts in new ways.[1]

As its title suggests, Walter Ong's *Orality and Literacy* is primarily concerned with the contrasts between oral and literate modes of thought and language. But his work and his argument rely on a supplementary classification in which literate thought and language itself falls into three distinct phases: the phase of the manuscript which gives rise to chirographic cultures; the phase of the printed book which we associate with typographic cultures; and the phase of the electronic text or document which we associate with a computer culture, or an electronic culture.

This classification of the modes of literacy is similar to that of Marshall McLuhan in his book *The Gutenberg Galaxy*. But there is an important difference in the way in which they apply this schema. McLuhan was perhaps unlucky in writing his book at a time when it seemed the technology of the television was to be the basis and exemplar of an electronic culture. The computer or computing is scarcely mentioned in the book.[2] This is a remarkable omission. Computer scientists have been talking about machine *codes* and programming *languages* since the early development of the technology and the language of computing is riddled with literary terms: computers have editors, compilers, read only memory, words, and so on. But the technology was well advanced before it became obvious, to humanists at least, that computers are in some sense linguistic machines. The point is made in an arresting fashion by Joseph Weizenbaum:

Texts are written in a language. Computer languages are languages too, and theories may be written in them . . . we need not restrict our attention to machine languages or even to ... 'higher level' languages . . . We may include all languages, specifically also natural languages, that computers may be able to interpret. The point is precisely that computers do *interpret* texts given to them, in other words, that texts determine computers' behaviour. (1984: 144-5)

It is now almost uncontroversial to assert that computing is the technology which is having and will continue to have a profound effect on the written word. But, as Weizenbaum points out, the written word will also have a profound effect on the computer.

In considering the effects of this new technology on the written word, it may be useful to distinguish three stages. First, there may be some effect on the process of composition or writing. Second there may be effects on the process of reproduction or distribution. Third, there may be effects on the reader or consumer. These are approximate distinctions. We may feel the need to question or subvert them, but they draw our attention to the fact that the publisher is the middle term in a relation between the writer and the reader. The publisher is not essentially concerned with the physical production of books—that is the printer's speciality. Nor is he primarily concerned with retailing books—that is the province of the bookseller. But he is fundamentally concerned with identifying and establishing a market in books. This specialist role for the publisher is a relative innovation. For example, in 1885 Oxford University Press was already well known as a printer and publisher of books. It was one of the largest employers in the city, but fewer than ten members of the staff were employed in what we would now recognize as publishing; the others were printers and paper-makers. There is a similar pattern with every other long-established and well-known publisher, for example: Macmillan, Collins, Elsevier, Longman, and Cambridge University Press. In the nine-teenth century the reputation and business of these publishers was very largely dependent on their activities as printers or booksellers. One of the reasons why publishers are now more numerous and necessary is that the market for books is very much more sophisticated and highly differentiated. In 1949 11,924 new titles were published in this country; in 1984 there were 40,246 new titles.

The publisher, in consort with printers and booksellers, attempts to create a market which will match the output of authors or writers with the resources and demands of readers. There are types of publishing in which the supply side is dominant—scientific journal publishing would be an example. There is, by contrast, a type of publishing in which market considerations are so dominant that the author barely gets a look in—one thinks here of the 'generic' fiction which has been sold in American supermarkets under no author's name in much the same way as own-label baked beans and washing powder. But to recognize that there are forms of publishing which are primarily impelled by the producer and forms which are slavishly subservient to the whims of the consumer is not to deny that publishing can only work with authors, editors, or creators. Similarly there can be no point or justification in a publishing process which has no readers.

Before considering the new technologies we should perhaps establish what we understand by the 'old technology'. The most useful working definition is that the old technology is comprised of those printing techniques which are natural developments of Gutenberg's invention of printing texts, on paper, in alphabetical scripts from movable metal types. The transition between old and new technology obviously cannot be fixed with chronological precision. In some parts of the world books are still printed from metal type. But very few of the new books published in Oxford this year will be printed by this method. Twenty-five years ago the overwhelming majority were. In itself this suggests that in one respect the printing industry at least has moved into a post-Gutenberg era.

Many writers have noted the extraordinary continuity and vitality of Gutenberg's invention.[3] Gutenberg invented one of the first industrial processes and 450 years later the printing industry still bore Gutenberg's stamp: the metal he used was remarkably similar to the compound in use in 1950. Little has been found to better the ink with which the incunables were printed, some of our most popular typefaces date from the seventeenth and eighteenth centuries. Many of the conventions which regulate our conception of good typography are inherited from the earliest printed books, and since the earliest printed books were aping and inheriting the tradition of the medieval manuscripts, there are many features of typographic culture which can only be explained by reference to earlier scribal customs and requirements. But the strands of continuity should not blind us to the adaptability of the printing tradition. In the last hundred years printers have developed techniques for accurate colour printing, and for marrying photographic with printed reproduction. Above all the printing factory has seen great advances in automation and mechanization. The pace of change has quickened but there is every sign that it will continue to accelerate.

There is an important general feature of the new technologies which are today beginning to have profound effects on the publishing process and on the world of print. Publishers and printers are having to learn to cope with, to take advantage of, or to adapt to technologies which are being formed by vast investments from telephone companies, computer corporations, and the like. In consequence, one can only understand and assess the likely effect of the new technologies of computing and telecommunications on publishing and printing if one recognizes that publishing and printing are going to be affected in ways somewhat similar to other commercial and industrial activities. This is most obvious in the way in which personal computers are beginning to have an effect on the writer and the act of composition. There are plans in America to produce a 'scholar's work-station', which will bring to the scholar or scientist a terminal with the hardware and software which will help him in research. Big computer companies, such as Wang, are putting together 'reference shelves' which offer authors a range of automatic author-aids: computerized dictionaries, simple grammar and punctuation checkers, and statistical routines which will give some guidance to the complexity of a document. These products are specifically aimed at the requirements of authors or office workers but they are put together from the standard technologies of the computer business, in determining the course of which authors, publishers, and printers collectively have little muscle.

In the first four centuries of printing the vast majority of texts to be printed were written by the hand of authors or their secretaries.[4] The typewriter was invented in the 1880s and gradually transformed the physical characteristics of the texts or copy with which printers and publishers are supplied. It has meant that publishers and printers deal with copy of greater legibility, more uniformity, and greater predictability—it is much more possible to form a reliable estimate of the extent of an author's typescript than of his handwritten text. It is now most unusual for publishers to accept handwritten texts for publication. Perhaps no more than one book in the next thousand published by Oxford University Press will be set from manuscript. Publishers' contracts now specify that the author should deliver a typescript.

One should be careful not to overstate the completeness of this gradual shift in the mechanics of written composition. Handwriting continues to play a part in the composition and publication process. Many authors continue to delegate the preparation of typescripts to their secretaries, and of those that type their own work many draft in pen or pencil. Within the publishing or printing house, an author's 'manuscript' will have many handwritten emendations and marks added to it. This shift from pen to typewriter has been in several respects less thoroughgoing than might at first blush appear.

A more profound change in the technology of writing has recently been sprung on us. Ten years ago, few editors had seen texts generated by an author using a computer. Today a significant proportion of authors are using word processors, and within five or ten years almost all authors will be using word processors—the American Publishers Association conducted a survey of authors in 1983 and discovered that 80 per cent of them expected to deliver word-processed texts to their publishers in 1985. Authors are moving from typewriters to word processors much more rapidly than they moved from manuscript to typewriter two generations ago. It is possible that in ten or fifteen years typewriters will be museum pieces in much the same way as slide rules are now. The word-processing micro-computer will also drive handwriting from some of the niches in which it still survives. In the very recent past software houses have begun to produce so-called 'ideas processors'— packages which are designed to assist the process of outlining, drafting, and note-taking as word-processing programs assist the typing function. These and other sorts of computerized author aids make it increasingly attractive for writers to work directly on to their computers, thus cutting out the need for pencil and paper work. As publishers and printers process an increasing proportion of their texts in electronic form there will be a diminishing requirement for the use of handwritten mark-up, proof corrections, and so on. Publishers have already begun to devise standard codes which allow an editor, author, or designer to 'mark up' the text with generic codes implemented on a keyboard.

A friend of mine thinks that one of the insidious consequences of the word-processing mode is that it encourages writers to compose and revise many, many drafts of a piece of work, *none of them any good.* This may be too gloomy a view, but in making the switch from handwriting to typing, and then to word processing, one is encouraged to reflect on the unexpected ways in which the technology of writing influences the writing act.

From one point of view, changes in the mechanics of the composition process may seem rather trivial and superficial. And it would be a crass reductionism to try to explain or understand literature or philosophy in terms of the author's method of composition. Nevertheless there can be pervasive if subtle consequences following from the choice of writing tool. Writing with a computer is quicker than writing with a typewriter, as writing with a typewriter is quicker than writing with a pen. The present generation of micro-computers save time over the typewriter primarily in the way in which they facilitate the making of revisions, fair copies, etc. But the micro-computers of the future will probably contain devices which accelerate the process of simple inputting, for example by the use of speech processing. Another background feature of an author's writing which is constrained in quite a direct way by his choice of writing tool concerns the errors of execution he makes. The errors of the scribe, the omission or repetition of letters or words, or the simple problem of illegibility are very different from the kinds of error to which the typist is prone. The typical errors of the typist reflect the layout of the keyboard, by the mistaken depression of an adjacent key, or come as a consequence of the serial process of typing one key after another: the scribe who goes too fast runs his letters together, whereas the typist who goes too fast tends to make errors of transposition.

Since micro-computers have keyboards, they tend to inherit some of the ways in which typewriters are error-inducing. However, many micro-computers now have software which checks spelling against a computerized dictionary, and this greatly cuts down the risk of errors of the kind which printers refer to as 'literals'. But word processors do encourage or permit errors of a novel kind. One of the main attractions of a word-processing program is that it makes it extremely easy to move sentences and paragraphs from one context to another, or to delete passages and insert new matter. An author who uses a word processor is able to have a rather interactive relation with his text—the stream of text moves on his screen, and the cutting edge of his cursor can be relocated to revise any part of the working document. In consequence, texts revised on a word processor sometimes have sentences with pronouns which no longer have a reference in the document. The order of the sentences and paragraphs may no longer reflect the order in which they were thought and there may be no logic in the order in which they appear. Errors and infelicities of this kind may be difficult to detect, and they will not easily be rectified by improved software.

Does it matter that different writing technologies have a propensity to encourage different sorts of mistake? There are at least two reasons why the subject deserves some attention. First, it matters in a strictly practical way for editors, publishers, printers, and readers. In reading the work of a scribe we must guard against illegibility, elision, and the compounded errors that come from copying the work of a copyist. In proofing the work of a typist we need to watch out for transposition and repetition. We are learning that in vetting the work of the computer operator one needs to take account of a propensity towards removing sentences from their true context and for the catastrophic garbles that come from a misplaced code, as when a whole paragraph is set in Greek. There is a second reason for not lightly dismissing the parapraxes or unintended mistakes of the writer. The different sorts of mistake may be indicative of a deeper level of difference associated with the writing technology.

The nature or ambition of the books we choose to write may be constrained by the writing method. The use of micro-computers may have a more radical effect than the use of typewriters. The technology of the typewriter brought the author rather close to the possibilities of print for, in Steinberg's phrase, the typewriter is 'essentially a one-man printing press' (1974: 291). In a sense it restricted the author to the possibilities of traditional hot-metal print. The typographical repertoire of the typewriter is a considerably restricted subset of the repertoire of a printing press—there is no result you cannot better achieve on a printing press. Computers are not nearly so restrictive. As authors begin to realize the graphic and multi-dimensional possibilities of micro-computers they will surely begin to subvert and challenge some of the formal constraints of the printed literary or scientific text. For example, one of the most striking innovations in the latest micro-computer software involves the use of 'windows' through which a user can allow one piece of writing to blend into or overlay another. Once texts are regularly delivered and read electronically, authors will be very tempted to use windows as a formal device within the text.

The computer's typographical potential is improving so quickly that it has already overtaken the printed page in some respects. The earliest computers were so typographically restricted that their screen display looked like a telegram, and they could not even discriminate between upper and lower case; within fifteen years the terminal screen was able to give a convincing approximation of a single page of typescript; and now the latest screens simulate a crowded desk and allow a good mix of print-like sizes and styles of typeface. It is difficult to imagine these new possibilities for textual form but they will no doubt take advantage of the capacity of a computer to present data to a reader in ways which have not been anticipated by the author, of the computer's great potential for graphic representation (a computer display can immeasurably improve on the page as a way of reproducing three-dimensional images), and of the great economy and efficiency of computers at low-level information processing. Some of these possibilities are hinted at by Andries Van Dam in this passage:

Hypertext is a term coined . . . to describe nonsequential writing. Think of a directed graph, with sections of text, pictures, and even sound at the nodes, and with cross-references between materials and pointers to footnotes and marginalia, etc., at the edges. With this easy availability of information, hypertext allows us to manipulate not only individual materials but also the associations between them. We can deal explicitly with the structure of the entire corpus of material. (Van Dam 1984: 648.)

I am not sure that I can see exactly what this term 'hypertext' and this explanation would amount to in practice.[5] But there is something in the idea that the exploitation of the information-processing characteristics of the computer will lead to new developments in the forms of texts. As the invention of printing led to the development of tables of contents, headlines, title pages, indices, or to the production of dictionaries, encyclopaedias, atlases, and gazettes, so the use of the computer will lead authors to present texts in new ways and surround them with a novel apparatus.[6] The 'book' which is not merely written on a computer but written *for* a computer, may be given a structure which has loops and branches and thereby subverts the linearity of the printed book. Since authors have not yet written such books one cannot cite convincing examples. But some intimations of novelty, taken from the world of print, can be mentioned; for example the novel *Hopscotch* by the Argentine novelist Julio Cortazar. This unusual work strains against the possibilities of the printed book in a form which anticipates a serious possibility with computerized texts. There are two sets of page numbers. At the top of the page are the ordinary sequence of page numbers, numbers which correspond to the order in which the leaves are bound, and at the foot of the page are placed the numbers which determine the alternative order in which the book could be read—if you find '123' at the bottom of the page you know that Cortazar intended you to turn to page 123, and so on. It may be contrived, experimental, or artificial to write a book, printed on paper, whose pages can be read in two different orders, but there are serious artistic or practical possibilities in books, written for a computer, whose order and structures can be modified or recomposed by the reader on the screen.

One point about the author's involvement in the technology of composition should be made explicit. In employing the threefold classification of literate cultures with which we began, it is natural to suppose that the chirographic 'period' ends in the late fifteenth century, and the electronic 'period' begins in the late twentieth century. But if we look simply at the technology of the act of composition we find that Ong's typology has been telescoped on to the modern author. One hundred years ago all authors used pen or pencil; within the space of two generations the typewriter was widespread and it seems likely that the computer will shortly become a universal writing tool. From the narrow standpoint of the author's technique, the timescale for the chirographic/typographic/electronic modes is very different from those of the publisher or reader. Long after the invention of printing the author retained a strong foothold in the world of the scribe. Books were handwritten by authors until the end of the nineteenth century, and yet authors are now entering the electronic world at a faster rate than publishers, printers, and readers. Personal computers were designed for professionals, intellectuals, or 'knowledge workers', not for printers or publishers. Personal computers have become a popular consumer item, and word processing is their most popular software application.

As authors have begun to write books on computers, the precise allocation of function between publisher and author has come into question. Authors, publishers, and printers, all have an interest in using the author's electronic version of his text as a basis for reproducing his book. By so doing some money can be saved, there is some hope of simplifying and speeding the publisher's in-house editing, and there should be greatly reduced risk of errors being introduced in the publication process by the typesetter. An increasing number of books are being produced in this way, but for several reasons the process is rarely completely straightforward. Printers, publishers, and authors still have much to learn about electronic production methods. Some of the obstacles are of a practical kind likely to attend any new manufacturing process. But some of the more intractable difficulties come from a lack of certainty about the appropriate division of labour between author and publisher.

One of the clearest practical difficulties confronting anyone in the business of transforming an author's floppy discs into typeset books is the variety of word-processing equipment in everyday use. It is relatively unusual for the output of one micro-computer to be immediately compatible with another system. You can see what sort of problem the publisher faces if you imagine that radio disc jockeys were required to play every request on a different turntable running at a different speed, often with no sign on the disc as to what the correct speed is. This problem of nonstandard inputs is compounded by the fact that the printer's output devices, computerized typesetting machines, are equally nonstandard. This excessive consumer choice is an instance of the generalization I mentioned earlier—printers and publishers are learning how to take advantage of a technology which they did not invent. If the micro-computer had been invented simply for writing books we should have insisted that there should be one design. Fortunately the computer industry is gradually solving the problem. First, by *de facto* standardization on IBM specifications, and second by an increasing accent on the importance of 'communications'—as a rule it is sufficient for typesetting if a text can be communicated, or transmitted down a telephone line. It is not necessary that the physical memory, or floppy disc, be moved from one machine to another.

The second difficulty of a practical nature which confronts the publisher who is in the business of processing texts in an electronic form is that the technology is very rapidly improving; a new generation of word-processing micro-computer appears every two years and a new generation of typesetting computer arrives every four to six years. These continuing improvements are in part the cause of the lack of standardization mentioned earlier, but they are also a consequence of the extraordinary vitality and innovativeness of the micro-electronics industry.

The third, and in many respects the most intractable obstacle to the rapid introduction of techniques of electronic text production lies in the spheres of management and industrial relations. Machines can be obsolete within two years, but most of us take four to five years to learn a new job thoroughly and cannot learn many in our working life. But it is right to point out that some of these human and managerial difficulties are less acute in the book-publishing industry than in the newspaper industry: the unions are less powerful, the ownership is less concentrated, and international competition is a factor. For all these reasons the book-publishing industry is more open to technological change than the newspaper industry in Fleet Street.

These practical obstacles are all surmountable, and they are to varying degrees of success being overcome. But the eventual character of electronic production methods will depend on the ways in which the author is given, or assumes, fuller responsibility for the final production of his text. One can already discern three different types of role.

One approach places the author in a position in which he supplies the printer or publisher with a text which is an electronic stream of letters and spaces with a few content-related codes incorporated in the text. These content-related codes would mark such features of the text as the end of a paragraph, the beginning of a chapter, the position of a footnote, and so on. The publisher or typesetter who accepts a text of this kind adds further codes which build up the typographical complexity of the text. He adds codes which turn some of the characters in the text into 8 point Baskerville roman, others into 8 point italic, and others into 6 point superscripts. These additional codes, and decisions about line-endings and an arrangement on the page, need to be inserted by someone because a book, printed in the traditional way, is a much more tightly organized package of information than the traditional typescript. To give one example of this: a typewriter can produce approximately 94 distinct letter forms or symbols, a reasonably good typesetting system may be able to reproduce from 10,000 to 100,000 distinct letter forms. It is perhaps not surprising that publishers and printers tend to favour this model of electronic production, in which the author supplies letters and spaces, with the mysteries of print being reserved for the expertise of the book designer and compositor. But authors may feel that they are capable of supplying more than a stream of letters and spaces.

A more ambitious view of the author's function would give him sufficient control of the typography of his text for him to produce a coded data stream which will drive a remote typesetting system with very little intervention from a professional compositor. Early attempts to give the author direct control of the typesetting function involved passing to the author the actual codes which would drive the typesetting machine. This could never be a general solution since there is no uniform typesetting language in use in computerized typesetters. So there have been efforts to create a standard language. The most elaborate, impressive, and powerful one known to me is Donald Knuth's TEX.[7] TEX was developed for the special purpose of setting mathematics, which is, with tabular work and some foreign languages, the most difficult sort of setting. The author can type his coded text at any standard keyboard, and the codes or commands are reasonably mnemonic. The flavour of TEX can be gathered from the following example:

$$\ sum-[p \ rm \ ;prime]f(p) = \ int-[5 \pm 1]f(t) \ ,d \ pi(t).\$$

which TEX uses to generate:

$$\sum_{p \text{ prime}} f(p) = \int_{t>1} f(t)\, d\pi(t).$$

It is no trivial matter to master TEX. The handbook exceeds 490 pages. Knuth is one of the founders of software science and he has discovered much of the mathematical basis of traditional typography. TEX is an impressive scientific achievement, but I doubt that it will be an enduring method for writing books, even in mathematics where the author has a level of expertise which is, to his frustration, not widely shared by professional compositors.

One reason why TEX may not command lasting allegiance is that its general strategy is orientated towards *commands* rather than *image forms* or the user's screen. The style of attack is to overcome the screen limitations of an old-fashioned computer and the restricted range of characters on a standard typewriter keyboard by the use of codes. This is at odds with the underlying design philosophy of the micro-computer industry, which eschews codes and attempts to make the computer screen increasingly rich in design possibilities. The aim is to make the computer more 'user-friendly' and to avoid codes so that What You See (on the screen) Is What You Get (on the printer).

The WYSIWYG philosophy leads to another view on the division of labour between author and compositor. According to this view the software and printers available for use with micro-computers are improving so rapidly that within a few years it will be possible for authors to deliver to the publisher camera-ready copy which is almost of conventional typeset quality. This optimism may be well placed, and it is likely that authors will be increasingly able to deliver good camera-ready copy, particularly by using relatively cheap laser printers. But one may doubt whether all authors will relish this additional responsibility, and if standards are to be maintained it will be increasingly incumbent on the author to seek out and heed the publisher's advice, for example on matters of design and copy-editing. As Knuth remarks:

There is a danger that authors—who are now able to typeset their own books with TEX—will attempt to do their own designs without professional help. Book design is an art that requires considerable creativity, skill, experience, and taste; it is one of the most important services that a publisher traditionally provides to an author (1984: 413).

There is a continuum between these three positions and I expect that we shall see all of them developed for particular kinds of book. Authors and publishers will be particularly attracted by the method of author-supplied camera-ready copy for the most specialist publications. But in the case of many books, and most of the most important ones, publishers and authors will continue to have an interest in the publisher having some control over the final electronic form of the text. A principal reason for this will be that publishers will be required to reproduce and distribute electronic versions of the text. This they will only be able to do if they hold the text in an electronic or machine-readable form.

In considering this matter of electronic reproduction we should note two technologies which had begun to disturb the equilibrium of traditional print before the arrival of the computer. First came a decisive shift in the method of printing through the use of photo-lithography. This printing method, which relies on the chemical properties of ink rather than the bite of metal to transfer an impression, began to be widely used in book production in the 1950s. Few laymen can tell whether a book is printed lithographically or from metal, but the decisive consequence of the new method was that any image became printable. If Gutenberg had invented this printing technique, rather than typesetting all our books would be facsimiles of manuscripts. It may be a sign of our collective conservatism about books that the widespread use of lithographic printing did not lead to a revival of interest in reproducing books from manuscript, and even books reproduced from a typescript image have been surprisingly unpopular.

The second striking, new, reproductive technology of recent years is the technique of photocopying. This invention has been scarcely used by printers and publishers to publish books, but it has had an important effect on the dissemination of texts and has broken the practical reproductive monopoly of the printing press. Anyone can now reproduce typeset matter, and we all do. Publishers are prone to exaggerate the threat to their business posed by photocopying, but it is obvious that this is a technology which can be used for unscrupulous or piratical ends. It is also obvious that photocopying can assist the dissemination of knowledge and has considerable advantages for the consumers of print.

Photocopying is like several other new technologies in the extent to which it distributes and democratizes the ability to reproduce documents. It is no accident that totalitarian regimes view typewriters, xerox machines, and micro-computers with suspicion. But photocopying is not a particularly cheap way of reproducing texts. It only has the illusion of cheapness because many of us do not pay for our photocopying and, even when we do, we are inclined to compare the cost of a photocopy with the published price of a book, overlooking the fact that the largest share in the price of a book is attributable to the cost of marketing and distributing it. At present the physical costs of reproducing data for use in a micro-computer are roughly comparable with the costs of printing that data, but the cost of computer memory is falling so rapidly that it will soon be very much cheaper to store large amounts of text in computer memory rather than in paper form. The compact disc which is used in modern audio systems can also be used as a digital store in a micro-computer memory. A single compact disc, which costs a pound or so to manufacture, can hold as much text as the largest multi-volume dictionaries or encyclopaedias. The complete *Oxford English Dictionary* is printed on paper which costs nearly £100 and yet will fit on a piece of plastic which will slip in a pocket. This laserdisc technology is still under development, but it is already much cheaper and easier to copy a floppy disc than it is to photocopy a comparable packet of printed text.

One of the radical consequences of photocopying is that it has undermined the exclusiveness of print. The realm of print, of publication, and of copyright is no longer so sharply separated from the realm of correspondence. Before 1950 there were roughly two reproductive possibilities for a text: it could be reproduced in twos or threes, by handwriting or typewriter; or it could be reproduced in runs of several hundred or more by printing processes. The invention of xerography has led to a reproductive technology which provides a continuum between the draft, the working paper, or lecture notes on the one hand, and the short-run monograph on the other hand. In most subjects one can now find texts of outstanding quality, which are widely circulated and extremely influential—more so than many a monograph—and yet these texts remain provisional, uncitable, and inevitably lack the authority of full-scale publication. But if the invention of xerography has facilitated the *samizdat* circulation of works of genius or extreme topicality, it has also replicated many more texts of inferior quality, which have never passed through a referee's or an editor's hands. Indeed, the exclusiveness, the authority, and the quality of the world of print was created behind a double tariff and both tariffs have been lowered. The text needed to be of sufficient interest to promise a market of several hundred buyers and it needed to be of sufficient value for it to be worth while for somebody to go to the labour and expense of setting it up in metal. It was against the background of limited resources, and costly investments that publishers were bound to focus on questions of quality, neutral refereeing, and, *in extremis*, market research. The profligacy and availability of computer-based publishing may lead to a renewed emphasis on quality control, and refereeing practice, not because it is difficult or expensive to reproduce texts, but as the best hope of offering the consumers of print protection from the growing problems of information overload.

Perhaps the clearest way in which computerized technology will assist the consumers of texts is in the task of searching for, and locating, texts with relevance to a reader's interests. Since 1970 a significant new information service has grown up in the form of computerized on-line data bases. These data bases permit a user to search huge libraries at great speed. The earliest data bases often consisted entirely of bibliographic information, or abstracts. Data bases of this kind make for very gruelling reading, but they are clearly of use in pointing a researcher to material which *might be worth reading.* But in recent years the tendency has been for very large files of pure text, for example legal reports, or verbatim news stories, to be placed directly on the data base. Chunks of these data bases can be read on a computer screen and the data base suppliers usually provide the user with the opportunity to print out, locally, passages which interest him. At first these 'full-text' data bases could only be searched by means of a literal-minded, and narrowly logical, sieving technique. If you asked for all the contexts in which 'disc' occurs in some data base, the system would not be able to tell you that this word is spelt in two different ways. You might in consequence miss just those contexts that interested you, or your search might be cluttered up with many occurrences of the sense in which a disc comes between two vertebrae. The newest data base systems can circumvent problems of this kind by supplying the user with a thesaurus or a dictionary which helps to give a more intelligent search. With software of this sort data bases of the future may be able to offer readers the equivalent of a personalized news cuttings service.[8]

It is one of the more striking features of a print economy that publishers, booksellers, and librarians can have rather exact notions of the number of copies of a book that are printed, sold, or borrowed, without having a clear idea of how much their publications are *read.* Many forms of electronic distribution keep a much tighter hold on 'readership' since the consumer pays not only for the privilege of accessing a data base, but additionally and *pro rata* for those parts of it he displays on his screen or 'downloads' to his printer or computer memory. It may be that most printed matter is not read at all. It has been estimated that 3,000,000,000 copies of academic, scientific, and technical journal articles were distributed in the USA in 1984.[9] Since there are probably fewer than a million serious consumers of technical journal articles in the USA one is bound to conclude that the system of publishing research articles on paper exhibits a high degree of redundancy. But, as elsewhere in the theory of communication, a high level of 'redundancy' is a means of ensuring effective communication. The electronic age will almost certainly lead, is already leading, to a great multiplication in the number of copies and variety of texts *available* to readers, but our ability to read and understand texts or literature shows little sign of increasing at a similar rate, and is probably not susceptible to technological improvement.

E. P. Goldschmidt (1943: 89–90) reminds us how protracted and precarious must have been the medieval author's task of assembling his sources and reading matter. The modern reader's problem is more one of superabundance than of scarcity. The on-line data base is a crude example of the ways in which the computer can help in the location of *relevant* reading matter. Computers are good at routine and efficient low-level information processing and we are beginning to discover ways in which they can assist in the reading of texts as word processors assist in the writing of texts. They will obviously not *relieve* us of the necessity to read, but they may make it easier for us to deploy our reading time efficiently. From a publisher's point of view one of the interesting features of this sort of development is the way in which the reading and writing machines become a new sort of market for some of the traditional publisher's products. Oxford University Press has found that there is a strong demand among computer companies for word lists, dictionaries, and other sorts of reference books to be sold by the computer manufacturer as an integral part of his system.

At the beginning of the chapter I suggested that we see the publisher as the middle term in a relationship between the author and the reader. One of the snags with this generally unexceptionable model is that it can suggest an unrealistically linear view of the publishing process. One of the most striking features of specialist academic publishing is that the pool of readers in a particular field can be assumed to be reasonably co-extensive with the pool of potential authors. The more specialist the field the more likely this is to be so. The linear model may also suggest that the success of the publishing process is to be measured in terms of its ability to amplify or multiply the text which is the author's input to the system. Individual authors and editors are invariably disposed to view the success or failure of their own contributions in this way—as though success in publishing was like shouting loudest in a noisy party. But there are very different considerations which determine the success or failure of the system of publishing as a whole. The success of the system as a whole may have much more to do with the extent to which it permits the publication of obscure, unpopular, or highly original works, and also with the degree to which it allows obscure and difficult works to be found and read by those who need them. The system as a whole is only successful if the quieter guests can be heard.

This in the end may be the final justification and rationale for the publisher in an era of ever more powerful information technologies —technologies which tend to place more power in the hands of writers and readers, the consumers and producers of information. These new technologies make it easier and cheaper to write, to copy, to distribute, and to consult texts; but the task of regulating and making an efficient market will fall to publishers or their equivalent. The reader and author will still look to a middleman who can create a list, a market place, a refereeing procedure, an archive, or an imprint, within which new ideas can be launched.[10]

NOTES

1. Papert (1980: 17) notes that the point of using computers in schools is not to save money, or shave a year off the time a child spends in school, but rather that computational ideas can give children new possibilities for learning.
2. The book contains no index. It is therefore difficult to be sure that the, to me obscure, discussion of computers in relation to sense 'ratios', is the *sole* instance in which computers are discussed: McLuhan 1962: 183.
3. For example Jennett 1967: 30 and McLean 1980: 14–17.
4. Some fascinating case studies are presented in an accessible way in Gaskell 1978.
5. Directed graphs have been used by psychologists as a means of summarizing conceptual relations in small areas of knowledge. Buzan (1974: 102) discusses the ways in which directed graphs, or 'brain patterns', can be used to organize note-taking and thinking.
6. The most convenient and detailed summary of our knowledge of the

formal and textual innovations of print in the fifteenth and sixteenth century is to be found in Eisenstein 1979.

7. Knuth's deep interest in typography extends to the mathematics of font design, for which purpose he has developed his METAFONT programs.

8. Hammond 1984 is a practical guide to data bases.

9. This estimate was given at the London On-line conference in 1984 by Donald W. King.

10. I am grateful to Marise Cremona, Robin Denniston and Andrew Rosenheim for their comments on a draft of this lecture.

REFERENCES

Buzan, T. 1974: *Use Your Head*. London: BBC Publications.

Eisenstein, E. L. 1979: *The Printing Press as an Agent of Change*. Cambridge: Cambridge University Press.

Gaskell, P. 1978: *From Writer to Reader*. Oxford: Clarendon Press.

Goldschmidt, E. P. 1943: *Medieval Texts and Their First Appearance in Print*. Oxford: Clarendon Press.

Hammond, R. 1984: *The On-Line Handbook*. London: Fontana.

Jennett, S. 1967: *The Making of Books*. London: Faber.

Knuth, D. E. 1984: *The TEXbook*. Reading, Mass.: Addison-Wesley.

McLean, R. 1980: *The Manual of Typography*. London: Thames & Hudson.

McLuhan, M. 1962: *The Gutenberg Galaxy*. Toronto: Toronto University Press.

Ong, W. J. 1982: *Orality and Literacy*. London: Methuen.

Papert, S. 1980: *Mindstorms*. Brighton: Harvester Press.

Steinberg, S. H. 1974: *Five Hundred Years of Printing*. Harmondsworth: Penguin.

Van Dam, A. 1984: 'Computer Graphics Comes of Age', in *Communications of the Association for Computing Machinery*, vol. 27, no. 7: p. 638.

Weizenbaum, J. 1984: *Computer Power and Human Reason*. Harmondsworth: Penguin.

ON AUDIO AND VISUAL
TECHNOLOGIES: A FUTURE
FOR THE PRINTED WORD?

ANTHONY SMITH

OUR language at the present time does not offer a ready-made
or aptly turned phrase which sums up the way in which a new
technology exercises its impact upon society. We can take from
economics the notion of the multiplier, or from scientific discourse
Thomas Kuhn's notion of the broken paradigm. We can borrow
from engineering and from telecommunications all sorts of thrusts
and forces and scatterings, but nothing which conjures up at all
quickly a useful and transposable conceptualization of the causal
influences which pass in both directions between a new technique
or technology and a human society.

In the case of systems of communication the gap is all the more
acute since it is difficult in practice to talk about them at all without
starting to suggest a cause-and-effect process. The historian of a
single medium can almost by accident leave behind an excessive
sense of that medium's influence. Elizabeth Eisenstein, in her
remarkable books about the coming of print (1979), leaves one with
a mental picture of the printing press as the supreme turning-point
in Western history, altering as it did all forms of government, all
social and cultural institutions, all ways of thought. We, too, are
living through a period of considerable technological change, and
in this decade it seems that information and communication are at
the very centre of all innovation. And so it has become easy both to
exaggerate or, through sheer contrariness, to dismiss the impact of
modern media upon the lives of both individuals and societies. A
debate in the House of Lords transmitted via television looks very
much as it did a century ago, but the impact of television upon the
peerage and the reverse impact of the peerage upon the evolving
medium are both very great. All kinds of extended influence upon
institutions and upon the public view of the political system are at
work, and historians will no doubt long argue about the level of

importance to attach to the arrival of television in Parliament. What we have failed to evolve—and I certainly am not going to remedy the omission in this chapter—is a general theory of such instances of technological impact, even an easily memorable metaphor for these complicated clusters of change.

What I thus want to do is to concentrate upon the way in which perceptual revolutions take place through the agency of new media, with a view to saying something about the specific nature of the changes now under way within the printed word, which may well alter institutions and perhaps structures of thought in future decades.

Many years ago I met a man who told me that he had prepared as script-writer the first documentary ever made for British television. He had previously worked in radio and for magazines. On receiving his commission he visited the contracts section of the BBC and argued his case for extra payment. The official, to his surprise, offered him a sum not more but less than that he received for comparable work in the medium of radio. When he remonstrated the answer was: 'Oh, no, surely we pay more for radio than television for the writer in radio has to create the pictures, but in television we, the BBC, create the pictures and add them to the writer's work'. Certainly, whatever the contracts clerk had failed to grasp, she had at least identified the essentially collaborative nature of the new medium. Television was going to conjure into being, as cinema had done, a whole new range of crafts and skills, intellectual, artistic, organizational, and technical, but no single one of them, in practice, would ever successfully assert its primacy. In the technology of moving letters the printer had rapidly come to play a supporting role to the author. In the era of Gutenberg, society had developed a logocentric individualism at the heart of all its intellectual work. The printed text centred upon the author; all methods of study and instruction, the organization of libraries, the laws of copyright, all systems of censorship and control were predicated upon the idea of textual composition as the work of named authors. The immense structural changes in society which were facilitated by the advent of moving letters occurred in a world in which the composition of text assumed the crucial moral role. Text had passed from being a mental to being a physical object; it became personal property. The distribution of text could be controlled through the licensing of printing. Industrially, text passed into the specialist hands of publishers, but the book culture of the last five centuries has been essentially a culture of authors. The film and television cultures, on the other hand, are definable more in terms of companies and institutions, production teams and partnerships. The texts, so to speak, of the age of moving images are the results of industrial processes—and these are themselves of course based ultimately upon the primary enabling function of the written word. The moving image media consist of a series of artefacts and illusions which bear the marks of an infinity of deals and compromises between an array of parties. All of these are in some sense creative (in that they involve the application of judgement as well as skill); all of them entail moral and often legal responsibilities; all of them are engaged, in some sense, in the act of communicating. To say, as the film critics of the 1950s did, that the film director was or could be simply the author is to make an extremely controversial statement. The main British films of our time are producer-led rather than director-led, and in other times and places the writer or the editor could acquire the chief authorial role. It seems to me that it is the industrial nature of the technologies of audio and visual communication which provides their essential character. We are building in film, radio, the gramophone, and television a vast and new apparatus for creating and distributing meaning in society, an apparatus which is in constant evolution, but which must, in time, exert upon the sensorium a shift at least as great as that exerted by the printing press. The psychic changes are gradual and haphazard. They are observed by people whose own perceptual apparatus has itself passed through the change concerned. Each layer of change in a medium is influenced by the current perceptions of it, each leaving a residual impact, a sediment of latencies, possibilities within the consciousness, echoes within the self.

It is interesting to look back at the first reception of moving images in the world, and to ask how someone immersed in the culture of the written word envisaged the changes wrought by the new medium. 'Last night I was in the Kingdom of the Shadows,' wrote Maxim Gorky on 4 July 1896 after seeing Louis Lumière's films at the Nizhni-Novgorod Fair. 'If you only knew how strange it is to be there. It is a world without sound, without colour. Everything there—the earth, the trees, the people, the water and the air— is dipped in monotonous grey. Grey rays of the sun across the grey sky, grey eyes in grey faces, and the leaves of the trees are ashen grey. It is not life but its shadow, it is not motion but its soundless spectre' (Leyda 1959: 407). This is not the excited discovery which one might have expected. Gorky was not the enthusiastic recipient of a revelation, but a rather disappointed sceptic. The Franken-steinian dream which had occupied many nineteenth-century minds, the dream of a medium which would reproduce life itself through a device of illusion, had been part of the attempt to break through the barriers of Victorian naturalism; the cinema pioneers had wanted to discover the secret of duplicating life, as Noël Burch (1981) puts it. The Lumière brothers were doing something more than developing a mechanical device for making familiar photo-graphic images move; they were, like many of the pioneers of cinema, trying to examine the nature of perception with a view to structuring or restructuring it. Marey had created various means for *describing* perception rather than reproducing images. Marey thought that Lumière had 'stripped away none of our illusions, added nothing to the potency of our vision' (Sadoul 1953: 100). Marey thought that the research 'should abandon the representa-tion of phenomena as we see them' and he concentrated thereafter on reproducing motion in slow form and on perfecting various kinds of stroboscopic photography. Edward Muybridge himself was attempting in his moving images of the running horse and the naked oarsman to analyse human perception rather than create a new device of entertainment or illusion. The first ten years or so of cinema were dominated by a desire to do what Walter Ong has told us printing did to restructure thought. Lumière's craft developed from amateur photography; his films were an emanation in aesthetic terms from 1890s picture postcards, unposed street scenes, contrast-ing with the posed photographs taken by professionals and found in the home. The early film, like the postcard, was to be stared at, to be seen again and again until all the various elements converged in the mind. It was viewed quite differently from the later narrative film which was made to be seen once only. Primitive cinema was not a consumer culture. Lumière's projection began from a still frame. Gorky noticed and stressed this fact at his own viewing of the films:

When the lights go out in the room . . . there suddenly appears on the screen a large grey picture, shadows of a bad engraving. As you gaze at it you see carriages, buildings and people in various poses, all frozen into immobility . . . but suddenly a strange flicker passes through the screen and the picture stirs to life. Carriages coming from somewhere in the perspective of the picture are moving straight at you, into the darkness in which you sit . . . all this moves, teems with life, and, upon approaching the edge of the screen, vanishes somewhere beyond it. (Leyda 1959: 407.)

It was not so much a case of Lumière not having learned how to frame correctly his picture of the workers leaving the factory, or the train entering the station, in order to make the information offered clear at first glance; it was a case of deliberate pursuit of a different aesthetic, according to Noël Burch, of offering a deliberately different mode of representation which was a decade later to be rejected by the new commercial cinema industry. Primitive cinema made you look at the world differently—differently from the photograph, differently from the medium which later emerged.

How different was the memory of the silent cinema in its classical period. Richard Griffith in his introduction to the post-war edition of Paul Rotha's *The Film Till Now* writes of the 'singular completeness' which silent cinema had acquired by that fateful year of 1929 when the medium was just about to disappear with the arrival of the talkies. 'To walk into a darkened theatre,' says Griffith, 'to focus upon a bright rectangle of moving light, to listen somewhat below the level of consciousness to music which was no longer good or bad in itself but merely in relation to what was on the screen, and above all to watch, in a kind of charmed hypnotic trance, a pattern of images which appeared and disappeared as capriciously as those pictures which involuntarily present themselves to the mind as it is dropping off to sleep—but which, also like those of the mind, gradually amount to a meaning of their own—this was an experience complete and unique, radically unlike that provided by the older arts or by the other new media of mass communication' (Rotha 1944). As Béla Balázs wrote, looking back on the same moment in media history:

The birth of film art led not only to the creation of new works of art but to the emergence of new human faculties with which to perceive and understand this new art . . . Now the film is about to inaugurate a new direction in our culture . . . words do not touch the spiritual content of the pictures and are merely passing instruments of as yet undeveloped forms of art. Humanity is already learning the rich and colourful language of gesture, movement and facial expression. This is not a language of signs as a substitute for words—it is the visual means of communication, without intermediary of souls clothed in flesh. (Balázs 1952: 41.)

I am suggesting that a medium of communication is both an industrial technology and an attempt to reconstruct the process of cognition. In part each new technology is based upon an attempt to learn how human mental processes work but it ends invariably by reorganizing those processes and thereby, I would add, influencing works of art or communication performed through other, earlier processes. The media have one history; they are an accumulation of cultural projects, not a mere succession. Within each medium there exists a series of genres and each of these has also in effect come into existence to reorganize thought or to appeal to latent emotional patterns or to satisfy a newly structured facility to absorb narrative or argument. Since the arrival of printing Western mankind has attempted through new apparatus of observation and representation to possess the world ever more securely; the equipment for seeing the world has also been the equipment for coming to terms with it, for unravelling its mysteries, for co-opting the environment. Consider Pudovkin on film editing:

If we consider the work of the film director, then it appears that the active raw material is no other than those pieces of celluloid on which, from various viewpoints, the separate movements of the action have been shot . . . And thus the material of the film director consists not of real processes happening in real space and real time, but of those pieces of celluloid on which these processes have been recorded. This celluloid is entirely subject to the will of the director who edits it. (Pudovkin 1933: 56.)

Cinema has passed through a number of major technical watersheds, each of which has enabled a different kind of structuring of reality to take place; for example, with the development, under the directorial eye of Orson Welles, of deep focus, or the technique of *ciné-vérité* of the 1950s. Each stage has suggested an intensification of the fidelity with which the resulting illusion mirrors or suggests 'reality' but each has been a new illusionism, based upon a technical development in production and a new training of the eye on the part of the intended audience. We can today accept ways of arranging a narrative—see the extraordinary methods used by writer/director David Hare in the film *Wetherby*—which would have puzzled, perhaps dismayed Pudovkin or Eisenstein.

The Gutenbergian printing press had offered a similar restoration of seeming reality. It produced for simultaneous audiences the *ipsissima verba* of an original work. It offered an exact multiplication of knowledge. Through reproduction it offered a library without walls, as Erasmus put it, the complete restoration for one generation of the entire corpus of ancient work, which was previously available only in copies painfully constructed in the effort to preserve the information faster than the ravages of time consumed the material which held it. Knowledge ceased to be focused upon the restoration of that which had been known but lost or almost lost and became subject to a process of progressive augmentation through the easy comparison of available versions of texts. Where knowledge had been a matter of search, it became a matter for research. The roles of memory, imagination, speculation, and reasoned argument all shifted. Different mental qualities came to be prized. The intellectual skills were differentially revalued. Education has gradually caught up with new social tasks based upon the prevailing methods for storing and distributing information. 'Reading' and 'literacy' have become dominant terms, ever-expanding metaphors which we are obliged to use when describing other cognitive skills, including the observation of moving image media. We speak today of 'film literacy' and 'reading pictures', suggesting that somehow the air of legitimacy acquired by the older skill should apply with appropriate amendment to the new medium. Each new technology since printing has realigned the senses and altered the nature of the images collected by the memory. Printing with its control over the language has not lost its supremacy.

The trouble with the bulk of public discussion of the media is that it is combined inexorably with discussion of social effects. Each new medium appears to possess, in the eyes of the generation whose perceptions were shaped by a previous medium or rather a previous formation of media, an uncanny and incalculable power over behaviour. The structure of public argument over cinema and over television has not been dissimilar to that over the fluoridation of water. These media—and others—have been presumed to be autonomous agents acting coercively upon the public, necessary, and sufficient causes of stated consequences. Social science has rather tended to run after the discussion in search of something to do and has become inextricably caught up in the endless regressions, analysing increasingly subtle interactions between direct media effects and gratifications.

Radio, cinema, and television have all taken so firm a grip upon our culture that it is easy to assign too great a causality to them, indeed to 'blame' them too automatically for every other discernible phenomenon within society. So pervasive is this easy rhetoric of social causation that it has become today almost impossible to find a way in which to discuss these media without automatically contributing to the loose but accumulating reservoir of conjecture. Every medium and every genre together with every stage within their evolution leave their impact upon the sensorium, even those which precede literacy and which therefore leave no physical reminder. But that is merely to say that they alter the opportunities of thought and feeling, not the conclusions. One may try out a very distant example, drawn from the dawn of the chirographic age. Eric Havelock (1963) shows how the pre-Homeric epic worked as a tribal encyclopaedia, expressed through formulaic language and repetitions; a complete perceptual apparatus was allowed to linger into the age of the scribal culture and indeed engaged in confrontation with the new educational philosophy of the age of Plato; Homer's versified bardic encyclopaedia survives today, still metaphorically powerful while interacting with millennia of further modes of thought, feeling, and imagery. The process of change is one of circularity rather than displacement. A media system exists within a set of social purposes and offers its own structure of feeling, designed to intermesh with a perceptual system.

Rather than visualizing media history as a series of technological breakthroughs one might choose to envisage it as a series of technical breakdowns as the apparatus of memory and cognition fails to cope within the genres, forms, and devices available. Havelock describes the revolution in Greek culture which made Platonism inevitable: the sheer social necessity to move from concrete to abstract modes of thought exerted its impact upon the old poetic form and upon the techniques of inscription. He describes the break with the poetized tradition 'with its habit of emotional identification with persons and stories of heroes, and with the play of action and episode. Instead the "philosoph" is one who wants to learn how to restate these in a different language of isolated abstractions, conceptual and formal: a language which insists on emptying events and actions of their immediacy, in order to break them up and arrange them in categories, thus imposing the rule of principle in place of happy intuition . . .' (Havelock 1963: 287). There was a need, perhaps driven by conscious economic requirement, for a new kind of thinking, a new psychic activity which the intellectual techniques of the bardic age prohibited or inhibited. 'In the Homeric or pre-Homeric period,' writes Havelock, preservation of the corpus of knowledge 'had to rely on the living memories of human beings, and if these were to be effective in maintaining the tradition in a stable form, the human beings must be assisted in their memorisation of the living word by every possible mnemonic device which could print this word indelibly upon the consciousness. The devices that were explored were first the employment of standard rhythms engaging all possible bodily reflexes, and second reduction of all experience to a great story or connected series of such stories.' (Havelock 1963: 198.)

It is possible to track the shifting of consciousness from medium to medium only with great difficulty, since it is that very point of psychic change that those directly concerned are keenest to deny. One may cite the way in which oral traditions were repressed at the point of the introduction of printing and substantially lost. The new cognition appears at a different point in the society. The cineasts despise television at first. Newspaper journalism scorns radio until their professionalisms merge. The new medium arrives as toy or irritant, usurper or rebel. Over thirty years ago Béla Balázs wrote of the coming of silent cinema a generation before that:

The forms of expression of the silent films developed gradually, but the rate of development was fast enough and together with it the public developed the ability to understand the new form-language. We were witnesses not only of the development of a new art but of the development of a new sensibility, a new understanding, a new culture in its public . . . Many million people sit in the picture houses every evening and purely through vision, experience happenings, characters, emotions, moods, even thoughts, without the need for many words. For words do not touch the spiritual content of the pictures and are merely passing instruments of as yet undeveloped forms of art. (Balázs 1952: 41.)

The evidence for such change in the sensorium is hard to track down, even harder to establish in the form of satisfactory proof. One would have to say, in the case of film and television, that constant evolution in directorial technique, in the social and economic context of these media and in their inner and outer technologies (that is, the means both of production and distribution) are reflected in a number of concomitant changes in perception. The addition of sound to cinema for example transformed the medium's imagistic possibilities. Colour, anamorphic lenses, computer animation, each has opened up a whole further range of visual possibility, and left audiences trained to apply to the world a growing repertoire of modes of seeing.

Television as a domestic medium has altered all the dimensions of distance within the communications processes of today, in absorbing within itself the whole international archive of cinema; television and video wrestle with partially rival cognitive systems, each frequently taking a step towards convergence, each discovering a new exclusive potentiality. I am not certain that I agree with all of Walter Ong's list of resemblances between the new orality, as he labels our age, and primary orality: he lists 'its participatory mystique, its fostering of a communal sense, its concentration on the present moment, and even its use of formulas' (Ong 1982: 136). The moving image media can operate also without a participatory sensibility and their formulae can shift and change very rapidly. They foster a sense of their own continuousness; their works follow in cumulative succession as if in mutual response. Television is a continuous process of transmission, almost a single text in itself, urging us to remain with the flow or be somehow excluded from the essence of what is really happening. Its essential trick—and that of radio before it—is to imply that it represents the completer version of reality, from which one's absence can only be exceptional. It is the opposite of escapist. It is the absent member of the audience who is the absconder. Perhaps it was rather like that if one missed the public recitals of pre-Homeric bardic culture. Victor Hugo argued that the printed book supplanted the role of the cathedral because it took over the task of carrying the spirit of the people. But it was the book which in a sense splintered the medieval cathedral, as a message-bearing medium into the opiniated diversity of the printed word. To quote from Béla Balázs again, printing 'made the faces of men illegible . . . So much could be read from paper that the method of conveying meaning by facial expression fell into desuetude' (1952: 41). In cinema and television the psyche is being offered a return to cathedral, forum, pre-printed text, a return to the reading of human feature and gesture, to the transcultural rather than the intra-cultural dissemination of signs. But the return is within the spiral. We are the cognitive heirs of an accumulating sign tradition. And it is the specific nature of the prevailing electronic media of today which must be influencing us by altering the prevailing modes of perception.

Let me try to pull together my argument so far. We belong in the world by virtue of our ability to perceive it through a variety of sensing apparatus converging on the memory. The communications systems taken together constitute a great marshalling of the facilities of perception of individuals and of societies, but among them they entail the placing of the senses in a hierarchy: in other words the media impose a bias upon the relative status of the senses and thus influence the content of memory, which in time further amplifies the prevailing patterning of the sensorium. As subjects of experience, as potential knowers of that which is to be known, we are to that extent pre-structured, though in a context of constant change. Human perception thus enjoys its own history, of which media history is a part.

The media strain and filter the information which passes through them and to some extent our non-media experience is rechecked by us through the filter of the media—and other institutions of society. But each medium has its own special experiential mesh and these have been applied in practice not separately but successively in history. Our senses learned to cope with the narrative structure of a Henry James novel and absorbed it through the multi-sensing apparatus of Henry James's sentence structure. Today the Henry James vision is available, in the case of several of his novels, by way of cinema, which completely reorganizes the narrative but still offers us the characters of James and something of his artistic intention. Our memories generally can differentiate the two experiences; we might forget in which novel a character appears but we seldom mistake the memory of the film for the memory of the novel. We might decide that both are independently excellent. We might completely reshape our view of the novel under the impact of the remembered faces and costumes of the actors in the film. But though one experience is laid upon the other, they remain memories of separate media experiences, which have passed through a different arrangement of the senses, a different programming of the senses.

A number of students of communication history have compiled great historiographic systems mapping out the media epochs into three or four grand stages. Walter Ong's is certainly the most developed of these and in his book *The Presence of the Word* (1967) he labels four great ages, oral, chirographic, typographic, electronic, each of them framing the epistemic possibilities of its time. What I would wish to emphasize is the extent to which each has completed a task, a complete human perceptual project, while opening up new tasks. Printing, for example, enabled us to acquire a cumulative view of knowledge, to learn the techniques of comparative criticism of different versions of the same information. With printing the whole world was quickly to acquire a calendar, a time system, inter-language dictionaries, maps and sailing charts, and, more to the point, an enduring certainty about the necessity of such things. Printing provided us with a certain training of the senses, an accepted filtering and arrangement of the knowledge that resulted and a set of permanent needs and latencies which later media have not and cannot displace or expunge. There may—or may not—be fewer people who can read today than fifty years ago but typographic culture has left its mark none the less, not just upon the skills of the senses but ineradicably upon human culture.

To dismiss the standardizing power of typographic culture as 'the middle-class literacy approved by the American establishment' as Robert Pattison does in his book entitled *On Literacy* (1982), is to miss the point. The standardization of language was an achievement without which the technologies of the electronic era would have been impossible. Pattison says: 'Electronic media are a powerful stimulant to the development of a literacy centered on the spoken word. They threaten established literacy by offering a continuous stream of vernacular raised to the level of popular art—an art without the constraints of correct English . . . Established American literacy with its emphasis on mechanical skills and its assertion of the limitations of language thwarts man's desire to feel himself fully represented in words' (Pattison 1982: 202). Let me pass over the curious modern tendency to use the word 'Americans' when the word 'people' is possibly what is meant. Pattison is guilty as are many of the apostles of the 'new literacy' or 'new literacies' of a misapplication of their liberationist instincts. The culture of voice and sound, of natural language in what Pattison calls the age of rock is built upon the culture which arose from the standardization of language and of writing. The genitive apostrophe may be as dead as a dodo, as he says, but only in a society which has acquired other linguistic means, just as secure, for establishing the relationship between objects. A language can go off the Latin standard, as a currency can go off the gold standard, but there exists some substitute machinery for setting up norms if the language is to survive on being taught to people with other tongues. The dictionaries have been written and someone needs to use them—without necessarily imposing a tyranny upon others. Literacies, so called, live in succession and new ones depend upon old ones even if careless of them.

The quest for objective knowledge—of which typographic culture was an essential prerequisite—has not departed nor will it, however many decide to opt for the 'literacy of the ear', as Pattison calls it. Chirographic culture, as Havelock shows us in his account of pre-Homeric society, never managed quite to cut the link between the knower and the known. Writing arrived as an extension of speech; it was print that offered a substitute for speech. It imposed a standardized system, for ever, upon the task of communicating knowledge. The knowledge thus acquired and stored became accessible in other times and places and, moreover, set up expectations that the defining essence of knowledge was thus.

It could be argued that our rapidly accumulating repertoire of electronic gadgetry—from the telegraph and radio to videodisc, digital computer, and satellite—places us in a kind of transitional era between the typographic and some super-electronic stage of communication. It seems to me that the implications of the electronic stage are already becoming clear, though its hardware is far from complete. The essence of the new stage in communications is digitization, the breaking down of all information into the basic unit of the bit, a mathematical standardization applicable to all things which can be reduced to the condition of information. It is not dissimilar in some ways to the Gutenbergian discovery of moving letters, though it is much simpler. All objects of the senses can be labelled in terms of strings of ones and zeros, and so can phenomena of nature such as signals passing through the electromagnetic spectrum. The striking difference between the Gutenbergian and the binary-digital system is that the latter is content to register the certain from the probable. The perfection of a digital recording to the human ear is in fact constructed from readings of the waves produced by the instruments through equipment which is content to calculate the resulting sound on the basis of statistical sampling. Marey's primitive cinema devices were based upon the exploitation of Plateau's discovery of the persistence of vision, the use of a human weakness to produce a perfect illusion. Digitization offers a similar illusion of perfection of information based upon registering the approximate.

Before the beginning of the electronic era, the various mechanical techniques of communication extended our senses in range, but did not, as it were, offer us a new sense. In the era of primary orality hearing was the chief of the five senses, where perhaps previously the sense of touch had been predominant. Hearing operates across space, beyond the line of sight, around corners, through physical substances. Writing, of course, placed emphasis upon the sense of sight; the exchange of information by way of writing was a substitute for speech and hearing in certain circumstances, and with the arrival of printing, both of words and pictures, very large quantities of information could be made available without physical presence. The various media of communication of course work through a combination of senses and refer back constantly to the data provided by other senses than the one that may predominate at a given moment. The reproduction of images through still and moving photography provides a substitute storage for visual memory, but also offers the evidence of vicarious seeing, just as typography offers the evidence of vicarious knowing: the media enable us to employ the senses of others, but linked to our memory. No medium before telecommunications, however, that is, prior to the electronic stage, could offer us through our senses information which is carried only by means of a sense which human beings do not possess: the sensing of the electromagnetic spectrum beyond the range of frequencies registered as sight, hearing and touch. The electronic therefore offers us a new set of dimensions to information, by transmuting that information back into data retainable in the human memory and accessible through the human senses. It is the principle of digitization married to the science of telecommunications which offers the particular extension of or substitution for the senses which is occurring in the electronic age. We are in transition to that age but are far enough into it to register at least the theoretical implications.

The mechanics of the Renaissance helped to recalculate the world for us. The universe which the perceptual tools of recent centuries helped us to compile offers a completely different conceptualization of the environment of time and space within which the senses—and the memory and imagination to which they are tied—operate.

Where in medieval thought the human being had been microcosm, the epistemic link with the macrocosm, the new sense order of the typographic world left mankind as a perceptual apparatus, self-conscious but lost within a different, now an infinite universe designed by Newton with the help of Galileo. The human sensorium, freed from the constraints of both concentric and anagogic views of the world reached out for one perceptual artifice after another with which to explore the new spatial extension. That left the self to expand upon the newly enfranchised senses. The instruments of knowledge which now filtered the world's data both trained the senses and offered it new categorizations of knowledge, from biology to economics, from physics to psychology.

That reconstruction of the individual-in-the-universe was completed within the confines of typographic culture, before the electronic revolutions of the twentieth century. The medium of print had helped to structure the senses in such a way as to pave the way for a new preoccupation with the self. The idea of the personality was the logical extension of the sensorium of the typographic age. Freud could later discover a new enabling substratum, the foundations of the new self, in the unconscious.

The structuring of the senses which the knowledge techniques of the twentieth century facilitated has been aided by sources of information which go beyond the senses. The moving image technologies, radio, the gramophone, have continued the work of extending sight and sound, but the electronic media of the latter part of the century are offering something more. The new apparatus which reconstructs information in terms of binary oppositions changes the nature of the whole environment of information.

The new aesthetic discoveries of the early years of the century prepared the senses for the multi-perspectives of electronic culture; in Morse code there had been a rehearsal of the great digital transformation of codes which has arrived now in the 1980s. Mathematics and physics underwent transformations under the impact of Einstein, Heisenberg, Russell, Hilbert, which urged new conceptions of time and space to take over in the realm of memory and imagination as much as in the laboratory. The innovation in art of the early years of the century accelerated the process of transferring the new concepts to the realm of the senses. The scheme of the Renaissance had shown how to reproduce the dimensions of space in illusion within rectangles of canvas, but now it became possible

for art to take on the task of offering a complete reconceptual-
ization of the world. Simultaneously in the field of language studies
nineteenth-century concepts of philology were being replaced and a
series of language analogies made themselves available in the human
sciences as models for the decoding of information. Being and consciousness separated, linked henceforth through language; consciousness came increasingly to be seen as a culturally constructed
phenomenon, functioning within these new conceptualizations.
Moreover, it was now accessible to the world of the economy
through advertising and publicity which came more and more to
be seen as central to these new cultural circumstances. Where a
nineteenth-century radical would see the physicality of work as
economically basic, the late twentieth-century counterpart would
increasingly emphasize the economic role of the senses; the emotional and cultural identity of human beings, as much as their
labour power, had become their link to society.

The new information machines and their attendant institutions
intrude deeply into the self, reshaping emotional and cultural outlook, redefining perceptual functions. Television and video arrived
not really as toys and distractions, as the cinema and phonograph
had done, but as workhorses of the psyche, offering as it were a
complete service, swamping the separate genres of information
with the sheer pervasiveness and omnipresence of the electronic
moving image, searching out every issue, every place, every event,
every personality, in order to build the new overwhelming perspective into the sensorium.

What is now offered in the information revolution, as the complex web of late twentieth-century changes are apt to be labelled, is
at root a digital revolution. And it is allied to the next set of changes
which are occurring as the medium of television itself undergoes the
process of digitization. If we are to envisage the impact upon print
culture of these alterations in the methods of information carriage,
storage, and transfer, we have somehow to put together in our
minds some of the issues of perceptual change, together with some
of the strands of technological evolution, and add some notion of
the dynamic forces causing both breakdown and demand in other
industries.

Digitization offers further exponential increases in the rapidity
of information processing, in the accuracy with which signals can be
transmitted. Students of computer development are now suggesting

that the 1990s will see a further leap forwards in the capacity of the simple data storage available domestically. With the use of cryogenically cool circuitry, computation times could be cut back to trillionths of a second. Furthermore, the arrival of such long predicted devices as Josephson Junction Computers could reduce really large-scale computer power to suitcase capacity, thus placing large computational power in the hands of individuals; thus opens up the possibility of the intelligent book, a portable device capable of access to great libraries of material, but capable also of interrogating that material, carrying out some of the tasks of critical comparison of data. These are all aspects of what has come to be labelled the fifth-generation computer. Such devices might also be capable of making full transposition between print and speech, thereby bringing about the final stages of convergence between the Gutenbergian and the electronic modes of information storage. It is always wise to be sceptical of too grandiose predictions, and the speech possibilities of the fifth-generation computer have perhaps begun to be over-canvassed. We need to hold back the technological predictions within an approach which concentrates upon the fundamental potentialities of digitization as a principle of organizing information, while permitting other questions to be treated as issues of quantitative rather than qualitative change.

Let us look again at the Gutenbergian system for reproducing text through moving letters. Essentially, it relied on placing identical blocks of information at different points in space and retaining them through time, almost indefinitely. The new survival ability of information meant that cataloguing became increasingly difficult but concomitantly necessary. During the typographic era the development both of new subject systems and classification systems took place on a scale suitable, at first at least, for catching up with the rate of evolution of knowledge itself. The progressive augmentation of knowledge accelerated through subject classification. The unit of information in the typographic era has been the book, retrievable under two or three keyboards such as author's name, title, subject-matter. Now, with digitization as the basic principle for capturing information, the possibilities for accessing information are increasing very considerably. The unit of information is reduced to a single nugget of knowledge, a word even, and this in an era when the search for information has been made increasingly difficult through the sheer quantity and flow of new data, not merely at the level of specialized research but also at the level of ordinary life. The search for an item of data to do with social welfare, the search for an address or a telephone number, for a medical record, or an insurance policy or a criminal's fingerprints, all such quests for information are becoming overwhelmed by the bulk of data available, at least where these functions have not already been subjected to the process of digitization.

Consider the history of the modern telephone directory. It is a printed volume, or set of volumes. That is, it looks like a book, is printed as a book and has to be produced, bound, and physically delivered to homes and offices. The quantities of information which it contains have grown very rapidly as the number of homes containing a telephone has increased from 40 per cent to 80 per cent in less than a quarter century. The data collected, however, go out of date faster than the most rapid and efficient available methods of production and distribution. In fact, while production has been speeded up, distribution has become all the more expensive and labour-intensive. And yet the users of the directory as individuals require each year an ever smaller proportion of the total quantity of information which it contains, and even that is likely to be out of date by the time the actual search is undertaken. The telephone directory is a typical example of the Gutenbergian mode of information: its existence is predicated upon the idea of multiplying the number of physical copies until they approximate to the size of the probable audience. It is still a convenient system for many genres of written material and will long remain so. It is a good distribution device for poetry, for the novel, for certain ranges of educational materials. It is not however any longer an appropriate device for disseminating perishable ranges of information including much scientific research. Digitization has already occurred at the production level; it is but one leap to transfer the digital signal to an electronic mode of distribution. And that is what, in due course, must happen. With the arrival of ever cheaper systems of information transfer—most probably the optic fibre attached to public videotex systems—the telephone directory is an urgent candidate for the Gutenbergian scrap-heap. So are timetables and classified data of many kinds—not all kinds, but many. Many of the ranges of information contained in the newspaper could be effectively transferred elsewhere and, indeed, are being developed through videotex.

We have now passed into the era in which every citizen is familiar with the principle of manipulating digital information, through the devices of teletext and videotex, in airline and travel offices, public libraries, schools, and elsewhere. Before the principle can be applied wholesale a further transformation in attitude and perspective must take place. For digitized information still runs counter to established habits of mind. In need we reach automatically for a book. The personal computer is still too small a thing to transform our attitudes to information—although it is training the imagination.

Technology is suggesting two possible directions, the first towards a merger of the printed word and the moving image, the second away from the printed word to the screen. The two are by no means mutually exclusive. Nearly all printed words, books, newspapers, magazines, or invoices, pass through at least one stage of digitization. Hot metal type is very rapidly disappearing and only in the conventional typewriter does the moving letter system survive significantly in the industrial economies. The word processor, as it transforms office work, will ensure that a further range of printed words will undergo this basic enabling process. The digitization of the moving image is still in its infancy, but certain elements of the television process are now changing to the digital mode. Gradually digitization will spread until it takes over all television, at the level of production. At the level of distribution the digitization of television will take much longer since the bulk of investment in the existing television system is held not in the studio but in the home and the transformation of reception will take a great deal of time, especially given the establishment of video. However, the digital 'compact' sound disc is becoming a familiar object; the distinction between high quality sound reproduction devices and high definition television images via disc is not a great one and at some stage these might merge, possibly within a decade. Already the videodisc, which has had a very slow and shaky start, has been identified as an equally good medium for text, still and moving image, as for a combination of all three. One can envisage within a very few years the arrival, perhaps in rather specialist areas of work, of a combined text and video disc, a circular video-book if you like.

The real problem in the information business is the lack of development of display systems. The cathode ray tube has not undergone a fundamental redesign for many decades, although various improvements to this bulky object have indeed taken place. During the last decade and a half there have been various crises in the newspaper industry, associated partly with the high cost of newsprint, a politically sensitive commodity at the best of times, which has now run foul of the ecological lobby also. It would not be beyond the bounds of feasibility before the end of the century for some kind of general merger of display systems to take place— the arrival of a flexible disc or rectangular screen which could display all of the digitalized materials. This would have considerable impact upon both the television and newspaper or publishing industries, but in the production area of both the change would be gradual. The impact upon booksellers, newspaper, and record distributors would be enormous and rapid. Happily for them, they seem all to be diversifying into one another's domains, so that publishers, independent video production companies, chains of bookstores, and newsagents are increasingly aware of their collective problems, aspirations, fears, and opportunities.

I am not predicting the arrival of some new object, the 'post-book', or 'post-television' medium. Rather, I am suggesting the evolution of a range of new objects for the carriage of information, some of them able to function as devices of interrogation, of access and input as well. I do not believe—exactly why would be difficult to say—that the book as such will disappear. In one important sense, of course, the book already has disappeared, in that its production system has been in recent years completely reconstructed through the use of computerized typesetting. But it continues to look like a book and to be used like a book. However, one can now begin to imagine a different object which, though perhaps still looking like a book, could combine moving images with readable text. It might even have pages though it is more likely to be some kind of semi-conductor slab.

I have not tried to predict or describe the future of the printed word, but to give an account of the context within which that future will be determined. As media change is accelerating, the apparently simple questions of the last ten years themselves seem to be changing. We used to ask, will the book survive television? We now find that the question is rather: in what forms will printed words, pictures, and moving images converge? What kinds of new media will be distributed widely, and what genres of material will they contain? The greatest determinant of the content of a new medium is, of course, the inherited culture of the previous ones. Typograhpic culture by its very nature has great survival power; its materials fill our world. The institutions of education, information, and government that emerged from the Gutenberg mode of information processing are equally resistant to change overnight.

There is a story that when Mr Attlee entered Downing Street in 1945, one of his younger aides suggested that No. 10 should acquire one of the new telex machines, just then on the market. Attlee dismissed the idea. The Foreign Office had plenty of clerks who could bring their telegrams across at any time. But he did agree to have one machine on a month's approval, and one afternoon noticed up-to-the-minute cricket scores clattering out of it. He proposed that the telex be retained, but always thereafter referred to it as 'the cricket machine'. We accept new modes and new technologies when they are justified by established needs. It takes time for them to generate new needs. The next generation of computers does indeed promise an intriguing fusion of the spoken and the written word, the ability to transmute languages from the written mode in one tongue to the spoken in another, and even to reverse the process. It offers us books that will converse with us, movie screens that behave like the pages of books. But such devices only emerge at a point of interaction, when the cultural and perceptual needs generated by established media stimulate more dimly felt new desires. It is an emotional as much as an industrial question that is raised. The real revolution in information is a revolution in perception.

REFERENCES

Balázs, Béla 1952: *Theory of the Film: Character and Growth of a New Art.* London: Dobson.

Burch, Noël 1981: 'Charles Baudelaire v. Dr Frankenstein', in *Afterimage*, 8/9: 4–23.

Eisenstein, Elizabeth 1979: *The Printing Press as an Agent of Change.* 2 vols. Cambridge: Cambridge University Press.

Havelock, Eric A. 1963: *Preface to Plato.* Oxford: Basil Blackwell.

Leyda, J. 1959: *Kino.* London: Allen and Unwin.

Ong, Walter J. 1967: *The Presence of the Word.* New Haven: Yale University Press.

—— 1982: *Orality and Literacy.* London: Methuen.

Pattison, Robert 1982: *On Literacy: The Politics of the Word from Homer to the Age of Rock.* London: Oxford University Press.
Pudovkin, V. I. 1933: *Film Technique.* London: George Newnes.
Rotha, Paul 1944: *The Film Till Now.* London: Jonathan Cape.
Sadoul, Georges 1953: *French Cinema.* London: Falcon Press.

INDEX